PowerScore® LSAT Logic Games Bible Workbook

The best resource for practicing PowerScore's famous Logic Games methods!

Published by
PowerScore Publishing, a division of PowerScore Incorporated
57 Hasell Street
Charleston, SC 29401

Author: David M. Killoran

Contributors:
Steven G. Stein
Jon M. Denning
Nicolay I. Siclunov
Ron Gore

Manufactured in Canada
02 11 20 16

ISBN: 978-0-9912992-1-8

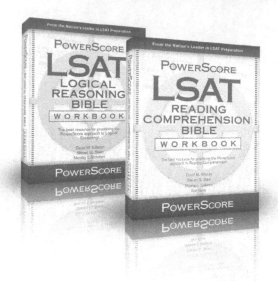

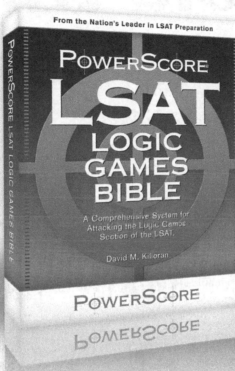

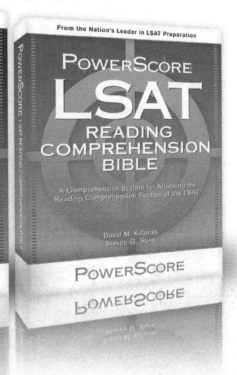

Contents

Introduction

Chapter One: Practice Drills

Chapter Two: Individual Logic Games

Appendix

Glossary

About PowerScore

PowerScore is one of the nation's fastest growing test preparation companies. Founded in 1997, PowerScore offers LSAT, GMAT, GRE, SAT, and ACT preparation classes in over 150 locations in the U.S. and abroad. Preparation options include Full Length courses, Weekend courses, Live Online courses, and private tutoring. For more information, please visit our website at www.powerscore.com or call us at (800) 545-1750.

For supplemental information about this book, please visit the Logic Games Bible website at www.powerscore.com/gamesbible. The website contains additional drills, expanded concept discussions and explanations, and answers to questions submitted by students.

About the Author

Dave Killoran, a graduate of Duke University, is an expert in test preparation with over 20 years of teaching experience and a 99th percentile score on an LSAC-administered LSAT. In addition to having written PowerScore's legendary LSAT Bible Series, and many other popular publications, Dave has overseen the preparation of thousands of students and founded two national LSAT preparation companies.

About PowerScore

[illegible]

About the Author

[illegible]

Introduction

Welcome to the *PowerScore LSAT Logic Games Bible Workbook.* This book is designed for use after you read the *PowerScore LSAT Logic Games Bible*; the purpose of this workbook is to help you better understand the ideas presented in the *Games Bible*, and to allow you to practice the application of our methods and techniques. This is not a how-to manual, but rather a traditional workbook designed to reinforce the skills and approaches that will enable you to master the games section of the LSAT.

If you are looking for a how-to manual, please refer to the *PowerScore LSAT Logic Games Bible*, which provides the conceptual basis for the setups, rule diagramming, and general strategies you will be practicing here. In the discussions of game approaches and techniques in this workbook, we will assume that you have read the *Logic Games Bible* and are familiar with its basic terminology.

To help you practice the application of your Logic Game skills, this book is divided into two sections:

<u>Section One: Practice Drills</u>

The first section of this workbook contains drills which test isolated analytical abilities, designed to reinforce and improve the specific skills necessary to successfully attack the Logic Games section. The set of drills is followed by an answer key explaining each item.

<u>Section Two: Individual Games</u>

The second section of this workbook contains eight individual LSAT Logic Games, each of which comes from an actual LSAT and is used with the permission of LSAC, the producers of the LSAT. At the end of the section is a comprehensive explanation of each game, including a discussion of the setup, each rule diagram, inferences, and a complete explanation of every question. This is an excellent section for testing and reinforcing your game skills on days when your time is limited.

Each part is easily located using the black sidebars that mark each section.

As you finish each item, we suggest that you carefully read the corresponding explanation. Examine the correct answer choice, but also study the incorrect answer choices. Look again at the problem and determine which elements led to the correct answer. Study the explanations and setups provided in the book and check them against your own work to assess and improve vital game skills. By doing so you will greatly increase your chances of performing well on the Logic Games section of the LSAT.

Finally, in our LSAT courses, in our admissions consulting programs, and in our publications, we always strive to present the most accurate and up-to-date information available. Consequently, we have devoted a section of our website to *Logic Games Bible Workbook* students. This free online resource area offers supplements to the book material and provides updates as needed. There is also an official book evaluation form that we strongly encourage you to use. The exclusive *LSAT Logic Games Bible Workbook* online area can be accessed at:

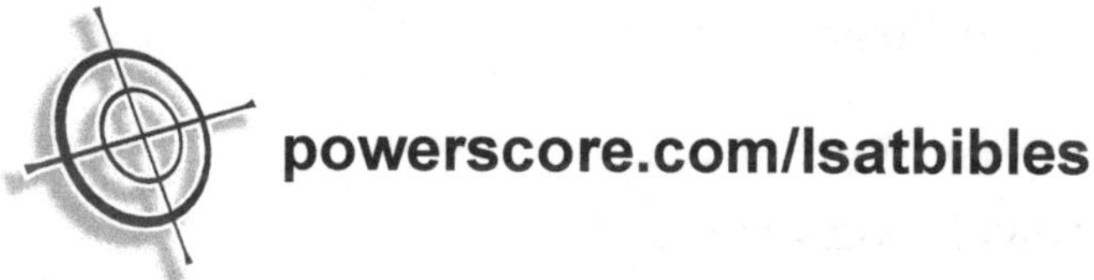

If you would like to discuss the LSAT with our experts, please visit our free LSAT discussion forum at:

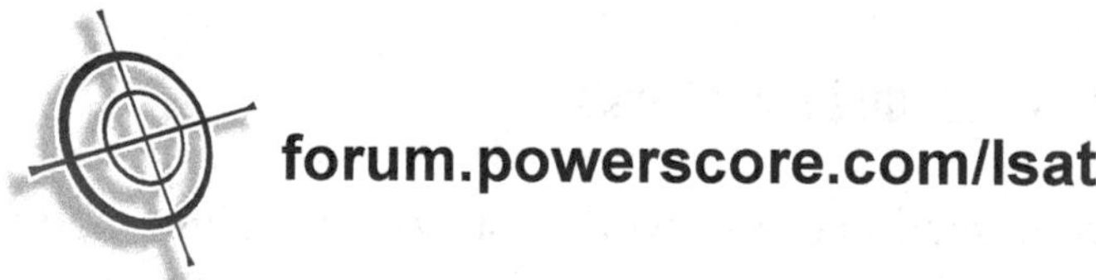

If we can assist you in your LSAT preparation in any way, or if you have any questions or comments, please do not hesitate to email us at:

We are happy to assist you in your LSAT preparation in any way, and we look forward to hearing from you!

1

Chapter One: Practice Drills

POWERSCORE
TEST PREPARATION

Chapter One: Practice Drills

POWERSCORE
TEST PREPARATION

Chapter Notes

This section contains a large set of drills designed to achieve the following goals:

1. To expand your knowledge of the language used in LSAT rules, and to further familiarize you with the correct representation for each rule.

2. To examine the interaction of variables and relationships, and the explain the different ways that the LSAT uses those elements.

3. To isolate and test certain skills that are used in Logic Games, and refresh and refine your abilities to apply those skills.

4. To expose you to a variety of game situations and overall game concepts.

We believe the best approach is to complete each drill, and then check the answer key in the back, examining both the questions you answered correctly and the ones you answered incorrectly.

These drills have no timing restrictions. Instead of worrying about speed, focus on a complete understanding of the idea under examination. Later in this book there will be timed exercises to give you practice with the timing element.

Rule Origin Drill

Each of the following items presents a Logic Game rule in final diagram form, followed by five lettered answer choices. Select the one answer choice that contains language that produces the *exact* rule diagram in the problem. In Linear diagrams, the position of variables is assumed to be ordered from left to right, first to last, highest rank to lowest rank, etc. Blocks and arrows could reflect Linear or Grouping relationships, so read the answer choices carefully to determine what language would produce the diagram. *Answers on page 82*

1. J ——→ W

   (A) Jin is selected unless Walter is selected.
   (B) Jin is selected if and only if Walter is selected.
   (C) Jin is selected if Walter is selected.
   (D) If Walter is not selected then Jin is not selected.
   (E) Either Jin or Walter must be selected.

2. R/S (block with R above S, crossed out)

   (A) Rena is not seated at the same table as Suki.
   (B) Rena is seated immediately next to Suki.
   (C) Neither Rena nor Suki is selected to attend the dinner.
   (D) If Rena is not selected to attend the dinner, then Suki is not selected to attend the dinner.
   (E) Rena and Suki are seated at the same table as each other.

3. G ←+→ H

   (A) Neither Greta nor Harrison speak at the fundraiser.
   (B) Greta and Harrison cannot speak in consecutive time slots at the fundraiser.
   (C) If Greta speaks at the fundraiser, Harrison cannot speak at the fundraiser.
   (D) If Greta does not speak at the fundraiser, Harrison speaks at the fundraiser.
   (E) Greta and Harrison cannot speak at any fundraiser with another speaker.

Rule Origin Drill

4.

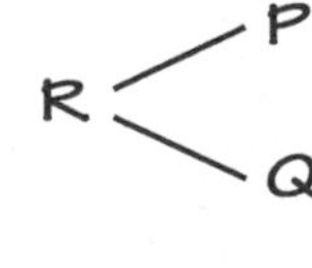

or

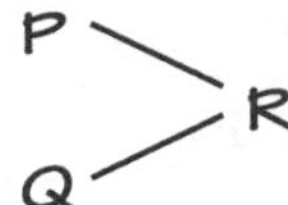

Assume no ties are possible.

(A) Neither P nor Q can depart earlier than R, unless they both depart earlier than R.
(B) R departs earlier than P or earlier than Q, but not both.
(C) P departs earlier than R if and only if R departs earlier than Q.
(D) Q cannot depart earlier than R unless P departs earlier than R.
(E) P departs later than R only if Q departs later than R.

5. | P | Q/R |

(A) Putnam must be seated in a chair adjacent to those of both Quince and Roe.
(B) Putnam must be seated in a chair adjacent to that of either Quince or Roe.
(C) Putnam and Quince must both be seated in chairs adjacent to that of Roe.
(D) Either Quince or Row must be seated immediately to the right of Putnam.
(E) Either Quince or Row must be seated immediately to the left of Putnam.

6. M —— N —— O

or

O —— N —— M

Assume no ties are possible.

(A) Either M is taller than N, or else N is taller than M, but not both.
(B) Either N is taller than O, or else N is taller than M, but not both.
(C) Either N is taller than O, or else O is taller than N, but not both.
(D) Either O is taller than M, or else O is taller than N, but not both.
(E) Either M is taller than O, or else M is taller than N, but not both.

Rule Origin Drill

7. 

(A) Grace is shorter than both Allison and Beth, whose heights are consecutive.
(B) Beth must be taller than Allison, who must be taller than Grace.
(C) Beth and Allison are the same height, but both are shorter than Grace.
(D) Allison must be taller than both Beth and Grace.
(E) Allison is taller than Beth, who is taller than Grace.

8. 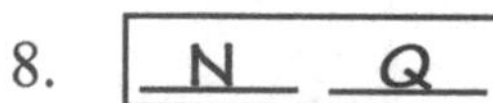

(A) Both Nairobi and Quito are visited.
(B) Nairobi and Quito are visited consecutively.
(C) Nairobi is visited earlier than Quito.
(D) Quito is the next city visited after Nairobi.
(E) Quito is visited immediately before Nairobi.

9. 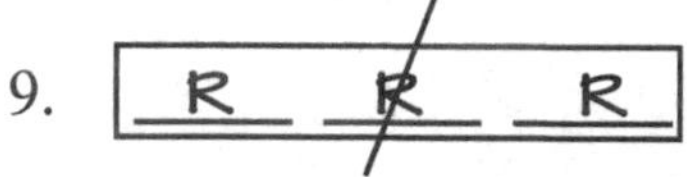

(A) At least two red lights must be consecutive.
(B) No two red lights can be consecutive.
(C) No more than three red lights can be consecutive.
(D) No more than two red lights can be consecutive.
(E) Any two red lights must be separated by at least one light of another color.

10. 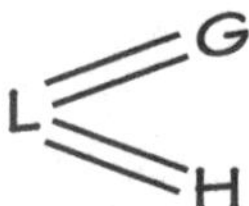

(A) Luisa finishes earlier than both Garrett and Henrietta.
(B) Garrett, Henrietta, and Luisa do not finish at the same time.
(C) Garrett and Henrietta finish at least as quickly as Luisa.
(D) Neither Garrett nor Henrietta finishes earlier than Luisa.
(E) Luisa finishes after both Garrett and Henrietta.

Rule Origin Drill

11. 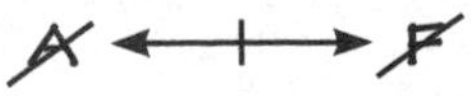 ~~A~~ ←|→ ~~F~~

(A) If A is not included in the competition, F cannot be included in the competition.
(B) A and F cannot both be included in the competition.
(C) Neither A nor F can be included in the competition.
(D) A cannot be included in the competition unless F is also included.
(E) Either A or F must be included in the competition.

12.

L	V
V	L

(A) Either L or V lives in an apartment on the fourth floor.
(B) L and V cannot live in the same apartment as each other.
(C) L lives in an apartment either directly above, or directly below, the apartment in which V lives.
(D) L and V live in apartments adjacent to each other.
(E) L and V live in apartments on separate floors.

13.  J ←——→ K

(A) Either K or J, but not both, must be painted.
(B) J is not painted unless K is painted.
(C) J is painted if and only if K is not painted.
(D) Either K is painted and J is painted, or K is not painted and J is not painted.
(E) K is painted only if J is painted.

14.  M_1 ——→ [MK]

(A) K cannot sing immediately after M unless M sings first.
(B) If M sings first, then K sings at some time after M.
(C) M cannot sing first unless K sings immediately after M.
(D) K sings immediately after M only if M sings first.
(E) M and K cannot sing consecutively unless M sings first.

Rule Origin Drill

15. C ═══ D

(A) Charlie ate more hotdogs than Daniel in the competitive eating championship.
(B) Daniel ate more hotdogs than Charlie in the competitive eating championship.
(C) Charlie and Daniel ate the same kind of hotdogs in the competitive eating championship.
(D) Daniel did not eat more hotdogs than Charlie in the competitive eating championship.
(E) Charlie did not eat more hotdogs than Daniel in the competitive eating championship.

16. 

(A) F and H cannot be selected together.
(B) At least one of F or H must be selected.
(C) F is selected if and only if H is selected.
(D) If H is selected, then F is selected.
(E) If H is selected, then F is not selected.

17. F ←——→ ~~G~~

(A) If Fran joins the team, Greg will not join the team.
(B) Fran will join the team only if Greg does not join the team.
(C) Either Fran or Greg will join the team, but not both.
(D) Fran will join the team if and only if Greg joins the team.
(E) Either Fran and Greg will both join the team, or neither of them will join the team.

18. A ——→ ~~B~~

(A) Alan will attend if Brad does not attend.
(B) If Alan does not attend then Brad will attend.
(C) If Alan attends, Brad will attend.
(D) Alan will attend if and only if Brad does not attend.
(E) Alan will not attend unless Brad does not attend.

Two Rule Inference Drill

In the space provided, supply the best symbolic representation of each of the following rules. Link the rules if possible, and, if applicable, show any corresponding inferences. Assume that each variable must occupy exactly one of the spaces provided, and that each space must be occupied by exactly one variable. If the diagram provides for more variables than the rules may suggest, assume the presence additional, unnamed variables. *Answers on page 97*

1. If Q is on the stage, then R is on the stage.
   R is not on the stage unless P is not on the stage.

2. The third car sold is either S or T.
   W is sold immediately before X.

cars = ___ ___ ___ ___ ___ ___
1 2 3 4 5 6

3. D's performance and E's performance are separated by exactly one performance.
   G performs immediately after F.

performances = ___ ___ ___ ___ ___
1 2 3 4 5

4. M cannot be in a group unless N is in the same group.
   Q and R cannot be in different groups.

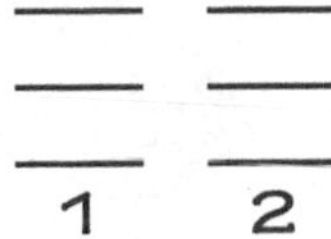

Two Rule Inference Drill

5. R's call is made at some point before S's call.
   T's call is made exactly two calls ahead of R's call.

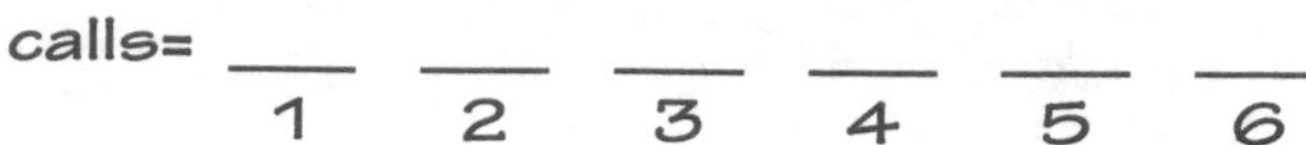

6. H cannot be in group 1 unless K is in group 1.
   J is in group 2 only if L is in group 2.

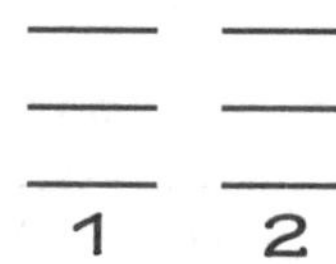

7. If A is not interviewed then B must be interviewed, and if B is interviewed then A cannot be interviewed.
   Of the six interviewees, if B is not interviewed then exactly two other interviewees cannot be interviewed.

Two Rule Inference Drill

8. J and K cannot audition together.
   When K auditions, L must also audition.

9. Q appears earlier than R but later than S.
   Q does not appear second.

appearances= ___ ___ ___ ___ ___ ___
1 2 3 4 5 6

10. Either Book R or Book S is written last.
    Book Y is written later than Book X.

books= ___ ___ ___ ___ ___
1 2 3 4 5

Two Rule Inference Drill

11. At least three deliveries are made before G is delivered.
    At least two deliveries are made after H is delivered.

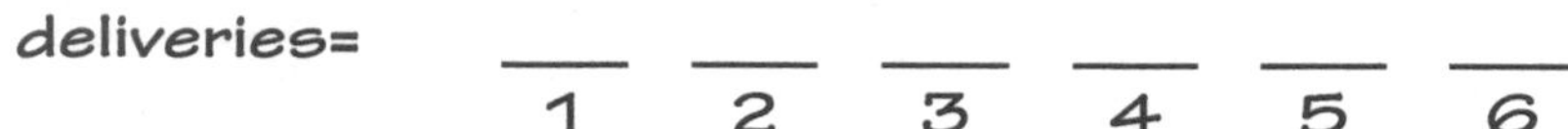

12. F is presented either immediately before or immediately after H.
    H is presented at some time before K is presented.

presentations= ___ ___ ___ ___ ___ ___
1 2 3 4 5 6

13. Either L or G reviews the site on day 3.
    R reviews the site exactly two days before X does.

days= ___ ___ ___ ___ ___
1 2 3 4 5

Two Rule Inference Drill

14. Exactly one lecture separates the lectures on Physics and Chemistry.
    If the Chemistry lecture is not the first lecture given, then it must be the last lecture given.

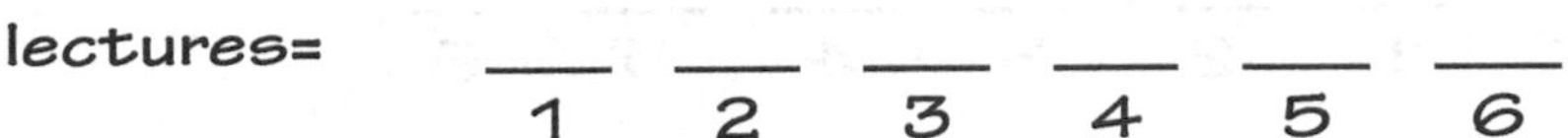

15. If K is not selected, then both F and H must be selected.
    Q is not selected unless only one other variable is selected.

16. In a row with five seats, L is seated immediately before S.
    L is seated before F but after U.

seats= ___ ___ ___ ___ ___
1 2 3 4 5

17. Without S, T will not be selected.
    R will be selected, unless T is selected.

Two Rule Inference Drill

18. M arrives on the second day, exactly three days before N arrives.
    Q arrives exactly three days after P arrives.

Days= ___ ___ ___ ___ ___ ___
1 2 3 4 5 6

19. Either A or B, but not both, joins Team 1.
    C and B are placed on different teams, and D and A are placed on different teams.

Team=
___ ___
___ ___
___ ___
1 2

20. Neither F nor G wins first place.
    D is ranked higher than C but lower than E.

Rank= ___ ___ ___ ___ ___
1 2 3 4 5

Linear Base Representation Diagramming Drill

Each of the following items contains a game scenario that features two separate variable sets. Using the given information, choose a base for the game and create a linear diagram. To the side, specify the variable set that will fill the linear slots. *Answers on page 112*

Example:

> Six sprinters—Hu, Natchez, O'Dell, Prince, Sato, and Tran—are assigned to six separate running lanes on a track. The lanes are numbered from 1 through 6.

Answer:

HNOPST[6]

___ ___ ___ ___ ___ ___
1 2 3 4 5 6

---

1. There are exactly six houses on a street. Each house is occupied by exactly one of six tenants—Alberto, Beatrice, Carmello, Drayton, Engrid, and Fong. All of the houses are on the same side of a street that runs West to East.

2. A highrise building has six residential floors, 32 to 37, containing a total of seven apartments. Each floor has exactly one apartment, except for the lowest of the six floors, which has two apartments. The residents of the building are G, J, L, R, T, U, and V, each of whom live in a different apartment.

Linear Base Representation Diagramming Drill

3. During a period of seven consecutive days, each of exactly seven warehouses—E, H, K, L, N, P, and T—will receive a delivery. During this period, each of the warehouses will receive exactly one delivery each day.

4. Six consecutive positions for a demo album, will be filled with exactly five rock songs—D, F, G, J, and O—and exactly one ballad. Each song will be assigned to a different position.

5. Five, colored flags—Blue, Green, Orange, Red, and Yellow—are all being raised up a flag pole, not necessarily in that order. No two flags can be raised at the same time.

Linear Base Representation Diagramming Drill

6. Three couples—Grace and Henry, Irene and Justin, and Kai and Lee—attend a concert together. The six attendees are seated in a single row, with one person assigned to each of six seats—103 to 108.

7. During the final round of a singing competition, six singers—Aretha, Barry, Celine, Dierdra, Evan, and Frank—are scheduled to perform, not necessarily in that order. The singers will be assigned to five time slots, with Aretha, Barry, Dierdra, and Evan each singing solos in four of the five slots, and Celine and Frank singing together in the remaining slot.

8. An exam proctor is assigning seats to four students—M, N, O, and P. The proctor has a single row of seven consecutive seats available, and cannot assign any two students to seats that are adjacent to each other.

Linear Base Representation Diagramming Drill

9. A personal trainer is planning a weekly schedule, Monday through Saturday, of individual training sessions for five clients—M, N, P, R and S. Each client will receive exactly one training session, with no two sessions scheduled on the same day.

10. On Thursday, a professor will have exactly one appointment with each of seven students—Edgar, Garrett, Hans, Juliette, Kristoff, Lorenzo, and Nadia—one student per appointment.

11. A computer algorithm generates a series of six-digit passcodes. Each passcode must include the numbers 0, 1, 2, 3, 4, and 5, and no others, with each of those six digits occurring exactly once per passcode.

Linear Base Representation Diagramming Drill

12. A gym is scheduling a four-hour block of exercise sessions beginning at 6 am. The sessions that are to fill this time block include three hour-long sessions—A, B, and C—and two half-hour sessions—F and H. The sessions will be scheduled one after the other, each session scheduled exactly once.

13. Six ski chalets—L, R, T, V, W, and Z—are arranged in ascending order up the slope of a mountain, not necessarily in that order.

14. Five people—Carver, Diaz, Esposito, Foley, and Grey—will be scheduled as participants in a game show that is aired once each day, Monday through Thursday. Each episode must have at least one participant, and no participant is scheduled for more than one episode.

Linear Base Representation Diagramming Drill

15. A tour group will view exactly seven artifacts—J, K, L, M, N, O, and P—displayed in five display cases. The first and the last cases viewed will each contain two artifacts. The remaining three cases will each contain a single artifact.

16. An accountant is scheduling five, day-long meetings over the course of five consecutive weeks. Each week will have a single meeting occurring on a single day—Monday, Tuesday, Wednesday, Thursday, or Friday. No two meetings can be scheduled on the same weekday over the five-week period.

Conditional Reasoning Mini-Diagramming Drill

Each of the following statements contains a sufficient condition and a necessary condition; therefore, each of the following statements can be described as a "conditional statement." In the spaces provided, write the proper arrow diagram for each statement, then write the contrapositive of that statement. Assume that no ties are possible. *Answers on page 120*

Example:

If Y is delivered second, then Z is delivered third.

Answer:

original diagram: $Y_2 \longrightarrow Z_3$

contrapositive: $\not{Z}_3 \longrightarrow \not{Y}_2$

---

1. If A is not delivered first, then B is delivered first.

original diagram: ____ ⟶ ____

contrapositive: ____ ⟶ ____

2. D performs fifth if E performs fourth.

original diagram: ____ ⟶ ____

contrapositive: ____ ⟶ ____

3. N is not interviewed on day 2 unless L is interviewed on the day 3.

original diagram: ____ ⟶ ____

contrapositive: ____ ⟶ ____

4. P precedes Q only if Q precedes R.

original diagram: ____ ⟶ ____

contrapositive: ____ ⟶ ____

5. If H is presented third, then either I or J must be presented fourth.

original diagram: ____ ⟶ ____

contrapositive: ____ ⟶ ____

6. If F is scheduled for 1:00, then G is not scheduled for 2:00.

original diagram: ____ ⟶ ____

contrapositive: ____ ⟶ ____

PRACTICE DRILLS

Conditional Reasoning Mini-Diagramming Drill

7. When D is taken in the Fall, then either E or F must be taken in the Spring.

original diagram: _____ ⟶ _____

contrapositive: _____ ⟶ _____

8. J doesn't ride in the third car if K rides in the second car.

original diagram: _____ ⟶ _____

contrapositive: _____ ⟶ _____

9. If the recipe includes either A or B, then it also includes C.

original diagram: _____ ⟶ _____

contrapositive: _____ ⟶ _____

10. V is selected for Team 1 if W is selected for Team 2.

original diagram: _____ ⟶ _____

contrapositive: _____ ⟶ _____

11. X is included if and only if Y is included.

original diagram: _____ ⟶ _____

contrapositive: _____ ⟶ _____

12. V appears only if it is presented first.

original diagram: _____ ⟶ _____

contrapositive: _____ ⟶ _____

13. If either G or H is invited, then I is also invited.

original diagram: _____ ⟶ _____

contrapositive: _____ ⟶ _____

14. B reads fourth unless C reads fifth.

original diagram: _____ ⟶ _____

contrapositive: _____ ⟶ _____

Conditional Reasoning Mini-Diagramming Drill

15. I conducts the session immediately before J if J conducts the session immediately before K.

original diagram: _____ ——→ _____

contrapositive: _____ ——→ _____

16. If S does not perform in the play, then T must be the third performer to appear on stage.

original diagram: _____ ——→ _____

contrapositive: _____ ——→ _____

17. If U is presented, it is presented neither immediately before, nor immediately after R is presented.

original diagram: _____ ——→ _____

contrapositive: _____ ——→ _____

18. If L is chosen or M is chosen then N is not chosen.

original diagram: _____ ——→ _____

contrapositive: _____ ——→ _____

19. K must compete immediately after J, whenever I competes second.

original diagram: _____ ——→ _____

contrapositive: _____ ——→ _____

20. O cannot play if both P and Q play.

original diagram: _____ ——→ _____

contrapositive: _____ ——→ _____

21. When J doesn't go second, K goes fourth.

original diagram: _____ ——→ _____

contrapositive: _____ ——→ _____

22. P is on stage only if O is on stage.

original diagram: _____ ——→ _____

contrapositive: _____ ——→ _____

Conditional Reasoning Mini-Diagramming Drill

23. C is not shown at the festival unless both D and E are also shown.

original diagram: _____ ⟶ _____

contrapositive: _____ ⟶ _____

24. Neither W nor X performs in any show in which Y doesn't perform.

original diagram: _____ ⟶ _____

contrapositive: _____ ⟶ _____

25. Every time A is displayed first, B is also included in the display.

original diagram: _____ ⟶ _____

contrapositive: _____ ⟶ _____

Basic Linear Games Rule Diagramming Drill

In the space provided, supply the best symbolic representation (if any) of each of the following rules. If applicable, show any corresponding implications (Not Laws, dual-options, etc.) on the linear diagram provided. Assume a one-to-one relationship for each problem, with no ties possible. *Answers on page 130*

1. G is recorded earlier than H and J.

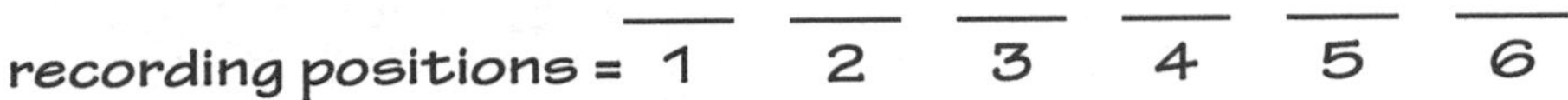

2. Exactly one day separates the interviews of Y and Z.

days = 1 2 3 4 5 6

3. C must sit three chairs behind D, and E must sit one chair before C.

chairs = 1 2 3 4 5 6

4. If S speaks, S speaks the day before T.

days = 1 2 3 4 5 6

5. The factory that is inspected second is also inspected first.

inspections = 1 2 3 4 5 6

Basic Linear Games Rule Diagramming Drill

6. If J performs, then K performs earlier than L.

performances = ___ 1 ___ 2 ___ 3 ___ 4 ___ 5 ___ 6

7. R's sole trip will occur between S's two trips.

trips = ___ 1 ___ 2 ___ 3 ___ 4 ___ 5 ___ 6

8. A sits in either the first or the last seat.

seats = ___ 1 ___ 2 ___ 3 ___ 4 ___ 5 ___ 6

9. Y is inspected after X is inspected but before Z is inspected.

inspections = ___ 1 ___ 2 ___ 3 ___ 4 ___ 5 ___ 6

10. M and T are not performed on consecutive days.

days = ___ 1 ___ 2 ___ 3 ___ 4 ___ 5 ___ 6

11. L is seated after N is seated.

seating order = ___ 1 ___ 2 ___ 3 ___ 4 ___ 5 ___ 6

Basic Linear Games Rule Diagramming Drill

12. Tan receives a higher score in Diving than in Gymnastics.

scores (lowest first) = 1 2 3 4 5 6

13. Priya is not faster than Rajit.

speed (fastest first) = 1 2 3 4 5 6

14. Gina is not selected first or last.

selection order = 1 2 3 4 5 6

15. F does not sit in an even-numbered chair.

chairs = 1 2 3 4 5 6

16. Either T or H has appointment 4.

appointments = 1 2 3 4 5 6

17. Lopez's visit is either on day 1 or day 6.

days = 1 2 3 4 5 6

Basic Linear Games Rule Diagramming Drill

18. P is seated immediately beside U, and also immediately beside O.

seats = ___ ___ ___ ___ ___ ___
1 2 3 4 5 6

19. If G is scheduled for Tuesday, Y is scheduled for Friday.

days = ___ ___ ___ ___ ___ ___
M Tu W Th F S

20. Cheese and Butter are not stocked on adjacent aisles.

aisles = ___ ___ ___ ___ ___ ___
1 2 3 4 5 6

21. The Harmons live next to the Pratts.

houses = ___ ___ ___ ___ ___ ___
1 2 3 4 5 6

22. The film *Tropos* is played either two or three days after the film *Exodus*.

days = ___ ___ ___ ___ ___ ___
1 2 3 4 5 6

Basic Linear Games Rule Diagramming Drill

23. Exactly three days separate Graham's appointment from Juarez's appointment.

days = M Tu W Th F S

24. If the site in London is inspected fifth, then the sites in London and Madrid cannot be inspected consecutively.

inspections = 1 2 3 4 5 6

25. U and V are both assigned either higher-numbered seats than T, or else they are both assigned lower-numbered seats than T.

seats = 1 2 3 4 5 6

26. If Gomez's visit is on Wednesday, then Park's visit must occur earlier in the week than Gomez's visit.

days = M Tu W Th F S

27. Competitors R and T place ahead of competitor M, and competitor M places ahead of competitors C and D.

order = 1 2 3 4 5 6

Basic Linear Games Rule Diagramming Drill

28. Neither P nor O is seated immediately beside S.

seats = ___ ___ ___ ___ ___ ___
1 2 3 4 5 6

29. If Chemistry is the second lecture scheduled, then the two lectures immediately following Chemistry must be Biology and Economics, not necessarily in that order.

lectures = ___ ___ ___ ___ ___ ___
1 2 3 4 5 6

30. Francois is assigned to run in the only lane between the lanes to which Javier and Natalia are assigned.

lanes = ___ ___ ___ ___ ___ ___
1 2 3 4 5 6

Question Stem Classification Drill

For each of the following items, classify the question stem as Global or Local, and then identify the truth characteristic of the correct answer and then the truth characteristic of the four incorrect answers. Also note any additional characteristics of the question stem, and remember to always convert false into true. *Answers on page 145*

Example:

Which one of the following must be true?

Answer:

Classification: Global, Must Be True
Four Incorrect Answers: Not Necessarily True

---

1. If L is the third car sold, then which one of the following could be true?

   Classification:

   ____

   Four Incorrect Answers:

   ____

2. Which one of the following could be false?

   Classification:

   ____

   Four Incorrect Answers:

   ____

3. Which one of the following is a list of all the musicians who could be in the band at any particular time?

   Classification:

   ____

   Four Incorrect Answers:

   ____

4. If more green shoes than yellow shoes are selected, then which one of the following cannot be true?

   Classification:

   ____

   Four Incorrect Answers:

   ____

Question Stem Classification Drill

5. If K is displayed fifth, then each of the following could be true EXCEPT:

   Classification:

   ____

   Four Incorrect Answers:

   ____

6. If T and R each received a rating of "excellent," then which one of the following cannot be false?

   Classification:

   ____

   Four Incorrect Answers:

   ____

7. Each of the following must be false EXCEPT:

   Classification:

   ____

   Four Incorrect Answers:

   ____

8. What is the minimum number of animals that could be in the barn at any given time?

   Classification:

   ____

   Four Incorrect Answers:

   ____

9. Suppose that the condition requiring W to perform earlier than Y is replaced by a new condition requiring that Y performs earlier than W. If all of the other original conditions remain in effect, which one of the following cannot occur?

   Classification:

   ____

   Four Incorrect Answers:

   ____

10. There is only one acceptable group of five speakers that can be selected if which one of the following pairs of speakers is selected?

    Classification:

    ____

    Four Incorrect Answers:

    ____

Question Stem Classification Drill

11. Which one of the following could be a list of the homes in the order of their scheduled inspections, from day 1 through day 7?

    Classification:

    ____

    Four Incorrect Answers:

    ____

12. If the fifth stone is a sapphire, then each of the following must be true EXCEPT:

    Classification:

    ____

    Four Incorrect Answers:

    ____

13. Which one of the following must be false?

    Classification:

    ____

    Four Incorrect Answers:

    ____

14. Each of the following is a day that must include an advanced session EXCEPT:

    Classification:

    ____

    Four Incorrect Answers:

    ____

15. Tennis can be scheduled for any day EXCEPT:

    Classification:

    ____

    Four Incorrect Answers:

    ____

16. If T lives on the fifth floor and O lives on the first floor, then which one of the following can be true?

    Classification:

    ____

    Four Incorrect Answers:

    ____

Question Stem Classification Drill

17. If P performs immediately before R, then each of the following must be true EXCEPT:

Classification:

____

Four Incorrect Answers:

____

18. If Felicia does not visit the same store on any two consecutive days, then which one of the following cannot be false?

Classification:

____

Four Incorrect Answers:

____

19. Each of the following could be false EXCEPT:

Classification:

____

Four Incorrect Answers:

____

20. Which one of the following CANNOT be the complete list of records sold at Daulton's?

Classification:

____

Four Incorrect Answers:

____

21. If three of the trucks are red, then each of the following could be the truck that arrives fourth EXCEPT:

Classification:

____

Four Incorrect Answers:

____

22. Which one of the following CANNOT be the songs scheduled for the second, third, and fourth performances, listed in that order?

Classification:

____

Four Incorrect Answers:

____

Question Stem Classification Drill

23. If T is not paired with L, then exactly how many sessions are there any one of which could be last?

    Classification:

    ____

    Four Incorrect Answers:

    ____

24. The question of which judges will be chosen to preside over the competition and in what order they will vote can be completely resolved if which one of the following is true?

    Classification:

    ____

    Four Incorrect Answers:

    ____

25. Which one of the following, if substituted for the condition that Raul cannot be selected third, would have the same effect in determining the order of the selections?

    Classification:

    ____

    Four Incorrect Answers:

    ____

Basic Linear Setup Practice Drill

Each of the following items presents a scenario and corresponding rules similar to those found in actual Logic Games. Using the space provided, diagram the setup and include a representation of all sequences, blocks, not-blocks, and Not Laws™. Occasionally, a problem will contain a corresponding question. Use your knowledge of the rules and the setup to answer the question. After you complete *each* item, check your work against the diagram in the answer key, and carefully read the comments concerning each diagram. *Answers on page 151*

1. A manager must schedule six employees—Kwame, Lars, Marina, Noriko, Oliver, and Paulo—to work during a single workweek, Monday through Saturday. Each employee must work on exactly one day, and no two employees can work on the same day. The schedule must observe the following constraints:

   If Noriko works on Tuesday, then Marina works on Saturday.
   Either Oliver or Paulo works on Wednesday.
   Kwame works on Monday or else on Saturday.

Basic Linear Setup Practice Drill

2. Five birds—a parrot, a quail, a raven, a sparrow, and a thrush—are being held in five different cages, numbered 1 through 5. Each cage holds exactly one bird in accordance with the following conditions:

   The raven is held in the second cage.

   There is exactly one cage between the cage holding the parrot and the cage holding the quail.

   Question 2.1. Which one of the following must be true?

   (A) Either P or Q is held in the first cage.
   (B) Either S or T is held in the first cage.
   (C) Either S or T is held in the fourth cage.
   (D) Either P or Q is held in the fifth cage.
   (E) Either S or T is held in the fifth cage.

3. Six speakers—B, C, D, F, G, and H—are scheduled to speak at a political rally. Each speaker will speak exactly once, and no two speakers will speak at the same time. The schedule must satisfy the following requirements:

   C speaks immediately after B.

   F must be the second speaker.

   B speaks at some time before D.

Basic Linear Setup Practice Drill

4. An opening act is selecting the songs for an evening's concert. Seven songs—G, H, J, K, N, O, and P—will be played one after another, not necessarily in that order. Each song will be played exactly once, according to the following conditions:

   G must be played exactly three songs before K.
   The fourth song played is either N or O.
   H must be played immediately before J.

5. A building manager must assign seven companies—Q, R, S, T, W, X, and Y—to seven different floors of the building—floors 1, 2, 3, 4, 5, 6, and 7. The assignments must comply with the following restrictions:

   Q must be assigned to the floor directly above R.
   S must be assigned to floor 2.
   X must be assigned to the floor directly below W.
   T must be assigned to floor 5.

Question 5.1. Each one of the following cannot be true EXCEPT:

(A) R is assigned to the floor directly below T.
(B) S is assigned to the floor directly below Q.
(C) R is assigned to the floor directly above W.
(D) T is assigned to the floor directly below R.
(E) Y is assigned to the floor directly above S.

Basic Linear Setup Practice Drill

6. Each of six tennis players—Gemma, Hiroko, Jun, Kurt, Lenisha, and Mahita—is assigned to exactly one of seven tennis courts in preparation for a tournament. The courts are consecutively numbered 1 through 7, and each court is assigned no more than one player. Court assignments must meet the following requirements:

   Kurt is assigned to a lower-numbered court than the court to which Hiroko is assigned.

   Courts 1, 2, and 3 must each be assigned exactly one player.

   Lenisha and Mahita must be assigned to higher-numbered courts than the court to which Hiroko is assigned.

   Jun cannot be assigned to court 1, 3, or 5.

7. There are exactly seven houses on a street, numbered 1 through 7. Each house is occupied by exactly one of seven families: the Pearsons, the Quarles, the Rodriguezes, the Sesays, the Tangs, the Valerios, and the Zolkins. All the houses are on the same side of the street, which runs from west to east. House 1 is the westernmost house. The following restrictions apply:

   Either the Quarles or the Rodriguezes live in House 4.

   The Rodriguezes and the Tangs do not live in consecutively numbered houses.

   The Quarles live to the west of the Tangs.

PRACTICE DRILLS

Basic Linear Setup Practice Drill

8. A researcher must test exactly eight products—B, C, D, F, G, H, J, and K—one product at a time, not necessarily in that order. The tests must be made in accordance with the following conditions:

    K is tested exactly two products before F is tested.
    Either J or K must be tested fourth.
    Either F or G must be tested sixth.
    Only if D is tested first is J tested fourth.

Advanced Linear Rule Diagramming Drill

In the space provided, supply the best symbolic representation (if any) of each of the following rules. If applicable, show any corresponding implications (Not Laws, dual-options, etc.) on the linear diagram provided. Assume a one-to-one relationship for each problem, with no ties possible, and assume that each variable is used in the game. *Answers on page 162*

1. Both green vehicles are inspected before the Ford car.

colors = ___ ___ ___ ___ ___ ___

cars = ___ ___ ___ ___ ___ ___

1 2 3 4 5 6

2. Martina reviews the Thai restaurant, which is reviewed immediately after the French restaurant.

cuisine = ___ ___ ___ ___ ___ ___

reviewer = ___ ___ ___ ___ ___ ___

1 2 3 4 5 6

3. An activity is assigned to each time period, and the activity selected for the afternoon of day 3 must be the same as the activity selected for the morning of day 4.

afternoon = ___ ___ ___ ___ ___ ___

morning = ___ ___ ___ ___ ___ ___

1 2 3 4 5 6

Advanced Linear Rule Diagramming Drill

4. Kim cannot compete in the morning sessions, and Rosen cannot compete in the afternoon sessions.

afternoon = ___ ___ ___ ___ ___ ___

morning = ___ ___ ___ ___ ___ ___

1 2 3 4 5 6

5. The Great Dane dog is shown before the Siamese cat, which is shown before the Calico cat.

dogs = ___ ___ ___ ___ ___ ___

cats = ___ ___ ___ ___ ___ ___

1 2 3 4 5 6

Advanced Linear Setup Practice Drill

Each of the following items presents an Advanced Linear game scenario. Using the space provided, diagram the game. Occasionally, a problem will contain a corresponding rule. Use your knowledge of rule representation to properly display each rule. *Answers on page 165*

1. A bicycle manufacturer produces six bike models—T, U, W, X, Y, and Z—in three different colors—black, red, and silver. Each bike is produced at a different time, and each bike is exactly one color. The production adheres to the following conditions:

   The only silver bike is produced immediately before the only red bike.
   The fourth bike produced is X or Y.
   Model W is silver.
   The second and fourth bikes are black.

2. K, L, N, O, P, R, and S are the only runners in a race. Four of the runners are male, and three are female. Each runner finishes the race, and no two runners finish at the same time. The following restrictions apply:

   P finishes immediately ahead of S.
   Either L or N finishes fourth.
   S is female.
   No two male runners finish in consecutive positions.

Advanced Linear Setup Practice Drill

3. A lawyer schedules the depositions of ten individuals—A, B, C, D, F, G, H, J, K, and L—over the course of five consecutive weekdays, Monday through Friday. There are exactly two depositions each day—one in the morning, and one in the afternoon. Each individual is deposed exactly once in accordance with the following conditions:

    Neither A nor B can be deposed in the afternoon.
    H must be deposed before K is deposed.
    D cannot be deposed on Monday afternoon.
    K and L must be deposed on consecutive mornings, with K deposed before L.
    H is deposed on the afternoon of the day immediately following G's morning deposition.

4. A design company displays artworks in two office buildings--A and B, each of which has six floors, numbered 1 through 6. Each artwork is made of glass, plaster, or steel, and each floor is used to display exactly one artwork. The following conditions govern the display:

    No two artworks made of the same type of material as each other can be displayed on identically numbered floors.
    The artwork on Floor 3 of Building A is identical to the artwork on Floor 4 of Building B.
    The artwork on Floor 6 of Building A is not made of plaster.
    No steel artwork can be displayed on a floor immediately above, or immediately below, a floor on which a glass artwork is displayed.

Advanced Linear Setup Practice Drill

5. A total of nine books occupies three shelves, with three books on each shelf. Three of the books are anthologies—M, N, and O. Three others are biographies—I, J, and K. The remaining three are children's books—F, G, and H. The books' arrangement is consistent with the following:
   No two biographies are on the same shelf.
   M and K are both on the same shelf.
   K is two shelves above F.

6. Four athletes—Don, Eddie, Frank, and George—compete in three separate events—Hammer Throw, Ice Ballet, and Javelin. The athletes are ranked from first through fourth based on the results. The following information is all that is known about the rankings:
   Don's rank in Javelin is lower than his rank in Ice Ballet.
   Frank ranks third in the Hammer Throw.
   Eddie ranks higher than George in all three events.

Advanced Linear Setup Practice Drill

7. During one week, from Monday through Thursday, a health inspector must inspect exactly eight restaurants—Q, R, S, T, U, V, W, and X. An inspection requires either an entire morning or an entire afternoon. No more than two restaurants can be inspected in a single day. The inspections for the week are scheduled in accordance with the following conditions:

   Q must be inspected in the morning, on the same day that X is inspected.
   S must be inspected in the afternoon.
   T must be inspected in the morning.

8. A movie Cineplex with four theaters—1, 2, 3, and 4—must screen eight films—O, P, Q, R, S, T, U, and V. Each theater screens exactly two films, and each film is screened in exactly one theater. The following conditions apply:

   Q is screened in Theater 2.
   O and P are screened in the same theater as each other.
   S is screened in a higher-numbered theater than T.

Advanced Linear Setup Practice Drill

9. An auto magazine ranks five cars—A, B, C, D, and E—from first to fifth in three categories—mileage, overall quality, and performance. The cars are ranked in accordance with the following conditions:

   All five cars are ranked in each category.

   In mileage, A is ranked third and B is ranked fourth.

   In performance, D is ranked second and E is ranked fifth.

   In overall quality, B is ranked higher than A.

10. Each of six passengers—Q, R, S, T, U, and V—will be assigned to exactly one of six airplane seats in two rows, O and P. There are three seats, numbered from 1 through 3, in each row. Only seats in the same row as each other are immediately beside each other, and consecutively numbered seats within each row are adjacent. Seat assignments must meet the following conditions:

    Q's seat is P3.

    R's seat is O2.

    S's seat is either directly in front of, or directly behind, T's seat.

Grouping Games—Unified Grouping Theory Classification Drill

Each of the following items provides a Grouping game scenario. In the space provided, supply the most accurate classification of the game using the categories defined by the Unified Grouping Theory (Defined/Partially Defined/Undefined, Fixed/Moving, Balanced/Unbalanced, Overloaded/Underfunded). *Answers on page 174*

1. A student must select college courses from a group of nine possible courses.

   Classification:

   ____

2. Nine research grants are allocated to three different universities—university H, university S, and university Y. Each university receives exactly three grants, and each grant is given to only one university.

   Classification:

   ____

3. Eight scientists attending a conference are assigned to two panels—the Policy Panel and the Research Panel. Each panel includes at least three members, and no scientist is assigned to more than one panel.

   Classification:

   ____

4. The members of four committees will be selected from among seven candidates. Each committee must select exactly two members, and each candidate must be selected for membership on at least one committee.

   Classification:

   ____

5. Exactly six of nine reviewers are selected to review four restaurants. Each selected reviewer must review exactly one restaurant, and each restaurant must be reviewed by at least one reviewer.

   Classification:

   ____

6. A dinner reservation for at least four people will be made at a local restaurant. The diners will be selected from a group of ten people.

   Classification:

   ____

7. Exactly six of eight weight lifters are assigned to two weight lifting teams of three weight lifters each.

   Classification:

   ____

8. A traveler must visit at least one of the following seven countries over the course of a year: Australia, Denmark, Guatemala, Kenya, Morocco, Thailand, and Venezuela.

   Classification:

   ____

Grouping Games—Unified Grouping Theory Classification Drill

9. A manager must select exactly five individual employees to attend a skills workshop. The employees under consideration are B, D, F, G, H, K, and L.

   Classification:

   ____

10. Antonio and Jun each take at least two art classes at a local art museum that offers only five types of art classes: contemporary, impressionism, modern, neoclassic, and realism.

   Classification:

   ____

11. A moving company employs eight workers: M, O, P, R, S, T, V, and X. Exactly five of the eight workers are selected to work three different jobs—jobs 1, 2, and 3. Each job is assigned at least one worker, and no worker is assigned to more than one job.

   Classification:

   ____

12. Five pilots—Bae, Chisholm, Dayani, Fang, and Gutierrez—are assigned to four separate flights. Each flight must be assigned exactly two pilots, and each pilot must be assigned to at least one flight.

   Classification:

   ____

13. A dog walker must walk eight dogs—F, G, H, J, K, L, M, and P—in three separate groups. Each group must be assigned at least two dogs.

   Classification:

   ____

14. A gardener is planting flowers in three separate flower beds. The gardener will use exactly six types of flowers: asters, daffodils, lilies, pansies, roses, and tulips. Each flower type will be used at least once, and each flower bed will contain at least three different types of flowers.

   Classification:

   ____

15. Four products—M, P, Q, and R—are each featured in a local store over a period of five weeks. Each product is featured on exactly two of the weeks, and each week features at least one, but no more than four, products.

   Classification:

   ____

16. A corporate retreat features confidence-building exercises. Six employees—Fung, Jackson, Narvaez, Patterson, Sandeep, and Williams—complete each exercise either alone or in groups with one another.

   Classification:

   ____

Grouping Games—Unified Grouping Theory Classification Drill

17. Ten rowers compete for membership on one of two rowing teams--Team A and Team B. Each team consists of exactly four members, and no rower can be a member of more than one team.

    Classification:

    ____

18. Each of seven students—Khan, Martin, Paulo, Qadira, Sara, Takeshi, and Uchenna—is assigned exactly one of two speech topics—freedom and liberty. Each speech topic is assigned to at least three students.

    Classification:

    ____

Grouping Games Rule Diagramming Drill

In the space provided, supply the best symbolic representation (if any) of each of the following rules. If applicable, show any corresponding implications on the diagram provided. *Answers on page 180*

1. Of the three applicants W, X, and Y, exactly two are interviewed.

2. W and Y cannot be selected together.

3. K and L cannot be assigned to the same group, and every salesperson is assigned to at least one of the two groups.

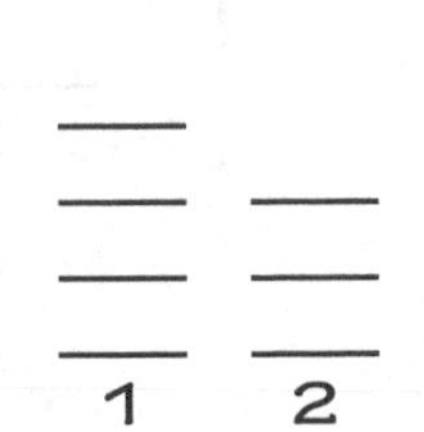

Grouping Games Rule Diagramming Drill

4. If D is assigned to group 2, then E is assigned to group 2.

5. If R is not selected, then S must be selected.

6. Either P or Q, but not both, must be selected.

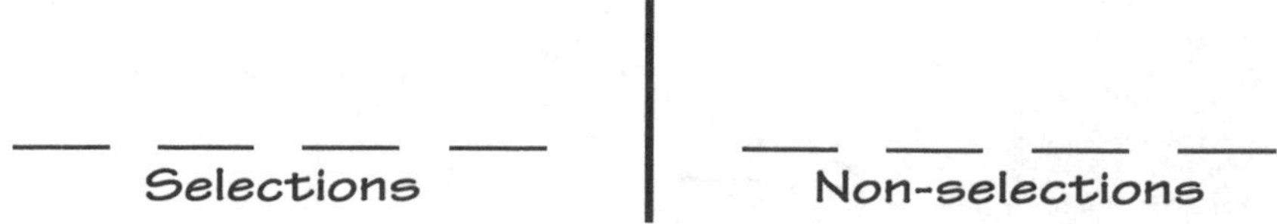

Grouping Games Rule Diagramming Drill

7. Group 2 and group 3 do not have any members in common.

8. R and S cannot be assigned to the same group as each other.

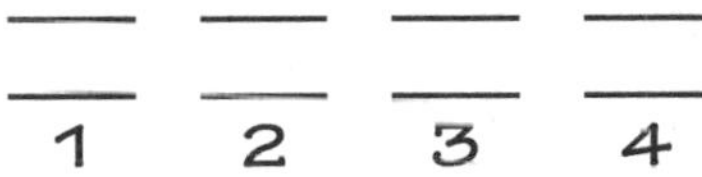

9. O is not assigned to group 2 or group 3, and every player is assigned to exactly one of the groups.

Grouping Games Rule Diagramming Drill

10. Neither F nor G works in Areas 2 or 3.

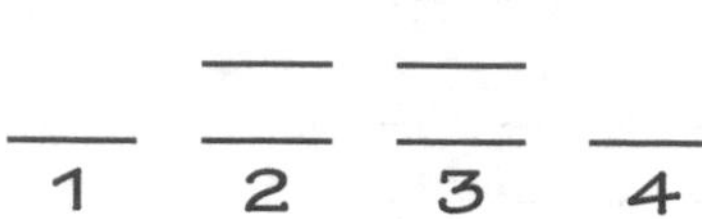

11. If M is hired, then O must be hired.

12. If Z is assigned, then Q and U must be assigned.

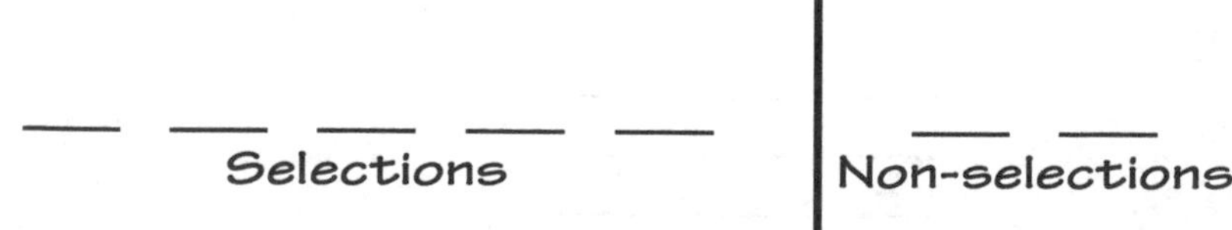

Grouping Setup Practice Drill

Each of the following items presents a scenario and corresponding rules similar to those found in actual Logic Games. Using the space provided, diagram the setup and include a representation of all rules and inferences. After you complete *each* item, check your work against the diagram in the answer key, and carefully read the comments concerning each diagram. *Answers on page 187*

1. Six waiters—S, T W, X, Y, and Z—are assigned in pairs to wait on four tables—tables A, B, C, and D. The assignment of the waiters will meet the following conditions:

   Each waiter is assigned to at least one table.
   S is not assigned to table A.
   W is assigned to table B only if Y is assigned to table D.
   S and T are both assigned to the same table.

2. Seven horses—A, B, C, D, F, G, and H—are in a horse paddock at various times. The horses are in the paddock in a manner consistent with the following conditions:

   If C is in the paddock, then D is not in the paddock.
   Every time F is in the paddock, C is in the paddock.
   D is in the paddock only when G is in the paddock.
   If A is not in the paddock, then B is in the paddock.

Grouping Setup Practice Drill

3. At a music festival, eight bands—Cage, Deadbolt, Fluster, Gravel, Hammer, Irony, Kernel, and Lunar—are assigned to two stages—the Main Stage and the Side Stage. Each band must be assigned to a single stage. The assignments are made in accordance with the following conditions:

   At least four bands are assigned to the Main stage, and at least three bands are assigned to the Side Stage.

   Kernel cannot be assigned to the Side Stage unless Deadbolt is assigned to the Main Stage.

   Fluster and Gravel are not assigned to the same stage.

4. Eight senators—J, K, L, M, O, P, Q, and R—serve on three subcommittees—Defense, Finance, and Policy. Each subcommittee has three members, except for the Finance subcommittee, which has two members. The following is known about the three subcommittees:

   P serves on the Defense subcommittee.

   Q serves on the Finance subcommittee.

   K and L serve on the same subcommittee.

   J serves on a subcommittee if and only if M serves on that subcommittee.

Grouping Setup Practice Drill

5. A window display consists of exactly three flowerpots. Each flowerpot contains at least three of the following six types of houseplants: forsythia, geranium, hibiscus, iris, jasmine, and kalanchoe. Each houseplant must be planted in at least one flowerpot, and no houseplant can be planted in all three flowerpots. The following conditions hold:

    Exactly two of the flowerpots contain hibiscuses.
    If a flowerpot contains geraniums, then that flowerpot contains forsythias.
    If a flowerpot contains irises, then that flowerpot contains neither jasmines nor kalanchoes.
    If a flowerpot contains no geraniums, then that flowerpot contains both jasmines and kalanchoes.

Question 5.1. Which one of the following CANNOT be the complete list of houseplants in one of the flowerpots?

(A) forsythia, geranium, iris
(B) hibiscus, jasmine, kalanchoe
(C) forsythia, hibiscus, iris
(D) forsythia, geranium, jasmine, kalanchoe
(E) forsythia, geranium, hibiscus, iris

Question 5.2. Which one of the following must be the complete list of houseplants in one of the flowerpots?

(A) hibiscus, jasmine, kalanchoe
(B) forsythia, geranium, iris
(C) forsythia, geranium, hibiscus
(D) forsythia, jasmine, kalanchoe
(E) hibiscus, iris, kalanchoe

Grouping Setup Practice Drill

Question 5.3. If each flowerpot contains exactly three houseplants, then which one of the following must be true?

(A) Exactly one of the flowerpots contains forsythias.
(B) Exactly one of the flowerpots contains geraniums.
(C) Exactly one of the flowerpots contains irises.
(D) Exactly one of the flowerpots contains jasmines.
(E) Exactly one of the flowerpots contains kalanchoes.

Question 5.4. Which one of the following lists the minimum and maximum possible numbers, respectively, of different houseplants in one of the flowerpots?

(A) 3, 3
(B) 3, 4
(C) 3, 5
(D) 4, 4
(E) 4, 5

Question 5.5. If two of the flowerpots contain exactly the same houseplants as each other, then which one of the following could be false?

(A) Exactly one of the flowerpots contains forsythias.
(B) Exactly one of the flowerpots contains geraniums.
(C) Exactly two of the flowerpots contain irises.
(D) Exactly two of the flowerpots contain jasmines.
(E) Exactly two of the flowerpots contain kalanchoes.

Question 5.6. If the complete list of houseplants in one of the flowerpots is forsythias, jasmines, and kalanchoes, then which one of the following houseplants CANNOT be planted in more than one of the flowerpots?

(A) forsythia
(B) geranium
(C) hibiscus
(D) jasmine
(E) kalanchoe

Grouping/Linear Combination Setup Practice Drill

Each of the following items presents a scenario and corresponding rules similar to those found in actual Logic Games. Using the space provided, diagram the setup and include a representation of all rules and inferences. Each problem contains a corresponding question or questions. Use your knowledge of the rules and the setup to answer the question(s). After you complete *each* item, check your work against the diagram in the answer key, and carefully read the comments concerning each diagram. *Answers on page 199*

1. During a five week period, an elementary school teacher will select exactly five students from among a group of eight to do class presentations. Exactly one student will be selected from among two first grade students—Alan and Bobby; two students will be selected from among three second graders—Charlotte, Debra, and Edward; and two students will be selected from among three third graders: Frankie, Greg, and Hank. The presentations are given in accordance with the following conditions:

   The student chosen from the first grade class will be the first to present.
   If Alan is selected, then Debra must also be selected.
   If Debra is selected, then her presentation is scheduled for the third week.
   If Edward is selected, then Frankie and Greg must both be selected, and both must present before Edward.
   Alan is selected only if Frankie is selected.

<u>Question 1.1</u>. If neither Alan nor Charlotte is selected, which one of the following could be true?

(A) Bobby is not selected to give the first presentation.
(B) Hank is selected to give the second presentation
(C) Debra is not selected to give the third presentation.
(D) Frankie is selected to give the fourth presentation.
(E) Edward is not selected to give the fifth presentation.

<u>Question 1.2</u>. If both Frankie and Debra are selected, which one of the following CANNOT be true?

(A) Alan is selected to give the first presentation.
(B) Bobby is selected to give the first presentation.
(C) Neither Charlotte nor Greg is selected to give a presentation.
(D) Alan is not selected to give a presentation.
(E) Neither Hank nor Edward is selected to give a presentation.

Grouping/Linear Combination Setup Practice Drill

2. In a dance competition, four co-ed teams (each comprised of one man and one woman) will be selected to compete, one team at a time. The players are paired at random, from among six women—I, J, K, L, M, N—and six men—O, P, Q, R, S, and T. The following is known about the day's selections:

   O is part of the team that dances first.
   M is part of the team that dances third.
   N is not selected unless P is selected.
   If R is selected, N and J are also selected, and either N or J, but not both, must precede R.
   S is selected if and only if Q is selected.

<u>Question 2.1</u>. If P and T are both selected to dance in the competition, which one of the following could be true?

(A) R is not selected to dance in the competition.
(B) S is selected to dance in the competition.
(C) J is not selected to dance in the competition.
(D) Q is selected to dance in the competition.
(E) L is not selected to dance in the competition.

<u>Question 2.2</u>. Which one of the following is an acceptable selection and order of the couples chosen to dance in the competition?

(A) O and N; R and I; T and M; S and J
(B) O and J; P and N; R and M; T and K
(C) O and L; S and N; P and M; Q and J
(D) P and J; O and K; R and M; T and N
(E) O and J; R and L, P and N; T and I

Grouping/Linear Combination Setup Practice Drill

3. On Saturday evening, six aircraft must land at Caledonia International Airport. Of the aircraft, two are short-haul, two are medium-haul, and two are long-haul. Each aircraft must use exactly one of two runways for landing: X and Y. Only one aircraft lands at a time.

   No short-haul aircraft lands on the same runway as any long-haul aircraft.

   No two medium-haul aircraft land consecutively on the same runway.

   No short-haul aircraft lands on runway X until at least one medium-haul aircraft lands on runway X.

   No medium-haul aircraft lands on runway Y until at least one long-haul aircraft lands on runway Y.

Question 3.1. Which one of the following could be a complete and accurate list of aircraft landing on runway X, listed in the order in which they land:

(A) short-haul, short-haul
(B) medium-haul, medium-haul, short-haul, short-haul
(C) medium-haul, long-haul, long-haul
(D) long-haul, medium-haul, long-haul
(E) medium-haul, long-haul, long-haul, medium-haul

Question 3.2. Which one of the following must be false?

(A) The number of aircraft landing on runway X is greater than the number of aircraft landing on runway Y.
(B) The number of aircraft landing on runway Y is greater than the number of aircraft landing on runway X.
(C) The number of aircraft landing on runway X is equal to the number of aircraft landing on runway Y.
(D) At least two aircraft land on runway X.
(E) At least two aircraft land on runway Y.

Question 3.3. If no two medium-haul aircraft land on the same runway, then each one of the following must be true, EXCEPT:

(A) A medium-haul aircraft lands second on runway Y.
(B) A medium-haul aircraft lands first on runway X.
(C) A short-haul aircraft lands second on runway X.
(D) A short-haul aircraft lands third on runway X.
(E) A long-haul aircraft lands first on runway Y.

Question 3.4. If a long-haul aircraft lands first on runway X, then which one of the following could be false?

(A) A short-haul aircraft lands first on runway Y.
(B) A short-haul aircraft lands last on runway Y.
(C) A medium-haul aircraft lands third on runway X.
(D) Exactly four aircraft land on runway X.
(E) Exactly two aircraft land on runway Y.

Pure Sequencing Diagramming Drill

Use the Pure Sequencing Diagramming Guidelines from the *LSAT Logic Games Bible* to set up sequencing chains for each of the following items. The rules may yield more than one chain per item, and ties are possible for the purposes of this drill. Use your diagram(s) to answer the corresponding questions for each item. For the questions, assume that the only variables in the game are the ones explicitly named in the rules. *Answers on page 215*

1. Rules: L is taller than M.
N is shorter than M.
L is shorter than J and K.
O is taller than N.

Question 1.1. Which one of the following could accurately list the three tallest variables, in order from first to third tallest?

(A) J, L, M
(B) J, L, O
(C) J, K, M
(D) K, O, J
(E) K, L, O

Pure Sequencing Diagramming Drill

2. Rules: T is larger than W.
W is smaller than V.
T is not larger than S.
X is larger than W.
X is larger than Y.

A. Which variables in the chain could be largest?

B. Which variables in the chain could be smallest?

3. Rules: B and D are heavier than E.
J is lighter than B.
C is heavier than D.
B is lighter than A.
E is heavier than F and H.
K is heavier than H.
G is lighter than F.

A. Which variables in the chain could be heaviest?

B. Which variables in the chain could be lightest?

Pure Sequencing Diagramming Drill

4. Rules: C is shorter than A and B.
B and D are taller than E.
F is taller than A.

Question 4.1 Which one of the following could be an accurate list of the two shortest variables in a lineup of all six variables?

(A) A, E
(B) B, C
(C) B, E
(D) C, D
(E) D, E

Pure Sequencing Diagramming Drill

5. Rules: R is faster than S.
U is slower than T.
Q is faster than R and T.
W is faster than R.
T is slower than X.
P is faster than Q.

Question 5.1 Which one of the following must be false?

(A) S is sixth fastest.
(B) W is sixth fastest.
(C) X is sixth fastest.
(D) Q is fifth fastest.
(E) P is third fastest.

Pure Sequencing Diagramming Drill

6. Rules: P and Q are both lower-rated than M.
Z is higher-rated than Y.
X is lower-rated than W.
Y is higher-rated than X.

A. Which of the variables could be the highest-rated?

B. Which of the variables could be the lowest-rated?

C. What is the highest-rated position that Y could occupy? What is the lowest-rated position that Y could occupy?

7. Rules: J is more popular than L, and L is more popular than P.
E and O are both less popular than D.
J is less popular than E and O.

A. Which of the variables in the chain could be most popular?

B. Which of the variables in the chain could be least popular?

C. How many solutions exist to this game if no ties occur?

Pure Sequencing Diagramming Drill

8. Rules: B arrives earlier than C.
F arrives later than C and E.
D arrives earlier than E.
F arrives earlier than G.
A arrives earlier than B and D.

A. Which of the variables in the chain could arrive earliest?

B. Which of the variables in the chain could arrive latest?

C. Assuming no ties are possible, if B arrives second, what is the earliest that D could arrive?

9. Rules: J is delivered after E.
K is delivered before O.
J is delivered before K.
K is delivered after L.

A. Which of the variables in the chain could be delivered first?

B. Which of the variables in the chain could be delivered last?

C. If E is delivered first, how many solutions exist to this game if no ties occur?

Pure Sequencing Diagramming Drill

10. Rules: T and W sit in the same row.
R sits in a row closer to the stage than T.
Y does not sit in a row closer to the stage than W.
W sits in a row further from the stage than S.
Z can sit in any row.

A. Which of the variables in the chain could sit in the first row?

B. Which of the variables in the chain could sit in the last row?

C. What is the minimum number of rows that must exist in the game?

11. Rules: P is taller than F and G.
C is taller than K.
M is shorter than C but taller than P.

A. Which of the variables in the chain could be tallest?

B. Which of the variables in the chain could be shortest?

C. If G is taller than F, how many solutions exist to this game if no ties occur?

Pure Sequencing Diagramming Drill

12. Rules: B and L are both lighter than G.
L and Y are both lighter than R.

A. Which of the variables in the chain could be heaviest?

B. Which of the variables in the chain could be lightest?

C. What is the heaviest that Y could rank?

13. Rules: F is higher-rated than D, L, and J.
N is higher-rated than D.
G is lower-rated than B and higher-rated than F.

A. Which of the variables in the chain could be the highest-rated?

B. Which of the variables in the chain could be the lowest-rated?

C. If N is the third lowest-rated variable, how many solutions exist to this game if no ties occur?

Pure Sequencing Diagramming Drill

14. Rules: N and S are both smaller than O.
H is larger than R.
L and O are both smaller than R.
E and V are both larger than H.

A. Which of the variables in the chain could be largest?

B. Which of the variables in the chain could be smallest?

C. If L is larger than O, how many of the variables are then limited to a single position in the chain?

15. Rules: T is less popular than X, and W is less popular than Z.
X and Z are both more popular than V.
Y is less popular than W.
Y cannot be the least popular.

A. Which of the variables in the chain could be most popular?

B. Which of the variables in the chain could be least popular?

C. If T and Z have the same level of popularity, then what is the highest popularity rank that V can achieve?

Pure Sequencing Diagramming Drill

16. Rules: W is delivered after V but before T.
O and X are both delivered before V.
R is delivered before T.
S is delivered before T.
No two deliveries occur at the same time.

A. Which of the variables in the chain could be delivered first?

B. Which of the variables in the chain could be delivered last?

C. If S is delivered second and V is delivered fourth, how many solutions exist to this game?

17. Rules: H arrives earlier than N.
D, O, and V arrive earlier than H.
V and R arrive earlier than L.
J arrives earlier than N.

A. Which of the variables in the chain could arrive earliest?

B. Which of the variables in the chain could arrive latest?

C. If L arrives earlier than H, what is the earliest position that H could arrive, assuming no ties occur?

Pure Sequencing Diagramming Drill

18. Rules: X is taller than J and Q.
N is taller than D.
X is shorter than A.
D is shorter than Q.

A. Which of the variables in the chain could be tallest?

B. Which of the variables in the chain could be shortest?

C. If N is shorter than J, how many solutions exist to this game if no ties occur?

Conditional Sequencing Diagramming Drill

Use the Pure Sequencing and Conditional Sequencing Diagramming Guidelines to set up diagrams for each of the following rules. The rules may yield more than one chain per item. Assume no ties are possible. Use the " —— " sign to represent each relationship so that:

Higher		Lower
More	——	Less
Before		After
Earlier		Later

Answers on page 228

1. Rule: If the N train arrives earlier than the Q train, then the R train does not arrive earlier than the Q train.

2. Rule: If Viva is more popular than Splash, then neither Wonk nor Therapy is more popular than Viva.

3. Rule: G is assembled later than both H and I if and only if H and I are both assembled later than J.

Conditional Sequencing Diagramming Drill

4. Rule: If neither Ngu nor Miuccia receives a higher score than Lilly, then both Giacomo and Jordan receive a higher score than Lilly.

5. Rule: Either the Klausen exhibit closes earlier than the Milo exhibit, or the Milo exhibit closes earlier than the Leonardo exhibit, but not both.

6. Rule: Both Cadaques and Girona are visited later than Barcelona, or else Barcelona is visited later than both Cadaques and Girona.

7. Rule: Rodriguez is interviewed earlier than Thompson only if both Sinclair and Velasquez are interviewed later than Thompson.

Conditional Sequencing Diagramming Drill

8. Rule: J cannot be delivered later than K, unless either L or M is delivered later than J.

9. Rule: M is written earlier than each of L and P, or else M is written later than each of L and P.

10. Rule: If J is lower in cost than K, then R is lower in cost than each of S and T; otherwise, R is higher in cost than each of S and T.

Numerical Distribution Identification Drill

Each of the following game scenarios contain rules that lead to one or more numerical distributions. For each problem identify each of the possible fixed or unfixed numerical distributions created by the rules. *Answers on page 235*

1. Eight books are assigned to three students. Each student is assigned at least two books.

2. Ten drinks are served to two bar patrons. Each patron is served at least one drink but no more than seven drinks.

3. Six bones are given to three dogs—a Greyhound, a Mastiff, and a Terrier. Each dog must be given at least one bone, and the Terrier is given exactly one less bone than the Mastiff.

4. Eleven cookies are placed in four jars. Each jar contains at least one cookie but no more than five cookies.

5. Eight tables are assigned to four different servers—servers A, B, C, and D. Each server is assigned at least one table. Server A is assigned exactly twice the number of tables as Server B.

Numerical Distribution Identification Drill

6. Twelve students are assigned to five different floors in a dormitory. At least two students are assigned to each floor.

7. Seven animals are placed into three cages. Each cage contains at most five animals.

8. Thirteen toys are given to four children—W, X, Y, and Z. Each child is given at least two toys, and Y is given exactly three times as many toys as W.

9. Twenty-one pills are placed into six bottles. At least three pills are placed in each bottle.

10. Seven appointments with a doctor are scheduled over four days—Monday, Tuesday, Wednesday, and Thursday. At least one appointment must be scheduled for each day, and there is exactly one more appointment on Wednesday than there is on Thursday.

Numerical Distribution Identification Drill

11. Each of seven lawyers is assigned to represent exactly one of four criminal defendants. Each defendant must be represented by at least one but no more than three of the lawyers.

12. Each of four horses is treated by exactly one of three veterinarians. No veterinarian treats more than three horses.

13. At a historically preserved home with seven rooms, there is exactly one computer terminal in each room. To avoid circuit overload, at most twice as many terminals can be turned on as can be turned off at any given time. At least two terminals must be turned on at any given time.

14. A movie reviewer screens five new releases in a given week, Sunday through Thursday, to prepare for her live radio interview. The reviewer screens at most two new releases on any given day.

15. A baseball card collector is adding fourteen new cards to his collection. Each card features exactly one of four baseball players—Jeter, Lasorda, Mantle, and Robinson, and each player is featured on exactly two, four or six cards. The number of Jeter cards is no less than twice the number of Lasorda cards.

Numerical Distribution Identification Drill

16. A company contracts with homeowners to pave exactly thirteen driveways in a given week, Monday through Sunday. The company must pave at least one but no more than four driveways each day.

17. Each of eight students receives tutoring from a single instructor during a given week, Monday through Friday. The instructor tutors at least one but no more than three students per day.

18. A tennis instructor gives nine balls to two children. Each child is given at least two balls.

19. A jeweler will use exactly five birthstones to create three rings. Each ring will contain exactly three different birthstones, and each birthstone will be used in at least one ring.

20. Each of four fashion designers, Q, R, S and V, will attend at least one of six fashion shows. S attends exactly one show.

Rule Origin Drill Answer Key—page 6

(A) Jin is selected unless Walter is selected.
(B) Jin is selected if and only if Walter is selected.
(C) Jin is selected if Walter is selected.
(D) If Walter is not selected then Jin is not selected.
(E) Either Jin or Walter must be selected.

The correct answer choice is (D). Answer choice (D) provides the contrapositive of the rule diagram, but as with any rule where both terms are negative, you should take the contrapositive and show the rule with both terms positive. Answer choice (B) would be properly diagrammed as J ←→ W, so although it would include the diagram in question, the diagram in question would be only partially correct, and thus (B) is not the correct answer. Answer choices (A) and (E) produce identical diagrams of ~~J~~ ⟶ W, and answer choice (C) produces the Mistaken Reversal of the rule in this problem.

---

2. R
S

(A) Rena is not seated at the same table as Suki.
(B) Rena is seated immediately next to Suki.
(C) Neither Rena nor Suki is selected to attend the dinner.
(D) If Rena is not selected to attend the dinner, then Suki is not selected to attend the dinner.
(E) Rena and Suki are seated at the same table as each other.

The correct answer choice is (A). Answer choice (A) leads to a rule representation that must reflect the fact that R and S cannot be together. In a Grouping game, one method of displaying that situation is through a Not-block. Answer choice (B) would likely produce a rotating horizontal RS block. Answer choice (C) would produce two Not Laws on the dinner group. Answer choice (D) would produce a S ⟶ R diagram. Answer choice (E) would likely produce a positive block.

3. G ←|→ H

(A) Neither Greta nor Harrison speak at the fundraiser.
(B) Greta and Harrison cannot speak in consecutive time slots at the fundraiser.
(C) If Greta speaks at the fundraiser, Harrison cannot speak at the fundraiser.
(D) If Greta does not speak at the fundraiser, Harrison speaks at the fundraiser.
(E) Greta and Harrison cannot speak at any fundraiser with another speaker.

The correct answer choice is (C). The rule representation indicates that G and H cannot be together. Answer choice (C) indicates that if G speaks at the fundraiser, then H does not. Via the contrapositive, if H speaks, then G does not, and so G and H cannot speak at the same fundraiser, which is best represented by the rule diagram in this problem. Answer choice (A) would best be shown by two Not Laws. Answer choice (B) would produce a rotating horizontal Not-block. Answer choice (D) produces a double not-arrow where both terms are negated (the polar opposite of the rule represented here). Answer choice (E) means that G or H must speak alone, which, although it is then true that G and H cannot speak together, would be better represented by a rule indicating that G and H are separately alone.

4.

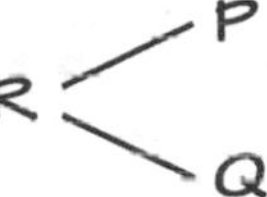

or

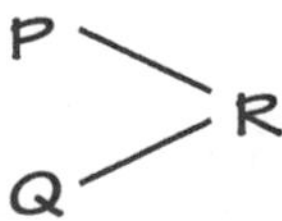

(A) Neither P nor Q can depart earlier than R, unless they both depart earlier than R.
(B) R departs earlier than P or earlier than Q, but not both.
(C) P departs earlier than R if and only if R departs earlier than Q.
(D) Q cannot depart earlier than R unless P departs earlier than R.
(E) P departs later than R only if Q departs later than R.

The correct answer choice is (A). After applying the Unless Equation, the clause modified by the word "unless" becomes the necessary condition (both P and Q depart earlier than R). The remainder must be negated to become sufficient: so, "neither P nor Q" becomes "either P or Q." Consequently, answer choice (A) can be represented as follows:

P — R

or ⟶ P, Q > R

Q — R

By the contrapositive:

R — P

or ⟶ R < P, Q

R — Q

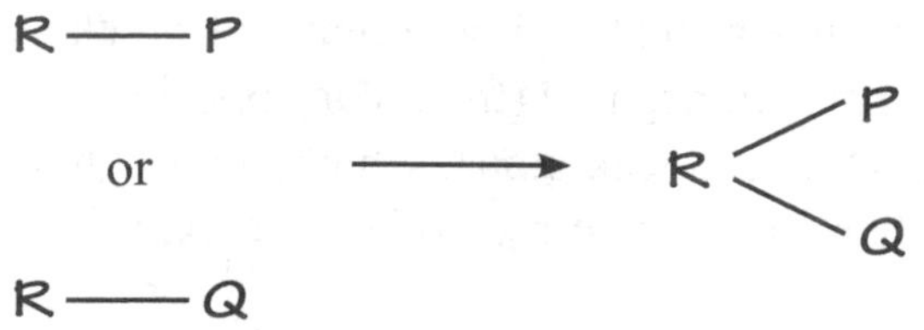

Since either of these sufficient conditions is always enacted, we can infer that there are only two possible sequences for P, Q, and R:

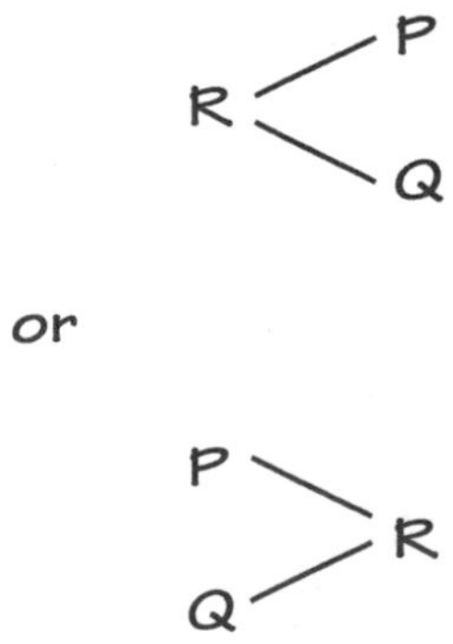

R < P, Q

or

P, Q > R

Answer choices (B) requires R to depart earlier than either P or Q, but not earlier than both. So, we have two possibilities for the order in which P, Q, and R depart, neither of which consistent with our rule diagram:

Rule Origin Drill Answer Key—page 6

Q — R — P

or

P — R — Q

Answer choice (C) can be diagrammed as follows:

(P — R) ←→ (R — Q)

Contrapositive: (Q — R) ←→ (R — P)

Consequently, the rule produces two options identical to those in answer choice (B):

P — R — Q

or

Q — R — P

Answer choices (D) and (E) produce identical diagrams, as described below. Neither answer contains language that produces precisely the dual option in the original problem:

Answer choice (D): (Q — R) ⟶ P, Q > R

contrapositive: (R — P) ⟶ R < P, Q

Answer choice (E): (R — P) ⟶ R < P, Q

contrapositive: (Q — R) ⟶ P, Q > R

Rule Origin Drill Answer Key—page 6

Although the necessary conditions in our diagrams of answer choices (D) and (E) are identical to the original rule diagram, neither answer choice contains a rule requiring that the necessary condition be met at all times. For instance, what if P departed before R? Or R departed before Q? Neither rule tells us what *must* be true in either of these two situations, leaving open the possibility that P, R, and Q form a sequence of P —— R —— Q. Such a sequence is not permitted by the original rule, making both answer choices incorrect.

---

5. | P | Q/R |
|---|---|

(A) Putnam must be seated in a chair adjacent to those of both Quince and Roe.
(B) Putnam must be seated in a chair adjacent to that of either Quince or Roe.
(C) Putnam and Quince must both be seated in chairs adjacent to that of Roe.
(D) Either Quince or Row must be seated immediately to the right of Putnam.
(E) Either Quince or Row must be seated immediately to the left of Putnam.

The correct answer choice is (D). The block representation indicates that Q *or* R is next to, *and behind* P (if Q or R were simply next to P, there would be a rotating block display, either with a circle or with both possible blocks shown). Answer choice (A) places P next to *both* Q and R, creating a QPR or RPQ block. Answer choice (B) places Q or R next to P, but not behind P. Answer choice (C) places P and Q next to R, creating a PRQ or QRP block. Answer choice (E) improperly reverses the order of the variables in the rule diagram.

---

6. M —— N —— O

or

O —— N —— M

Assume no ties are possible.

(A) Either M is taller than N, or else N is taller than M, but not both.
(B) Either N is taller than O, or else N is taller than M, but not both.
(C) Either N is taller than O, or else O is taller than N, but not both.
(D) Either O is taller than M, or else O is taller than N, but not both.
(E) Either M is taller than O, or else M is taller than N, but not both.

The correct answer choice is (B). The wording in the answer choice creates two separate and mutually exclusive chains. Because N is taller than O or M, but not both, when N is taller than one of the two, the other must then be taller than N. This creates two different chains, effectively breaking the game into two directions depending on which scenario applies. Since the two are mutually exclusive, one and only one of the chains is in operation at any given time, hence the "or" between the two sequences.

Answer choice (A) is incorrect because it never addresses O. Answer choice (C) is incorrect because it never addresses M. Answer choice (D) would produce the following diagram:

N —— O —— M
or
M —— O —— N

Answer choice (E) would produce the following diagram:

N —— M —— O
or
O —— M —— N

7. 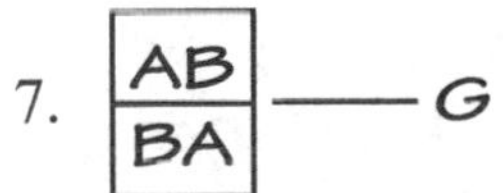

(A) Grace is shorter than both Allison and Beth, whose heights are consecutive.
(B) Beth must be taller than Allison, who must be taller than Grace.
(C) Beth and Allison are the same height, but both are shorter than Grace.
(D) Allison must be taller than both Beth and Grace.
(E) Allison is taller than Beth, who is taller than Grace.

The correct answer choice is (A). The diagram reflects that A and B are consecutive, but that their position relative to each other is unknown. In other words, A and B must be ranked immediately next to each other, but it is not clear whether A is taller than B, or B is taller than A. However, both A and B are taller than G. Answer choice (A) describes this relationship. Although answer choice (A) begins with Grace, the order of presentation of the description in the answer choice has no effect on the relationship given by the rule.

Answer choice (B) produces the diagram:

B —— A —— G

Answer choice (C) produces the diagram:

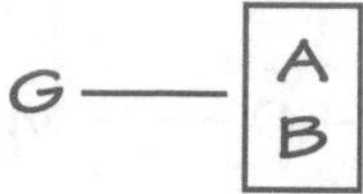

Answer choice (D) produces the diagram:

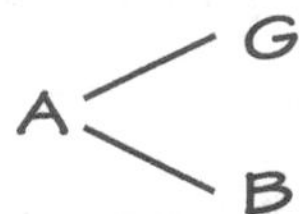

Answer choice (E) produces the diagram:

A —— B —— G

---

8. | N Q |

(A) Both Nairobi and Quito are visited.
(B) Nairobi and Quito are visited consecutively.
(C) Nairobi is visited earlier than Quito.
(D) Quito is the next city visited after Nairobi.
(E) Quito is visited immediately before Nairobi.

The correct answer choice is (D). The block representation indicates that Q is immediately after N.

Answer choice (A) is an attractive answer, but, if two variables were selected they would simply be placed on the diagram, and not necessarily in a block formation.

Answer choice (B) would create a rotating block of NQ or QN.

Answer choice (C) creates a N —— Q sequence.

Answer choice (E) improperly reverses the order of the variables in the rule diagram.

Rule Origin Drill Answer Key—page 6

9. 

(A) At least two red lights must be consecutive.
(B) No two red lights can be consecutive.
(C) No more than three red lights can be consecutive.
(D) No more than two red lights can be consecutive.
(E) Any two red lights must be separated by at least one light of another color.

The correct answer choice is (D). The block representation indicates that three consecutive Rs cannot occur.

Answer choice (A) would create an RR block, at the very least, and possibly more.

Answer choice (B) an "at least RR not-block" scenario. While that could include the block in this item, only an RR not block is needed to fulfill this rule wording.

Answer choice (C) is a very attractive answer, but this wording allows for RRR. It does *not* allow for RRRR.

Answer choice (E) would result in an RR not-block representation, which would then apply to all Rs in the game.

---

10. 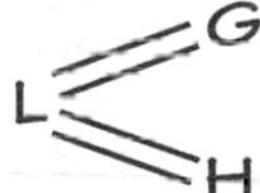

(A) Luisa finishes earlier than both Garrett and Henrietta.
(B) Garrett, Henrietta, and Luisa do not finish at the same time.
(C) Garrett and Henrietta finish at least as quickly as Luisa.
(D) Neither Garrett nor Henrietta finishes earlier than Luisa.
(E) Luisa finishes after both Garrett and Henrietta.

The correct answer choice is (D). Remember: the double dash indicates that a tie is possible between the variables connected with it. So, any answer choice that fixes the positions of the three people without allowing for a tie would be incorrect.

Rule Origin Drill Answer Key—page 6

Answer choice (A) produces the following diagram (note: no tie is allowed):

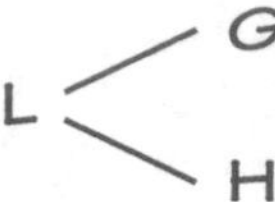

Answer choice (B) gives no particular order, and also disallows the possibility of a tie.

Answer choice (C) allows for a tie, but reverses the order:

Answer choice (D) is correct, as it tells us that Luisa is either ahead of, or tied with, Garrett and Henrietta.

Answer choice (E) is a reversal of answer choice (A), and once again disallows a tie:

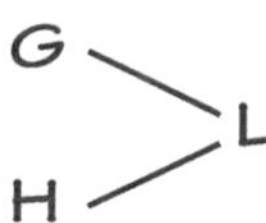

---

11. ~~A~~ ←+→ ~~F~~

- (A) If A is not included in the competition, F cannot be included in the competition.
- (B) A and F cannot both be included in the competition.
- (C) Neither A nor F can be included in the competition.
- (D) A cannot be included in the competition unless F is also included.
- (E) Either A or F must be included in the competition.

The correct answer choice is (E). The Double Not Arrow (←+→) between Not A and Not F tells us that those two conditions—A absent and F absent—cannot simultaneously occur. Since A and F cannot both be absent, then it must be the case that either A or F is included in the competition (and potentially both could be included). Note: for answer choice (B), that diagram would simply be "A ←+→ F" since that tells us A and F cannot both be included at the same time.

Rule Origin Drill Answer Key—page 6

12. 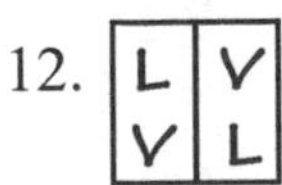

(A) Either L or V lives in an apartment on the fourth floor.
(B) L and V cannot live in the same apartment as each other.
(C) L lives in an apartment either directly above, or directly below, the apartment in which V lives.
(D) L and V live in apartments adjacent to each other.
(E) L and V live in apartments on separate floors.

The correct answer choice is (C). The rule diagram uses vertical blocks for L and V, meaning that L and V are grouped consecutively, with one immediately above the other. The presence of two blocks, one with L above V, and another with V above L, tells us that there is some uncertainty as to the exact order of the two variables, but they are vertically adjacent nonetheless. And that is exactly what answer choice (C) indicates. Note that answer (B) and (E) may well be true based on that diagram (under the rule provided in answer choice (C) they cannot share an apartment or be on the same floor), but neither of those two answer choices would produce this particular diagram.

---

13. J ⟷ K

(A) Either K or J, but not both, must be painted.
(B) J is not painted unless K is painted.
(C) J is painted if and only if K is not painted.
(D) Either K is painted and J is painted, or K is not painted and J is not painted.
(E) K is painted only if J is painted.

The correct answer choice is (D). The rule diagram in the problem connects J and K with a double arrow, which is typically introduced by the phrase, "if, and only if." However, this bi-conditional relationship can also be conveyed in other ways. Let's examine the implication of the double arrow: if either J or K is painted, then the other one must also be painted. Clearly, then, either both of them are painted, or else neither of them is painted. This is precisely what answer choice (D) entails: either K and J are both painted, or neither of them is painted.

Answer choices (A) and (C) produce identical diagrams of J ⟷ ~~K~~.

Answer choices (B) and (E) produce diagrams of J ⟶ K and K ⟶ J, respectively. Neither answer choice alone can produce the exact rule diagram in the problem.

Rule Origin Drill Answer Key—page 6

14. $M_1 \longrightarrow \boxed{MK}$

    (A) K cannot sing immediately after M unless M sings first.
    (B) If M sings first, then K sings at some time after M.
    (C) M cannot sing first unless K sings immediately after M.
    (D) K sings immediately after M only if M sings first.
    (E) M and K cannot sing consecutively unless M sings first.

The correct answer choice is (C). After applying the Unless Equation, the clause modified by the word "unless" becomes the necessary condition (K sings immediately after M). The remainder must be negated to become sufficient: so, "M cannot sing first" becomes "M sings first":

$$M_1 \longrightarrow \boxed{MK}$$

Answer choices (A) and (D) produce the following diagram, which is a Mistaken Reversal of the original diagram:

$$\boxed{MK} \longrightarrow M_1$$

Answer choice (B) does not require that K sing *immediately* after M. So, we would diagram answer choice (B) as follows:

$$M_1 \longrightarrow (M - K)$$

Answer choice (E) contains a rule that produces a rotating block (MK or KM), and is also a Mistaken Reversal of the original:

$$\boxed{MK\ /\ KM} \longrightarrow M_1$$

It should be noted that answer choice (E) precludes the formation of a KM block, because such a block would not allow M to sing first. As a result, the rule in answer choice (E) produces an inference of KM Not-Block, and a rule that is a Mistaken Reversal of the original:

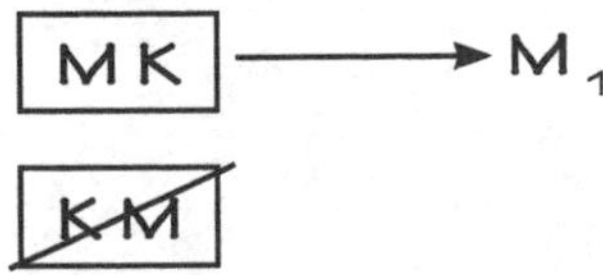

---

15. C ═══ D

(A) Charlie ate more hotdogs than Daniel in the competitive eating championship.
(B) Daniel ate more hotdogs than Charlie in the competitive eating championship.
(C) Charlie and Daniel ate the same kind of hotdogs in the competitive eating championship.
(D) Daniel did not eat more hotdogs than Charlie in the competitive eating championship.
(E) Charlie did not eat more hotdogs than Daniel in the competitive eating championship.

The correct answer choice is (D). It is important to remember that, unless you are expressly told otherwise, a tie is possible when ranking variables. The symbol " —— " shows the relative positioning of the variables, with the variable to the left of the " —— " being closer to the first position in the diagram than the variable following the " —— ". In this example, the competitor who ate the most hotdogs would be in the first spot, the position farthest to the left. The rule given indicates it may be the case that Charlie ate more hotdogs than Daniel did, or it may be that Charlie and Daniel tied, having eaten the same number of hotdogs. What is impossible, however, is that Daniel ate more hotdogs than Charlie.

Answer choice (A) produces the diagram:

C —— D

Answer choice (B) produces the diagram:

D —— C

Answer choice (C) produces no diagram, since it discusses which kind of hotdogs each person ate, rather than the relative number of hot dogs each person ate.

Answer choice (E) produces the diagram:

D ═══ C

Rule Origin Drill Answer Key—page 6

16. ~~F~~ ⟶ H

(A) F and H cannot be selected together.
(B) At least one of F or H must be selected.
(C) F is selected if and only if H is selected.
(D) If H is selected, then F is selected.
(E) If H is selected, then F is not selected.

Answer choice (B) is the correct answer. The conditional relationship reflected in this example is an often misunderstood and misapplied rule, which provides that at least one of F or H must be selected as stated in answer choice (B). This means there cannot be a valid solution in which neither F nor H is selected. People often misapply this rule by confusing it with the Double-Not Arrow, improperly inferring that F and H cannot both be selected. This inference is incorrect, since nothing in the rule prohibits F and H from being selected together.

Answer choice (A) produces the diagram:

F ⟷|⟶ H (double-not arrow)

Answer choice (C) produces the diagram:

F ⟷ H

Answer choice (D) produces the diagram:

H ⟶ F

Answer choice (E) produces the diagram:

H ⟶ ~~F~~; also H ⟷|⟶ F (double-not arrow)

PRACTICE DRILL EXPLANATIONS

Rule Origin Drill Answer Key—page 6

(A) If Fran joins the team, Greg will not join the team.
(B) Fran will join the team only if Greg does not join the team.
(C) Either Fran or Greg will join the team, but not both.
(D) Fran will join the team if and only if Greg joins the team.
(E) Either Fran and Greg will both join the team, or neither of them will join the team.

The correct answer choice is (C). The double arrow indicates a symmetrical conditional relationship between Fran and Greg, which amounts to two separate rules:

1. If Fran joins the team, then Greg will not join. By the contrapositive, if Greg joins the team, then Gran will not. Essentially, this rule stipulates that Fran and Greg cannot both be *present*: at most one of them can ever join.

Thanks to the double arrow, however, the rule can also be read in reverse:

2. If Greg does not join the team, then Fran will. By the contrapositive of that rule, if Fran does not join the team, then Greg will. This rule stipulates that Greg and Fran cannot both be *absent*: the absence of one requires the presence of the other. In other words, at least one of Fran or Greg must join the team.

The double arrow indicates that both of the above-mentioned rules must be enforced. Consequently, either Fran or Greg, but not both, must join the team.

Answer choice (A) and answer choice (B) both produce diagrams that closely resemble the one presented in the question; however, they both produce a diagram with a standard arrow (F ⟶ G̸). This is different from the diagram presented in the question (F ⟷ G̸), whose double arrow represents not only F ⟶ G̸, but also G̸ ⟶ F.

Answer choice (D) would produce a diagram that features a double arrow (F ⟷ G), but not one that matches the diagram from the question.

Answer choice (E) is incorrect because it dictates that either both join, or neither joins. Both of these scenarios are prohibited by the diagram presented.

Rule Origin Drill Answer Key—page 6

18. $A \longrightarrow \not{B}$

(A) Alan will attend if Brad does not attend.
(B) If Alan does not attend then Brad will attend.
(C) If Alan attends, Brad will attend.
(D) Alan will attend if and only if Brad does not attend.
(E) Alan will not attend unless Brad does not attend.

The correct answer choice is (E). Applying the Unless Equation, "Unless" introduces the necessary condition ("Brad does not attend"), and the sufficient condition ("A will not attend") gets negated (becoming "A will attend"). The result: $A \longrightarrow \not{B}$.

Answer choice (A) produces $\not{B} \longrightarrow A$, a Mistaken Reversal of the diagram as presented.

Answer choice (B) produces this diagram: $\not{A} \longrightarrow B$, which is a Mistaken Negation of the diagram from the question.

Answer choice (C) produces the diagram $A \longrightarrow B$, which can be quickly ruled out of contention.

Answer choice (D) produces the diagram $A \longleftrightarrow \not{B}$, a two-way relationship that includes the inference $\not{B} \longrightarrow A$; this is not an inference that can be validly drawn from the diagram presented.

Two Rule Inference Drill Answer Key—page 11

1. If Q is on the stage, then R is on the stage.
   R is not on the stage unless P is not on the stage.

Rule 1: Q ⟶ R

Rule 2: R ←+→ P

Combined: Q ⟶ R ←+→ P

Inference: Q ←+→ P

The first rule is a standard conditional rule. The second rule is a bit trickier to diagram because it features the indicator "unless" and two "nots." Using a single arrow, the diagram for the second rule is:

R ⟶ ~~P~~

This representation can be turned into the double-not arrow representation above.

When the two rules are combined, we can draw the very common grouping inference that Q and P cannot be on the stage at the same time:

Q ←+→ P

---

2. The third car sold is either S or T.
   W is sold immediately before X.

Rule 1: 3 ⟶ S/T

Rule 2: [WX]

On the diagram:

cars =			S/T			
	1	2	3	4	5	6
	~~X~~	~~W~~		~~X~~		~~W~~

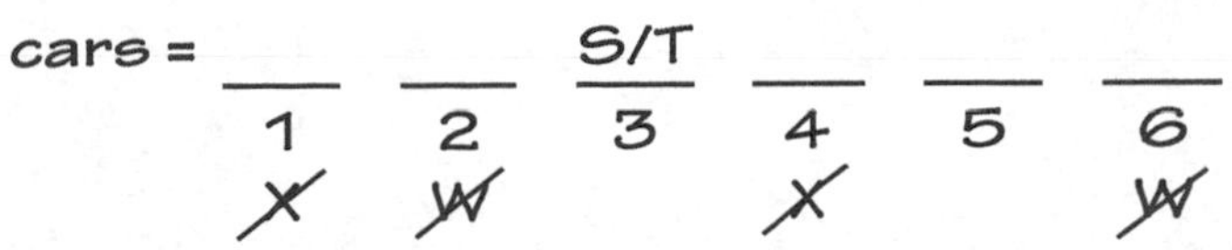

Two Rule Inference Drill Answer Key—page 11

The first rule is best displayed directly on the diagram, as an S/T dual-option on space 3. The block rule yields two Not Laws automatically: X cannot be the first car sold, and W cannot be the last car sold. The combination of the two rules also yields two more Not Laws: W cannot be sold second (no space for X to be sold third), and X cannot be sold fourth (no space for W to be sold third).

In fact, the WX block is very limited in this game, and can only be placed in spaces 1-2, 4-5, and 5-6. The presence of other rules might suggest attacking the game by Identifying the Templates or Possibilities.

---

3. D's performance and E's performance are separated by exactly one performance.

   G performs immediately after F.

Rule 1: D/E ___ E/D

Rule 2: FG

On the diagram:

performances = ___ ___ ___ ___ ___

1	2	3	4	5
~~G~~				~~F~~

The first rule is a rotating split-block, and the second rule is a standard block. The second rule yields two Not Laws: G cannot be the first performance, and F cannot be the last performance. At this point it may seem as if there are no further inferences that can be drawn, but the two blocks create a significant restriction in the game that should be explored further. For example, the DE split block can only be placed in three positions, and those positions then restrict the movement of the FG block:

	1	2	3	4	5
DE in 3-5:	F	G	D/E		E/D
~~DE in 2-4:~~		~~D/E~~		~~E/D~~	
DE in 1-3:	D/E		E/D	F	G

Two Rule Inference Drill Answer Key—page 11

As shown above, placing the DE block in spaces 2-4 does not allow for the placement of the FG block, and thus the DE block cannot be placed in 2-4. Therefore, the DE block must be in spaces 1-3 or 3-5 (meaning D or E is always in space 3), and the FG block must be in spaces 4-5 or 1-2. The final, unnamed variable would then fill in space 2 or 4.

---

4. M cannot be in a group unless N is in the same group.
   Q and R cannot be in different groups.

Rule 1: M / N

Rule 2: Q / R

Inference: M / N ←+→ Q / R

Although stated in conditional terms, the first rule has the functional effect of creating a block. If M cannot be in a group unless N is in the same group, then M and N must be in the same group together. Similarly, if Q and R cannot be in different groups, they must be in the same group.

The size of these two blocks makes it impossible for the two to be in the same group, and thus we can draw the inference that the two blocks cannot be together. This can be shown on the diagram:

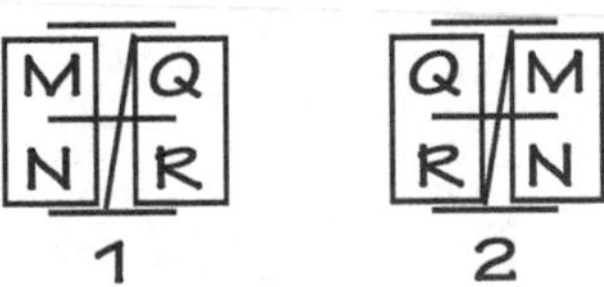

Of course, because the blocks take up two spaces in each group, there is only one space remaining in each group, and the other two, unnamed variables would have to be in separate groups as well.

Two Rule Inference Drill Answer Key—page 11

5. R's call is made at some point before S's call.
   T's call is made exactly two calls ahead of R's call.

Rule 1: R —— S

Rule 2: | T ___ R |

Combined: | T ___ R | —— S

On the diagram:

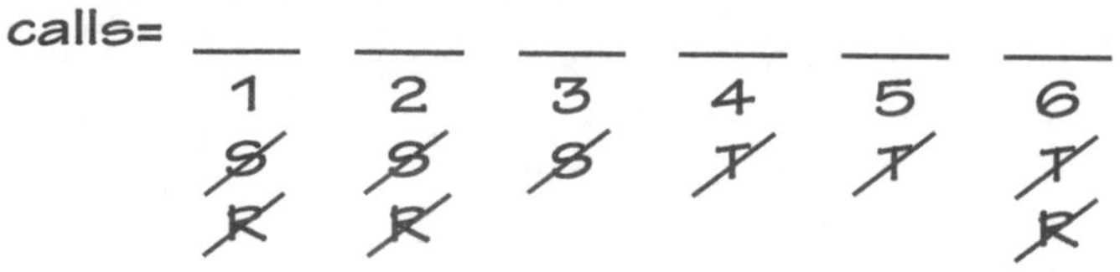

calls=	___	___	___	___	___	___
	1	2	3	4	5	6
	S̸	S̸	S̸	T̸	T̸	T̸
	R̸	R̸				R̸

The block-sequence configuration is fairly common in Logic games. Because the relationship involves three variables and four spaces, it produces a number of Not Laws. The configuration is also limited in placement, as the TR block has only three options: 1-3, 2-4, and 3-5.

---

6. H cannot be in group 1 unless K is in group 1.
   J is in group 2 only if L is in group 2.

Rule 1: $H_1 \longrightarrow K_1$

Rule 2: $J_2 \longrightarrow L_2$

As this is a two-value system game, the contrapositive of any conditional rule typically yields useful information. The contrapositives of the two rules above are as follows:

Contrapositive of Rule 1: $K_2 \longrightarrow H_2$

Contrapositive of Rule 2: $L_1 \longrightarrow J_1$

Because there are only three spaces in each group, any combination of the two rules that produces four variables in a group would be a violation. Thus, H and L cannot be in group 1 together because H requires K, and L in group 1 requires J. Similarly, J and K cannot be in group 2 together because J requires L, and K in group 2 requires H. These two inferences can be shown as follows:

7. If A is not interviewed then B must be interviewed, and if B is interviewed then A cannot be interviewed.
   Of the six interviewees, if B is not interviewed then exactly two other interviewees cannot be interviewed.

Rule 1: ~~A~~ ⟷ B

Rule 2: ~~B~~ ⟶ (B+2) out

Only two possible scenarios exist under the first rule: A is not interviewed and B is interviewed, or, via the contrapositive of the rule, A is interviewed and B is not interviewed. In other words, exactly one of A or B must be interviewed, and normally we would represent that fact with an A/B dual-option on the diagram.

However, the second rule creates a situation that impacts the first rule. If B is not selected, then two other variables are also not selected, for a total of three variables not selected. As the rules indicate that there are only six interviewees, and the diagram shows there are only four interviews, the second rule would create a situation where not interviewing B would leave only three interviewees for the four interviews. As this is unacceptable, we can conclude that B must be interviewed and A is not interviewed:

B ___ ___ ___	A ___
Group of 4 Interviews	Not interviewed

8. J and K cannot audition together.
When K auditions, L must also audition.

Rule 1: J ←+→ K

Rule 2: K ——→ L

Combined: J ←+→ K ——→ L

Inference: No useful inference

Compare this item to item #1. The rules involved are the same, but because the relationships are different, this pair of rules does *not* produce an inference that is useful during Games.

Unlike the chain in Item #1, this chain does not produce an additive inference because both rules share the same sufficient condition (K). We only know the fate of J and L if K auditions: in that case, L must audition but J cannot. However, if K does not audition, then neither L nor J would be bound by a conditional relationship.

For a chain relationship to produce an additive inference, the sufficient condition in one of the rules must be a necessary condition in another rule. This requirement is not met here.

---

9. Q appears earlier than R but later than S.
Q does not appear second.

Rule 1: S —— Q —— R

Rule 2: Q Not Law on 2

Inference: R Not Law on 3

On the diagram:

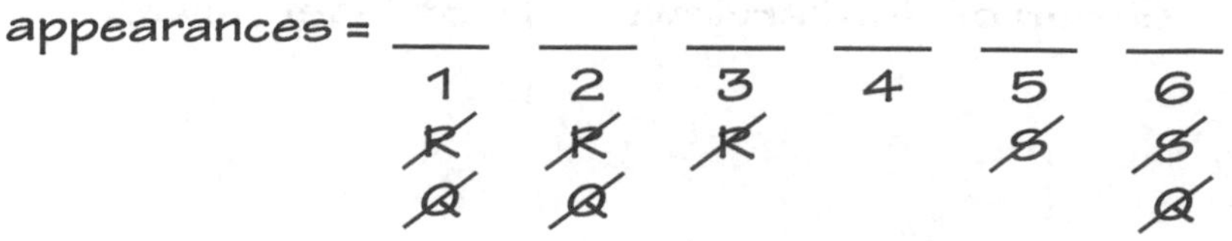

appearances =

1	2	3	4	5	6
~~R~~	~~R~~	~~R~~		~~S~~	~~S~~
~~Q~~	~~Q~~				~~Q~~

Two Rule Inference Drill Answer Key—page 11

The first rule creates a standard three-variable sequence, which then produces six Not Laws. The second rule has the effect of creating a Q Not Law on 2, and then also creating an R Not Law on 3 when the first rule is considered. The R Not Law on 3 would most definitely be tested during the game.

---

10. Either Book R or Book S is written last.
    Book Y is written later than Book X.

Rule 1: 5 ⟶ R/S

Rule 2: X —— Y

Inferences: X ⟶ 1/2/3, and Y ⟶ 2/3/4

On the diagram:

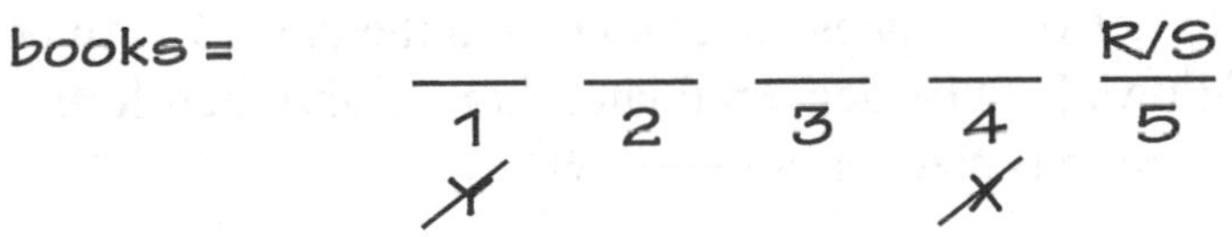

books =

1	2	3	4	5
				R/S
~~Y~~			~~X~~	

The first rule is best displayed directly on the diagram, as an R/S dual-option on space 5. The sequence rule yields two Not Laws automatically: Y cannot be the first book written, and X cannot be the last book written. But, because R or S is written last, we can infer that X cannot be fourth book written, and infer that X must be one of the first three books written, and that Y must be the second, third, or fourth book written.

Two Rule Inference Drill Answer Key—page 11

11. At least three deliveries are made before G is delivered.
At least two deliveries are made after H is delivered.

Rule 1: G Not Laws on 1, 2, 3

Rule 2: H Not Law on 5, 6

Inference: H —— G

On the diagram:

deliveries = ___ ___ ___ ___ ___ ___

1	2	3	4	5	6
~~G~~	~~G~~	~~G~~		~~H~~	~~H~~

The two rules may not initially appear to produce any inference because the Not Laws do not abut or overlap. However, G is limited to delivery spaces 4, 5, and 6, and the latest H can be delivered is 4th. Thus, there is no scenario that allows H to be delivered later than G, and therefore H must always be delivered earlier than G, which is represented as H —— G.

---

12. F is presented either immediately before or immediately after H.
H is presented at some time before K is presented.

Rule 1: [FH / HF]

Rule 2: H —— K

Inferences:

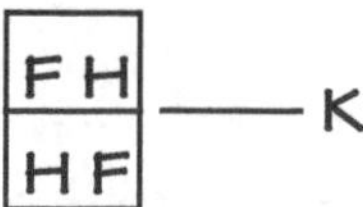

On the diagram:

presentations = ___ ___ ___ ___ ___ ___

1	2	3	4	5	6
~~K~~	~~K~~				~~F~~
					~~H~~

Two Rule Inference Drill Answer Key—page 11

The first rule creates a block where the exact order of F and H is uncertain, and the second rule can be connected to the first due to the shared variable H. Since H is in a block with F as well as ahead of K, it must be true that the entire FH block precedes K. Thus K can never be the first or second presentation, and neither F nor H could be the sixth presentation.

---

13. Either L or G reviews the site on day 3.
    R reviews the site exactly two days before X does.

Rule 1: 3 ⟶ L/G

Rule 2: [R _ X]

Inferences: R ⟶ 2, and X ⟶ 4

On the diagram:

	R	L/G	X	
days = 1	2	3	4	5

The first rule is best displayed directly on the diagram, as an L/G dual-option on day 3. This is a very common construction used by the test makers, where they fill the central space on an odd-numbered base (day 3 of 5 here), dividing the diagram into two even parts: one before and the other after the filled space. In this case, the second rule presents a large block with R two days before X, and, with day 3 filled, there is only one placement option for such a block: R must be day 2, and X day 4. R and X cannot be days 1 and 3, or days 3 and 5, because in both cases day 3 must be L or G. This is a very powerful inference and serves to firmly establish two of the five days.

14. Exactly one lecture separates the lectures on Physics and Chemistry.
If the Chemistry lecture is not the first lecture given, then it must be the last lecture given.

Rule 1:

P _ C
C _ P

Rule 2: C ⟶ 1 or 6

Inference: P ⟶ 3 or 4

On the diagram:

	C/		P/	/P		/C
lectures =	1	2	3	4	5	6

The first rule provides a block for C and P, with one day between and no knowledge of their order. This type of rule, with its uncertain order, typically does not yield any immediate inferences, however the second rule here gives more information about C: it is either 1 or 6. Many people diagram Rule 2 as conditional as follows:

$$\not{C}_1 \longrightarrow C_6$$

While that representation is technically correct, it fails to capture the true meaning of Rule 2: C will always be either first or sixth. That is, if we do not put C in 1, it must be in 6, and from the contrapositive if C is not in 6 then it must be in 1. Hence we have a split option for C, and since P is separated from C by just a single lecture, then P must either be 3 (if C is 1) or 4 (if C is 6). These split options can be shown on the diagram itself, with slashes reflecting the "either/or" nature of the placements.

Two Rule Inference Drill Answer Key—page 11

15. If K is not selected, then both F and H must be selected.
    Q is not selected unless only one other variable is selected.

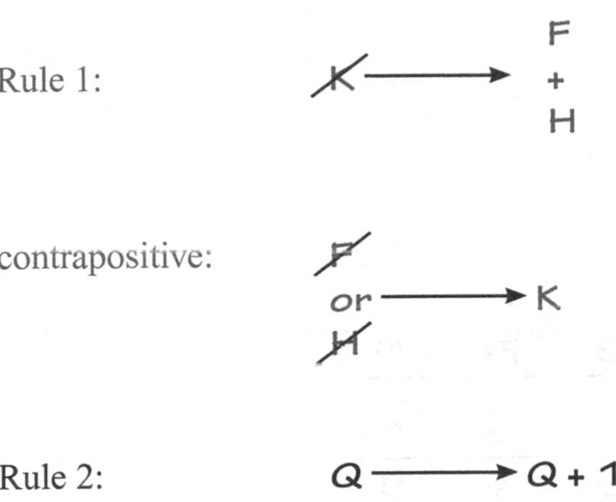

According to the first rule, the absence of K requires the selection of two other variables (F and H). By the contrapositive, if either F or H is not selected, then K must be selected. Note that it is possible for all three of these variables to be selected, as the selection of K has no bearing on either of the other two variables. To conclude otherwise would be a Mistaken Negation of the first rule, or a Mistaken Reversal of its contrapositive.

The second rule creates a situation that impacts the application of the first rule. If Q is selected, then only one other variable must also be selected. If that variable were *not* K, however, then the first rule would require us to select two variables (F and H), not one. To avoid this outcome, we must select K whenever we select Q:

Two Rule Inference Drill Answer Key—page 11

16. In a row with five seats, L is seated immediately before S.
L is seated before F but after U.

Rule 1: [LS]

Rule 2: U —— L —— F

Combined: U —— [LS] —— F

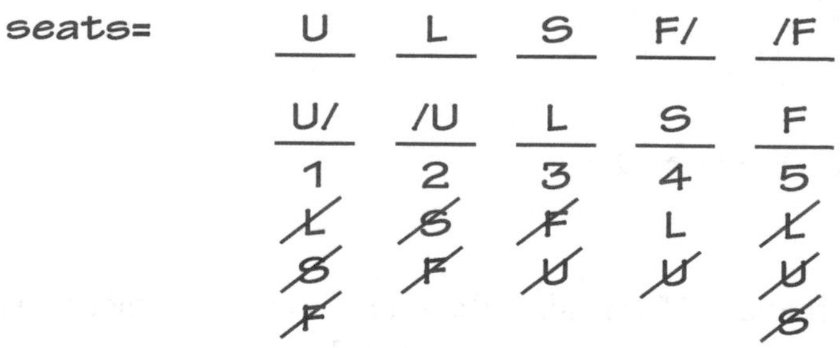

seats=

U	L	S	F/	/F
U/	/U	L	S	F
1	2	3	4	5
~~L~~	~~S~~	~~F~~	L	~~L~~
~~S~~	~~F~~	~~U~~	~~U~~	~~U~~
~~F~~				~~S~~

The first rule produces a block that reflects the relationships both sequencing and adjacency: L is not simply earlier than S, but immediately before it. The second sequencing rule includes L as well as two new variables, F and U. Combining the two rules together yields a Power Block that has limited space within which to move. This tension between the block and the limited space produces several Not Laws. It also results in multiple either/or options for variables and for spaces. At the ends of the base, U can only be in seats 1 or 2, and F can only be in 4 or 5. In the middle of the base, L can only be in seats 2 or 3, while S can only be in seats 3 and 4.

The presence of a Power Block in a short base is a strong indicator that this is a game where Identifying the Templates or Identifying the Possibilities may be appropriate.

Two Rule Inference Drill Answer Key—page 11

17. Without S, T will not be selected.
    R will be selected, unless T is selected.

Rule 1: T ⟶ S

Rule 2: ~~R~~ ⟶ T

Combined: ~~R~~ ⟶ T ⟶ S

Inference: ~~R~~ ⟶ S

Both of these rules contain language implying an exception to a general rule. When a conditional relationship contains language such as unless, except, until or without, use the Unless Equation to quickly and accurately diagram these often difficult relationships. Whatever is modified by the words unless, except, until, or without is the necessary condition. The remainder of the sentence you negate, and that becomes the sufficient condition.

In the first rule, the word "without" modifies S, so S being selected is the necessary condition. Negate the remainder, such that "T will not be selected" becomes "T will be selected," and this term is the sufficient condition.

In the second rule, the word "unless" modifies T, so T being selected is the necessary condition. Negate the remainder, such that "R will be selected" becomes "R is not selected." This term becomes the sufficient condition.

Because T being selected is the sufficient condition in Rule 1 and the necessary condition in Rule 2, it is possible to chain the two relationships together, yielding the additive inference that if R is not selected, then S will be. By the contrapositive, if S is not selected, then R will be. In other words, at least one of R or S must always be selected.

18. M arrives on the second day, exactly three days before N arrives.
Q arrives exactly three days after P arrives.

Rule 1: M_2 __ __ N_5

Rule 2: P __ __ Q

Days =

P/	M	/P	Q/	N	/Q
1	2	3	4	5	6

The first rule can be displayed directly on the diagram, and since the rule provides the exact day of arrival for both M and N, respectively, there is no need to create an MN block to represent this rule (although we did so, simply to represent the rule for the sake of appearance). The second rule provides that Q arrives three days after P (note that this means they are separated by exactly *two* days). This rule creates a four-space block that is quite constrained, given the placements from the first rule, creating only two possibilities for the PQ block: Either P is on Day 1 and Q is on Day 4, or P is on Day 3 and Q is on day 6:

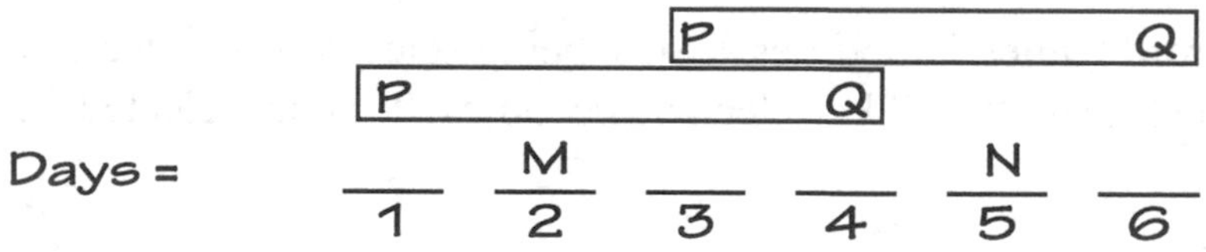

P Q (Days 3–6)

P Q (Days 1–4)

Days =

	M			N	
1	2	3	4	5	6

---

19. Either A or B, but not both, joins Team 1.
C and B are placed on different teams, and D and A are placed on different teams.

Rule 1: A ←|→ B,

Rule 2: C ←|→ B, D ←|→ A

Team=

1	2
C/D	D/C
A/B	B/A

Two Rule Inference Drill Answer Key—page 11

The first rule basically provides that A and B will be on different teams. The second rule provides that C and B will be on different teams as well. Since there are only two teams, and all variables join a team, this means that C and A must be teammates (as neither one will share a team with B). The second rule also provides that D and A will be on different teams, meaning that D and B will be teammates (neither one will share a team with A). This creates a vertical BD block and a vertical AC block, although the specific team placements are not determined.

---

20. Neither F nor G wins first place.
    D is ranked higher than C but lower than E.

Rule 1: F̸₁ G̸₁

Rule 2: E —— D —— C (all five variables ranked)

Rank =

E				
1	2	3	4	5
F̸	C̸		E̸	E̸
G̸				D̸
D̸				
C̸				

The first rule provides two Not Laws; in a game with only five variables, all of which are placed, this immediately narrows the options for first place to only three possibilities. These options are further narrowed by the second rule, which creates six Not Laws, and leads to the inference that the first place position can only be inhabited by E.

Linear Base Representation Diagramming Drill Answer Key—page 17

1. There are exactly six houses on a street. Each house is occupied by exactly one of six tenants—Alberto, Beatrice, Carmello, Drayton, Engrid, and Fong. All of the houses are on the same side of a street that runs West to East.

ABCDEF[6]

West ___ ___ ___ ___ ___ ___ East
1 2 3 4 5 6

This diagram should be represented horizontally, since East/West directions are horizontal when viewed on a map. Further, while not directly numbered, the houses can be listed from left to right as 1 to 6, where left is West and right is East. Rules would likely indicate housing arrangements in terms of these directions, such as, "Engrid lives to the east of Carmello," meaning Not Laws in house 1 for Engrid, and house 6 for Carmello.

---

2. A highrise building has six residential floors, 32 to 37, containing a total of seven apartments. Each floor has exactly one apartment, except for the lowest of the six floors, which has two apartments. The residents of the building are G, J, L, R, T, U, and V, each of whom lives in a different apartment.

GJLRTUV[7]

37 ___

36 ___

35 ___

34 ___

33 ___

32 ___ ___

Because the floors of the building have an inherent sense of order, they should be chosen as the base. And, because the floors of a building are vertically aligned, the diagram is vertical as well. The residents are then the variable set that is distributed over the seven apartments, with the two-apartment floor, floor 32, at the bottom.

Linear Base Representation Diagramming Drill Answer Key—page 17

3. During a period of seven consecutive days, each of exactly seven warehouses—E, H, K, L, N, P, and T—will receive a delivery. During this period, each of the warehouses will receive exactly one delivery each day.

E H K L N P T ^{7}

___ ___ ___ ___ ___ ___ ___
 1 2 3 4 5 6 7

Use the seven days as the base due to their inherent order, and then assign warehouses to the days in a 1-to-1 distribution. This represents a fairly basic linear game scenario.

---

4. Six consecutive positions for a demo album will be filled with exactly five rock songs—D, F, G, J, and O—and exactly one ballad. Each song will be assigned to a different position.

B D F G J O ^{6}

___ ___ ___ ___ ___ ___
 1 2 3 4 5 6

The song positions, 1 through 6, make for the appropriate base in this situation, as their order is fixed. Then the six songs can each be assigned to a unique position on that base. Note the inclusion of the variable "B" to signify the single ballad on the album. This sixth song balances the songs to the six positions, and should be represented as part of the song variable set.

Linear Base Representation Diagramming Drill Answer Key—page 17

5. Five, colored flags—Blue, Green, Orange, Red, and Yellow—are all being raised up a flag pole, not necessarily in that order. No two flags can be raised at the same time.

B G O R Y ^{5}

Top ___

___

___

___

Bottom ___

Because this is a flag pole, the base should be oriented vertically. Note: The flag raised first will naturally be the top flag, whereas the flag raised last will be the bottom flag. It is imperative to understand what is entailed by the directionality inherent in any vertical or horizontal setup.

---

6. Three couples—Grace and Henry, Irene and Justin, and Kai and Lee—attend a concert together. The six attendees are seated in a single row, with one person assigned to each of six seats—103 to 108.

GH IJ KL ^{6}

___	___	___	___	___	___
103	104	105	106	107	108

The seats make the ideal base for this scenario, since they are numbered. Note too that because the six people's relationships are given, incorporating that information into your variable list is important (here it is accomplished simply by spacing: the three couples are grouped together with larger spaces between). Be careful as well not to assume too much about the fact that the people are grouped in pairs! Just because they are a couple, does not necessarily imply that they must be seated next to one another; the rules may state something to that effect, but you cannot simply assume it.

Linear Base Representation Diagramming Drill Answer Key—page 17

7. During the final round of a singing competition, six singers—Aretha, Barry, Celine, Dierdra, Evan, and Frank—are scheduled to perform, not necessarily in that order. The singers will be assigned to five time slots, with Aretha, Barry, Dierdra, and Evan each singing solos in four of the five slots, and Celine and Frank singing together in the remaining slot.

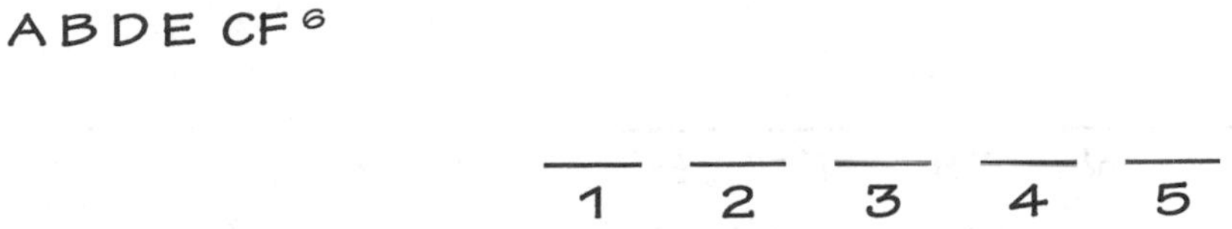

ABDE CF ^{6}

___ ___ ___ ___ ___
1 2 3 4 5

The five performance positions make the ideal base, as you know the exact order of the performances. We now have six singers to fill those five positions, however, because singers Celine and Frank are going to be singing together, they can be treated as a single performance. Thus there are really five "performances" (the four solos and the single duet) to fill the five positions, and the numbers are balanced. How you choose to represent the six singers is somewhat subjective, but it is necessary to show that C and F are grouped, whether it be in a single, vertical block, or as is shown above where they are simply written as a pair separated slightly from the other four, solo performers.

---

8. An exam proctor is assigning seats to four students—M, N, O, and P. The proctor has a single row of seven consecutive seats available, and cannot assign any two students to seats that are adjacent to each other.

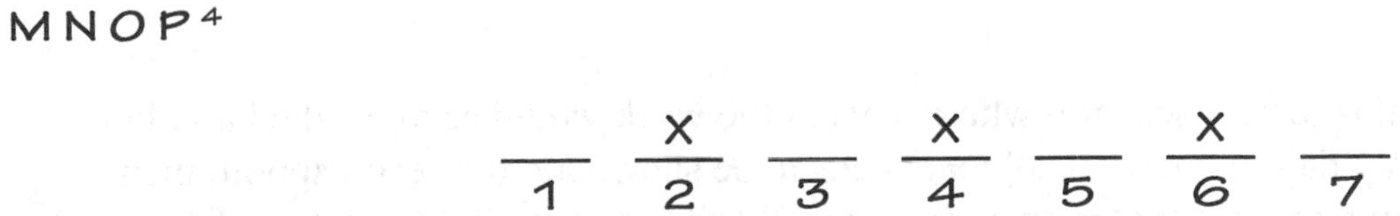

MNOP ^{4}

X X X
___ ___ ___ ___ ___ ___ ___
1 2 3 4 5 6 7

This scenario presents a unique situation because, while it is easy to choose the seven seats as the base (representing them vertically or horizontally is entirely your choice), the distribution of the four students into the seven seats carries a restriction: there must be separation between the students' seats. To accomplish this, think about how you could place four people into seven seats so that no two people are adjacent. You would have to position the four in seats 1, 3, 5, and 7, and then leave seats 2, 4, and 6 empty. To show this separation and the three empty seats, an "X" has been placed above the 2nd, 4th, and 6th seats, leaving the other four seats open to distribute the four students.

Linear Base Representation Diagramming Drill Answer Key—page 17

9. A personal trainer is planning a weekly schedule, Monday through Saturday, of individual training sessions for five clients—M, N, P, R and S. Each client will receive exactly one training session, with no two sessions scheduled on the same day.

MNPRSX^6

The days of the week, with their inherent sense of order, make for the appropriate base, and the five clients can then be assigned to the six days. Since there are five sessions to be scheduled over the course of six consecutive days, there must be a day on which the trainer schedules no sessions. Note the "X" listed in the client set to represent the trainer's day off. That additional variable balances this game as 6 into 6, and should definitely be included for that reason.

---

10. On Thursday a professor will have exactly one appointment with each of seven students—Edgar, Garrett, Hans, Juliette, Kristoff, Lorenzo, and Nadia—one student per appointment.

EGHJKLN^7

___ ___ ___ ___ ___ ___ ___
1 2 3 4 5 6 7

People initially believe this to be a scenario where days of the week would serve as the base, but since Thursday is the only day in question, all that needs to be shown are the seven appointment spaces, 1-7. Whether you represent the seven spots vertically or horizontally is a matter of personal preference.

Linear Base Representation Diagramming Drill Answer Key—page 17

11. A computer algorithm generates a series of six-digit passcodes. Each passcode must include the numbers 0, 1, 2, 3, 4, and 5, and no others, with each of those six digits occurring exactly once per passcode.

0 1 2 3 4 5 ^{6}

___ ___ ___ ___ ___ ___
1 2 3 4 5 6

This setup is challenging for many test takers, because both the base and the variable set are consecutive groups of numbers, and thus seem to have inherent order. However, the numbers in the passcode (0–5) are not ordered and can vary their positions, so the positions themselves—the six positions of the passcode, 1-6—make the more appropriate base. Put another way, you cannot know what the first digit of the passcode will be (it could be any of the numbers 0-5), but you do know it is first ("1"), and the second position second ("2"), etcetera. Thus 1-6 is the correct base to use.

---

12. A gym is scheduling a four-hour block of exercise sessions beginning at 6 am. The sessions that are to fill this time block include three hour-long sessions—A, B, and C—and two half-hour sessions—F and H. The sessions will be scheduled one after the other, each session scheduled exactly once.

AA BB CC F H ^{8}

___ ___ ___ ___ ___ ___ ___ ___
6 7 8 9

This is an initially confusing scenario, because three of the sessions are an hour long, while the other two are only a half hour. To compensate for this disparity, label the hour long sessions as double variables, thus making them appear as two consecutive half hours (effectively this makes them into hour long "blocks"). Then use the time slots as your base, separated into half-hour increments from 6 a.m. to 10 a.m. Note: there is no session scheduled for 10 a.m., as the final program ends at 10. So the last space represents the half hour from 9:30 to 10:00. Creating your setup in this fashion balances the variables to the positions, where the eight spots of the base are filled by the eight variables (with A, B, and C each counted twice).

Linear Base Representation Diagramming Drill Answer Key—page 17

13. Six ski chalets—L, R, T, V, W, and Z—are arranged in ascending order up the slope of a mountain, not necessarily in that order.

L R T V W Z ^{6}

High	___
	___
	___
	___
	___
Low	___

The ski chalets are described as appearing in ascending order, so this diagram should be set up vertically (unless the first position is dictated to be the one at the bottom or the top of the mountain, you can choose which is proper and label the diagram accordingly).

---

14. Five people—Carver, Diaz, Esposito, Foley, and Grey—will be scheduled as participants in a game show that is aired once each day, Monday through Thursday. Each episode must have at least one participant, and no participant is scheduled for more than one episode.

C D E F G ^{5}

___	___	___	___
M	T	W	Th

The four days of the week, with their inherent sense of order, make for the appropriate base, and the five participants can then be assigned to the four days. The key to this setup is to recognize the numerical distribution present: 5 people into 4 days, with no days empty and no people used more than once. That means that three of the days will have a single participant assigned, and one of the days will have 2 participants assigned. Hence we have a 2-1-1-1 distribution of people to days. While we cannot know at this point which day will have two people (the distribution is Unfixed), it is imperative that the imbalance be considered.

Linear Base Representation Diagramming Drill Answer Key—page 17

15. A tour group will view exactly seven artifacts—J, K, L, M, N, O, and P—displayed in five display cases. The first and the last cases viewed will each contain two artifacts. The remaining three cases will each contain a single artifact.

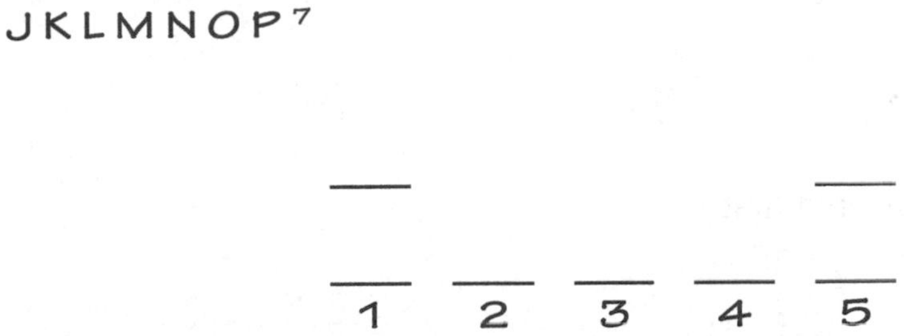

J K L M N O P ^{7}

___   ___

___ ___ ___ ___ ___

1 2 3 4 5

Assign the five cases as the base because you know they are being viewed sequentially, 1 through 5, and show two spaces for cases 1 and 5, since those cases contain two artifacts each. That gives seven spaces for the seven artifacts, and balances the variable-to-base relationship.

---

16. An accountant is scheduling five, day-long meetings over the course of five consecutive weeks. Each week will have a single meeting occurring on a single day—Monday, Tuesday, Wednesday, Thursday, or Friday. No two meetings can be scheduled on the same weekday over the five-week period.

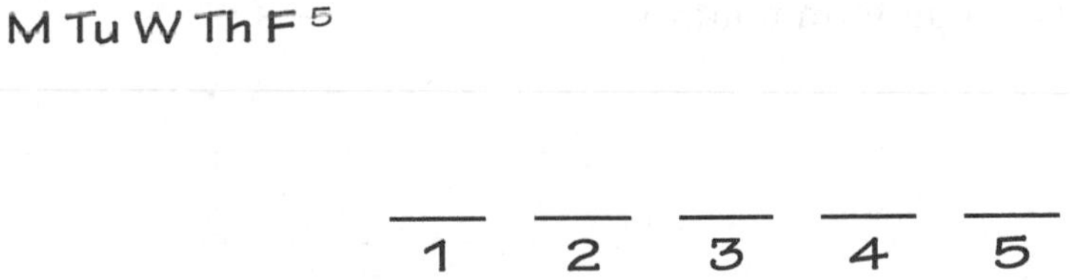

M Tu W Th F ^{5}

___ ___ ___ ___ ___

1 2 3 4 5

Choosing the appropriate base for this scenario is somewhat challenging, as you have both the five weeks (1 through 5), as well as the five weekdays (Monday through Friday). While weekdays normally make for an ideal base, as they are inherently ordered over the period of a single week, in this case it is the five weeks (1–5) that should be chosen as the base: we do not know on which day of the week the first meeting will be scheduled, but we know that week 1's meeting happens prior to week 2's meeting, which occurs before week 3's, and so on. Now we must simply assign the five different weekdays to the five numbered positions.

Conditional Reasoning Mini-Diagramming Drill Answer Key—page 23

1. If A is not delivered first, then B is delivered first.

original: $\not{A}_1 \longrightarrow B_1$

(If A is not delivered first, then B is delivered first.)

contrapositive: $\not{B}_1 \longrightarrow A_1$

(If B is not delivered first, then A is delivered first.)

Note: In a game, the most efficient way to diagram this rule would be as an A/B dual option in the first space.

---

2. D performs fifth if E performs fourth.

original: $E_4 \longrightarrow D_5$

(Reordered: If E performs fourth, then D performs fifth.)

contrapositive: $\not{D}_5 \longrightarrow \not{E}_4$

(If D does not perform fifth, then E does not perform fourth.)

---

3. N is not interviewed on day 2 unless L is interviewed on the day 3.

original: $N_2 \longrightarrow L_3$

(In other words, if N is interviewed on day 2, then L is interviewed on day 3.)

contrapositive: $\not{L}_3 \longrightarrow \not{N}_2$

(If L is not interviewed on day 3, then N is not interviewed on day 2.)

Conditional Reasoning Mini-Diagramming Drill Answer Key—page 23

4. P precedes Q only if Q precedes R.

original: (P —— Q) ——→ (Q —— R)

(P —— Q only if Q —— R.)

Note: "Only if" introduces a necessary condition.

contrapositive: (Q —/— R) ——→ (P —/— Q)

(If not Q —— R then not P —— Q.)

(In other words, if R —— Q, then Q —— P.)

---

5. If H is presented third, then either I or J must be presented fourth.

original: H_3 ——→ I/J_4

(If H is presented third, then either I or J must be presented fourth)

contrapositive: $\not{I}_4$ and $\not{J}_4$ ——→ $\not{H}_3$

(If neither I nor J is presented fourth, then H is not presented third.)

Note: The above could also have been diagrammed with conditional and/or statements, but in games, the dual option is an efficient way to reflect this relationship in the diagram.

As you may have noticed in the mini-drill, the contrapositive can yield some interesting insights into the relationship between the variables.

Conditional Reasoning Mini-Diagramming Drill Answer Key—page 23

6. If F is scheduled for 1:00, then G is not scheduled for 2:00.

original: $F_{1:00} \longrightarrow \not{G}_{2:00}$

(If F is scheduled for 1:00, then G is not scheduled for 2:00.)

contrapositive: $G_{2:00} \longrightarrow \not{F}_{1:00}$

(If G is scheduled for 2:00, then F is not scheduled for 1:00.)

---

7. When D is taken in the Fall, then either E or F must be taken in the Spring.

original: $D_{Fall} \longrightarrow E_{Spring}$ or F_{Spring}

(When D is taken in the Fall, then either E or F must be taken in the Spring.)

Note: "When," like "if," introduces a sufficient condition.

contrapositive: $\not{E}_{Spring}$ and $\not{F}_{Spring} \longrightarrow \not{D}_{Fall}$

(If neither E nor F is taken in the Spring, then D is not taken in the Fall.)

Conditional Reasoning Mini-Diagramming Drill Answer Key—page 23

8. J doesn't ride in the third car if K rides in the second car.

original: $K_2 \longrightarrow \not{J}_3$

(Reordered: If K rides in the second car, then J doesn't ride in the third car.)

contrapositive: $J_3 \longrightarrow \not{K}_2$

(If J rides in the third car then K does not ride in the second car.)

---

9. If the recipe includes either A or B, then it also includes C.

original: A or B $\longrightarrow$ C

(If the recipe includes either A or B, then it also includes C.)

contrapositive: $\not{C} \longrightarrow$ $\not{A}$ and $\not{B}$

(If the recipe doesn't include C, it includes neither A nor B.)

---

10. V is selected for Team 1 if W is selected for Team 2.

original: $W_2 \longrightarrow V_1$

(Reordered: If W is selected for Team 2, then V is selected for Team 1.)

Note: "if" introduces the sufficient condition.

contrapositive: $\not{V}_1 \longrightarrow \not{W}_2$

(If V is not on Team 1, then W is not on Team 2.)

Conditional Reasoning Mini-Diagramming Drill Answer Key—page 23

11. X is included if and only if Y is included.

original: X ⟷ Y

(X is included if and only if Y is included.)

contrapositive: 

(If X is absent, then Y is absent, and if Y is absent then X is absent.)

---

12. V appears only if it is presented first.

original: V ⟶ V_1

(In other words, if V is presented, then it is presented first)

contrapositive: ~~V_1~~ ⟶ ~~V~~

(If V is not presented first, then it is not presented at all. In other words, V cannot be presented anywhere else but first.)

---

13. If either G or H is invited, then I is also invited.

original: G or H ⟶ I

(If either G or H is invited, then I is also invited.)

contrapositive: ~~I~~ ⟶ ~~G~~ and ~~H~~

(If I is not invited, then G is not invited and H is not invited.)

(Alternate phrasing: If I is not invited, then neither G nor H is invited.)

Conditional Reasoning Mini-Diagramming Drill Answer Key—page 23

14. B reads fourth unless C reads fifth.

original: $\not{B}_4 \longrightarrow C_5$

(In other words, if B doesn't read fourth, then C reads fifth.)

(Applying the Unless formula, C_5 follows "unless" and is thus the necessary condition, while B_4 gets negated to become the sufficient condition.)

contrapositive: $\not{C}_5 \longrightarrow B_4$

(If C does not read fifth, then B reads fourth.)

---

15. I conducts the session immediately before J if J conducts the session immediately before K.

original: $\boxed{JK} \longrightarrow \boxed{IJ}$

(Reordered: If J conducts the session immediately before K, then I conducts the session immediately before J.)

Note: the outcome is that if J immediately precedes K, the $\boxed{IJK}$ block is formed.

contrapositive: $\not{\boxed{IJ}} \longrightarrow \not{\boxed{JK}}$

(If I does not immediately precede J, then J does not immediately precede K.)

---

16. If S does not perform in the play, then T must be the third performer to appear on stage.

original: $\not{S} \longrightarrow T_3$

(If S does not perform in the play, then T must be the third performer to appear on stage.)

Note: "must" refers to a necessary condition.

contrapositive: $\not{T}_3 \longrightarrow S$

(If T does not appear on stage third, then S does perform in the play.)

17. If U is presented, it is presented neither immediately before, nor immediately after R is presented.

original: U ⟶ ~~RU~~ and ~~UR~~

(If U is presented, then it appears neither immediately before nor immediately after R.)

contrapositive: Technically, there is no contrapositive; the RU & UR blocks are simply prohibited—neither can be a sufficient condition.

---

18. If L is chosen or M is chosen then N is not chosen.

original: L or M ⟶ ~~N~~

(If L or M is chosen, then N is not chosen.)

contrapositive: N ⟶ ~~L~~ and ~~M~~

(If N is chosen, then L is not chosen, and M is not chosen.)

(In other words: If N is chosen, then neither L nor M is chosen.)

---

19. K must compete immediately after J, whenever I competes second.

original: I_2 ⟶ JK

(K must compete immediately after J, whenever I competes second.)

Note: "whenever" introduces the sufficient condition.

contrapositive: ~~JK~~ ⟶ ~~I_2~~

(If K does not compete immediately after J, then I does not compete second.)

Conditional Reasoning Mini-Diagramming Drill Answer Key—page 23

20. O cannot play if both P and Q play.

original: $P \text{ and } Q \longrightarrow \not{O}$

(If both P and Q play, then O cannot play.)

contrapositive: $O \longrightarrow \not{P} \text{ or } \not{Q}$

(If O plays, then either P does not play, or else Q does not play. It is also possible that neither P nor Q plays.)

---

21. When J doesn't go second, K goes fourth.

original: $\not{J}_2 \longrightarrow K_4$

(In other words, if J does not go second, then K goes fourth.)

contrapositive: $\not{K}_4 \longrightarrow J_2$

(If K doesn't go fourth, then J goes second.)

---

22. P is on stage only if O is on stage.

original: $P \longrightarrow O$

(In other words, if P is on stage, then O is on stage.)

Note: "Only if" introduces a necessary condition.

contrapositive: $\not{O} \longrightarrow \not{P}$

(If O is not on stage, then P is not on stage.)

Conditional Reasoning Mini-Diagramming Drill Answer Key—page 23

23. C is not shown at the festival unless both D and E are also shown.

original: C ⟶ D and E

(In other words, if C is shown at the festival, then both D and E are also shown.)

contrapositive: D̸ or E̸ ⟶ C̸

(If D is not shown, or if E is not shown, then C is not shown.)

(In other words, if either D or E is absent (or both are absent), then C must also be absent.)

---

24. Neither W nor X performs in any show in which Y doesn't perform.

original: Y̸ ⟶ W̸ and X̸

(In other words, if Y doesn't perform, then neither W nor X performs.)

Note: "any" introduces a sufficient condition.

contrapositive: W or X ⟶ Y

(If either W or X performs, then Y must also perform.)

Conditional Reasoning Mini-Diagramming Drill Answer Key—page 23

25. Every time A is displayed first, B is also included in the display.

original: $A_1 \longrightarrow B$

(In other words, if A is displayed first, then B is also displayed.)

Note: "Every" introduces a sufficient condition.

contrapositive: $\not{B} \longrightarrow \not{A}_1$

(If B is not included in the display, then A cannot be displayed first.)

Basic Linear Games Rule Diagramming Drill Answer Key—page 27

Each item shows the appropriate rule representation, and then any relevant inferences or representations on the diagram.

1. G is recorded earlier than H and J.

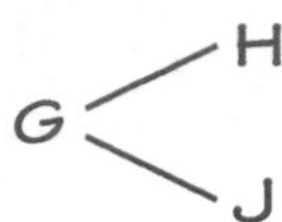

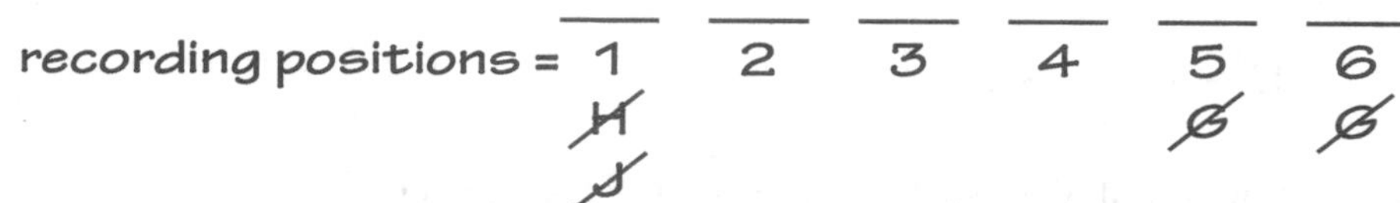

---

2. Exactly one day separates the interviews of Y and Z.

| Y/Z ___ Z/Y |

No Not Laws can be drawn from this rule.

days = ___ 1 ___ 2 ___ 3 ___ 4 ___ 5 ___ 6

---

3. C must sit three chairs behind D, and E must sit one chair before C.

| D ___ E C |

The diagram above is correct. If C sits *three* chairs *behind* D, then the diagram is | D ___ ___ C |. If E sits one chair before C, then the diagram is | E C |. Those two rules combined create the diagram above.

Due to the size of the block, it can only be placed in three different positions: 1-4, 2-5, or 3-6. Depending on the other rules in the game, you could show those three possibilities, or, alternately, show the Not Laws:

chairs =	1	2	3	4	5	6
	~~C~~	~~C~~	~~C~~	~~D~~	~~D~~	~~D~~
	~~E~~	~~E~~				~~E~~

Basic Linear Games Rule Diagramming Drill Answer Key—page 27

4. If S speaks, S speaks the day before T.

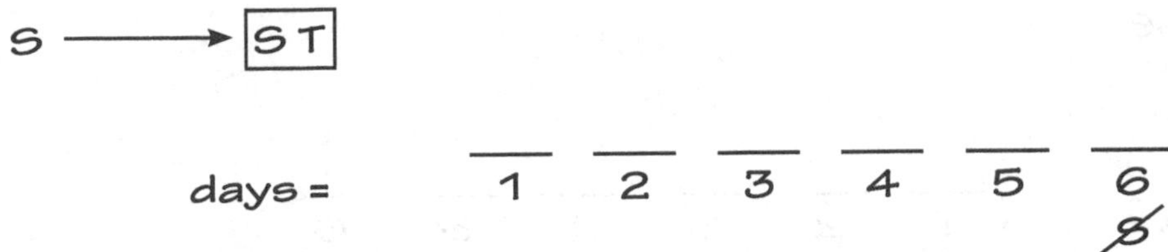

The rule indicates that "if" S speaks, then S speaks the day before T. Thus, S does not necessarily have to speak. As such, T could speak on day 1 as long as S does not speak. If S does speak, S could never speak on day 6, hence the Not Law on that day.

---

5. The factory that is inspected second is also inspected first.

2 ⟶ 1

Inspections = 1 ⟵ 2   3   4   5   6

The most useful representation is the one in the diagram itself. If we had more information about the game, we might be able to determine that seats 1 and 2 are in a block, but in the absence of that information the best representation is with an arrow.

---

6. If J performs, then K performs earlier than L.

J ⟶ (K —— L)   No Not Laws can be drawn from this rule.

performances = 1   2   3   4   5   6

Not Laws can be drawn only once J is known to perform. Otherwise, we cannot be certain that K —— L, and thus no inferences follow.

Basic Linear Games Rule Diagramming Drill Answer Key—page 27

7. R's sole trip will occur between S's two trips.

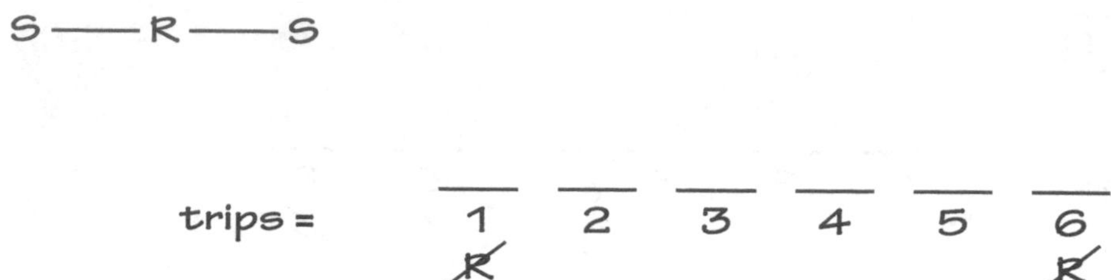

Because R is "bracketed" by S, R cannot go on the first or last trip. S could go on any trip, and thus no Not Laws can be shown for S. The only way to create Not Laws for S would be to use subscript designations for the first and second trip, as in S_1 and S_2. Then, an S_1 Not Law would be placed on trips 5 and 6, and an S_2 Not Law would be placed on Trips 1 and 2. However, due to the possibility of confusion we have elected not to show those Not Laws (you could—the choice is yours) and instead to use the S —— R —— S sequence.

---

8. A sits in either the first or the last seat.

A ⟶ 1/6

	A/					/A
seats =	1	2	3	4	5	6

Not Laws could be placed on seats 2, 3, 4, and 5, but since A is already shown in the diagram in seat 1 or seat 6, that would redundant.

Basic Linear Games Rule Diagramming Drill Answer Key—page 27

9. Y is inspected after X is inspected but before Z is inspected.

X —— Y —— Z

inspections =	1	2	3	4	5	6
	Z̸	Z̸			X̸	X̸
	Y̸					Y̸

The language of this rule can be confusing, but it is often used by LSAC. Let's take a closer look at the potential problem.

In the rule, some students do not realize that the phrase "after...but before" applies entirely to Y, the initial variable. Thus, the rule as stated actually contains two separate relationships:

X —— Y
and
Y —— Z

Combining the two produces the rule diagram: X —— Y —— Z.

The meaning would be clearer if LSAC restated the rule as, "Y is inspected after X, and Y is inspected before Z is inspected." Regardless, be on the lookout for confusing language, and read every rule carefully.

---

10. M and T are not performed on consecutive days.

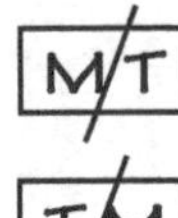

No Not Laws can be drawn from this rule.

days =	1	2	3	4	5	6

In most cases not-blocks (as in this item) and rotating blocks (as in item #2) do not allow you to make initial inferences. However, once other rules are added to the blocks, inferences often follow.

Basic Linear Games Rule Diagramming Drill Answer Key—page 27

11. L is seated after N is seated.

Rule diagram: N —— L

Diagram inferences:

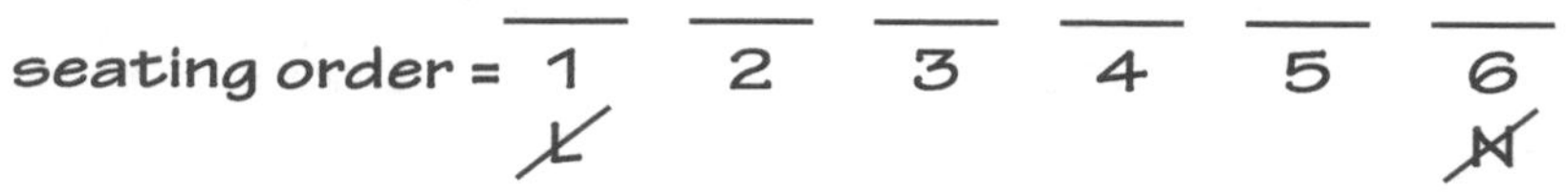

seating order =	1	2	3	4	5	6
	~~L~~					~~N~~

Because L is always seated after N, N can never be seated last and L can never be seated first.

---

12. Tan receives a higher score in Diving than in Gymnastics.

Rule Diagram: G —— D

Diagram Inferences:

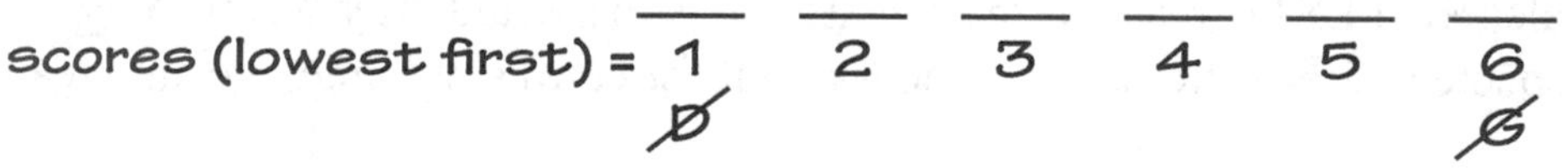

scores (lowest first) =	1	2	3	4	5	6
	~~D~~					~~G~~

Because Tan's score for Diving (D) is higher than her score for Gymnastics (G), and because scores increase from lowest to highest (1 to 6), G must always be placed to the left of D on the diagram. Hence, D can never be first (lowest score), and G can never be sixth (highest score).

Basic Linear Games Rule Diagramming Drill Answer Key—page 27

13. Priya is not faster than Rajit.

Rule diagram: R —— P

If this was *not* a one-to-one relationship (each variable assigned a single position), this would be a trick question with no Not Laws, and a diagram of R ═══ P. That is, according to the rule, while P is not faster than R, the two could still potentially be the same speed, and that tie possibility would undoubtedly be tested. However, in a one-to-one relationship where each variable completely fills a single space, R and P cannot be the same speed, and thus you can infer that P is not first and R is not last, and the proper diagram for this rule is R —— P.

Diagram inferences:

speed (fastest first) =	1	2	3	4	5	6
	~~P~~					~~R~~

Because R is faster than P, R can never be last and P can never be first.

---

14. Gina is not selected first or last.

Rule diagram: G ——→ Not 1 or 6

The rule is shown in conditional fashion since G cannot be selected in the first or last position.

Diagram inferences:

selection order =	1	2	3	4	5	6
	~~G~~					~~G~~

This is a fairly straightforward rule where we have Not Laws for G in 1 and 6, indicating that Gina cannot be selected for those two positions.

Basic Linear Games Rule Diagramming Drill Answer Key—page 27

15. F does not sit in an even-numbered chair.

Rule diagram: F ⟶ 1, 3, or 5

The rule is shown in conditional fashion since F cannot be seated in an even-numbered chair (chairs 2, 4, and 6), and thus must always be seated in an odd-numbered chair (chair 1, 3, or 5).

Diagram inferences:

chairs =	1	2	3	4	5	6
	F/		/F		/F	
		~~F~~		~~F~~		~~F~~

Note that you can represent this rule in your diagram either with Not Laws under the even-numbered chairs (2, 4, and 6), or by showing F above your diagram in the three possible chairs that she could take: the odd-numbered chairs, 1, 3, and 5. We have shown both to present the full scope of diagramming possibilities, however on the test showing either just the Not Laws or the split-options should be sufficient, and there is no need to show both.

---

16. Either T or H has appointment 4.

Rule diagram: 4 ⟶ T or H

The rule is shown in conditional fashion since appointment 4 must be assigned to either T or H.

Diagram inferences:

appointments =	1	2	3	4	5	6
				T/H		

Basic Linear Games Rule Diagramming Drill Answer Key—page 27

17. Lopez's visit is either on day 1 or day 6.

Rule diagram: L ⟶ 1 or 6

The rule is shown in conditional fashion since the placement of L tells us it must be in 1 or 6.

Diagram inferences:

	L/					/L
days =	1	2	3	4	5	6

Note that there is no need to put Not Laws for L on days 2–5.

---

18. P is seated immediately beside U, and also immediately beside O.

Rule diagram: [U P O]

[O P U]

Diagram inferences:

seats =	1	2	3	4	5	6
	P̸					P̸

This rule establishes that P is seated between U and O, however since we do not know the exact order of the three variables we must make two blocks, one for each possible seating arrangement. Since in either instance P has at least one person seated on either side of her, P can never be seated first or last, and Not Laws are shown to represent this.

Basic Linear Games Rule Diagramming Drill Answer Key—page 27

19. If G is scheduled for Tuesday, Y is scheduled for Friday.

Rule diagram: $G_T \longrightarrow Y_F$

$\not{Y}_F \longrightarrow \not{G}_T$

This is a fairly simple conditional rule, which is diagrammed with its contrapositive above.

Diagram inferences:

None. No Not Laws or variable placements can be drawn from this rule.

---

20. Cheese and Butter are not stocked on adjacent aisles.

Rule diagram:

Diagram inferences:

None. No Not Laws or variable placements can be drawn from this rule.

Final Note: In most cases not-blocks and rotating blocks do not allow you to make initial inferences. However, once other rules are introduced, inferences often follow.

Basic Linear Games Rule Diagramming Drill Answer Key—page 27

21. The Harmons live next to the Pratts.

Rule diagram:

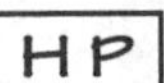

PH

Diagram inferences:

None. No Not Laws or variable placements can be drawn from this rule. Again, not-blocks and rotating blocks generally do not allow you to make initial inferences. However, additional rules often yield more powerful inferences.

---

22. The film *Tropos* is played either two or three days after the film *Exodus*.

Rule diagram:

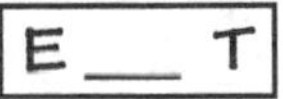

or

E ___ ___ T

Diagram inferences:

While there is some uncertainty as to exactly how many days separate T from E, and thus some limitations to the number of inferences that can be made, we can still show Not Laws based on the minimum amount of separation (T at least two days after E).

days =	1	2	3	4	5	6
	not T	not T			not E	not E

And knowing the placement of one of the two variables would yield additional inferences as well. For instance, if T is played third, then E must be played first (T two days after E). Similarly, if E is played fourth, then T must be played sixth (again, T two days after E).

Basic Linear Games Rule Diagramming Drill Answer Key—page 27

23. Exactly three days separate Graham's appointment from Juarez's appointment.

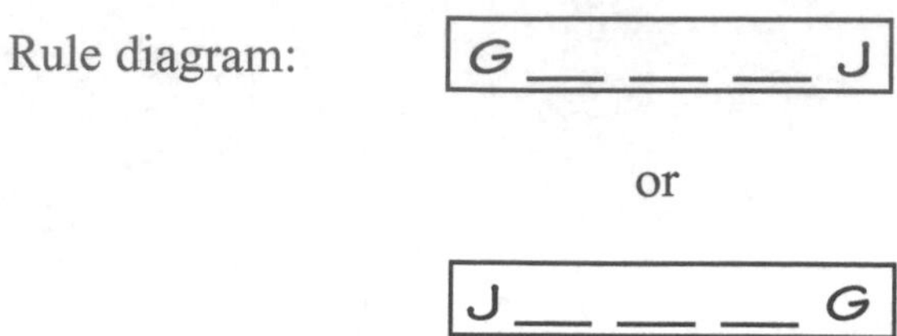

or

J ___ ___ ___ G

Note here that we do not know the specific order of G and J, but rather we are only told the number of days (3) between them. These large blocks often yield powerful inferences, as they are typically limited in their placement options. Here, G and J can either have appointments on Monday and Friday (although we do not know their order), or have appointments on Tuesday and Saturday (again, the person with an appointment on each day cannot be known).

Diagram inferences:

days =	M	Tu	W	Th	F	S
			~~G~~	~~G~~		
			~~J~~	~~J~~		

Due to the number of days between G and J, neither of them can have appointments on Wednesday or Thursday, as not enough room would exist for a three-day separation (for instance, only one day separates W from M, and only two days separate W from S).

---

24. If the site in London is inspected fifth, then the sites in London and Madrid cannot be inspected consecutively.

Rule diagram: L5 ⟶ ~~LM~~ / ~~ML~~ ⟶ ~~M4~~ / ~~M6~~

This conditional rule tells us that when L is the location of the fifth inspection, then L and M cannot be inspected consecutively. That means that placing L into 5 disallows M adjacent to it, so M could not be 4 or 6 in that scenario. Note, however, that showing Not Laws for M in 4 and 6 would be a mistake, since M could be placed in those positions any time the sufficient condition (L fifth) is not met.

From the contrapositive you can also infer that if M is inspected either fourth or sixth, then L cannot be inspected fifth (as that would make L and M consecutive). Always consider the effects of the contrapositive when working with conditional rules.

Diagram inferences:

None. No Not Laws or variable placements can be drawn from this rule, as it is conditional and only applies when L is inspected fifth.

---

25. U and V are both assigned either higher-numbered seats than T, or else they are both assigned lower-numbered seats than T.

Rule diagram: T < U, V or U, V > T

This type of three-variable sequence is fairly common in games, but the either/or nature of this rule actually creates a secondary inference, as it disallows two specific sequences from ever occurring:

cannot occur: U —— T —— V and V —— T —— U

Because both U and V must always be either after T or ahead of T, putting T between them violates this rule, regardless of the order of U and V.

Diagram inferences:

None. No Not Laws or variable placements can be drawn from this rule.

Basic Linear Games Rule Diagramming Drill Answer Key—page 27

26. If Gomez's visit is on Wednesday, then Park's visit must occur earlier in the week than Gomez's visit.

Rule diagram: $G_W \longrightarrow P_{M/T}$

$\not{P}_{M/T} \longrightarrow \not{G}_W$

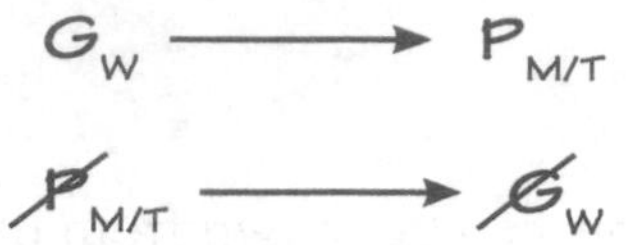

This conditional rule tells us that when Gomez visits on Wednesday, then Park's visit must occur earlier in the week than Wednesday. Hence Park's visit would have to occur on either Monday or Tuesday if Gomez visits on Wednesday.

From the contrapositive you can see that if Park's visit happens later in the week than Tuesday, then Gomez must visit on a day other than Wednesday.

Diagram inferences:

None. No Not Laws or variable placements can be drawn from this rule, as it is conditional and only applies when G visits on Wednesday, or P does not visit on Monday or Tuesday.

---

27. Competitors R and T place ahead of competitor M, and competitor M places ahead of competitors C and D.

Rule diagram:

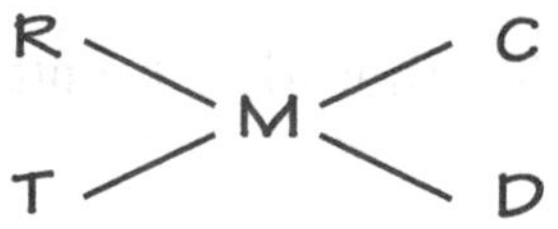

```
R         C
  >  M  <
T         D
```

This lengthy sequence is created by the common variable M, as all five variables can be positioned in a single chain due to their relationship with M. As such, a number of inferences and Not Laws are created.

Diagram inferences:

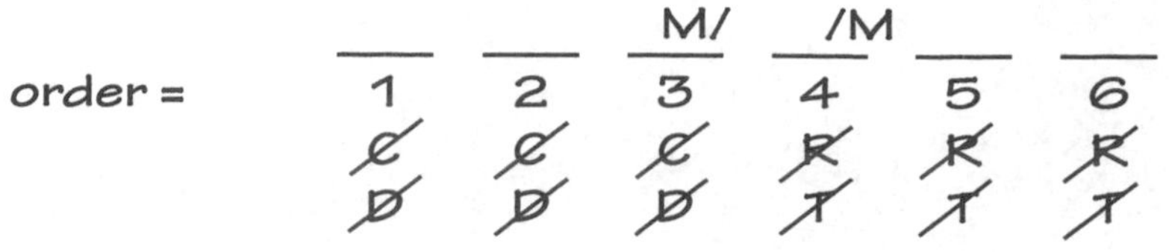

			M/	/M		
order =	1	2	3	4	5	6
	$\not{C}$	$\not{C}$	$\not{C}$	$\not{R}$	$\not{R}$	$\not{R}$
	$\not{D}$	$\not{D}$	$\not{D}$	$\not{T}$	$\not{T}$	$\not{T}$

Basic Linear Games Rule Diagramming Drill Answer Key—page 27

Note that since M is the most restricted variable, it can be placed above the diagram as a split-option in spaces 3 and 4. The other four variables are less well-defined, and are thus shown as Not Laws. However knowledge of the sixth variable in this scenario would likely prove sufficient to allow more definitive placement, or possibly even the creation of two templates: M in 3, and M in 4.

---

28. Neither P nor O is seated immediately beside S.

Rule diagram:

Diagram inferences:

None. No Not Laws or variable placements can be drawn from this rule.

---

29. If Chemistry is the second lecture scheduled, then the two lectures immediately following Chemistry must be Biology and Economics, not necessarily in that order.

Rule diagram:

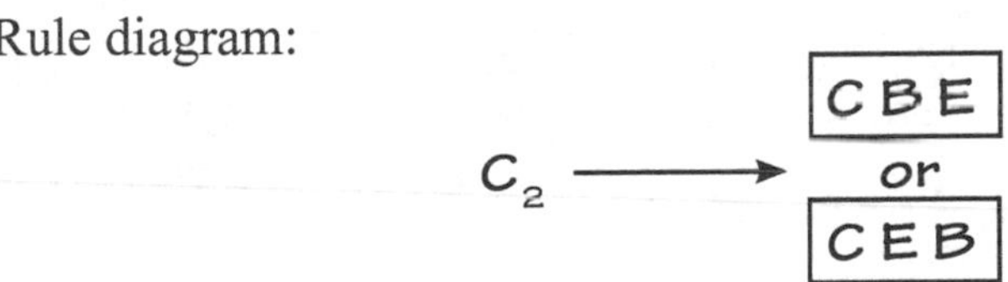

This is an interesting conditional rule and allows for some subjectivity in diagramming, as it can be shown like the above representation with two blocks reflecting the Chemistry, Biology, and Economics sequence (and the uncertainty of B and E's order), or it could be represented with numerical designations for B and E, as they would occupy spaces 3 and 4 under this rule. So long as you represent the uncertainty of which variable would be third and which would be fourth, either diagrammatic option is acceptable.

Diagram inferences:

None. No Not Laws or variable placements can be drawn from this rule, as it is conditional and thus only applicable under specific conditions.

30. Francois is assigned to run in the only lane between the lanes to which Javier and Natalia are assigned.

Rule diagram: | J F N |

| N F J |

Diagram inferences:

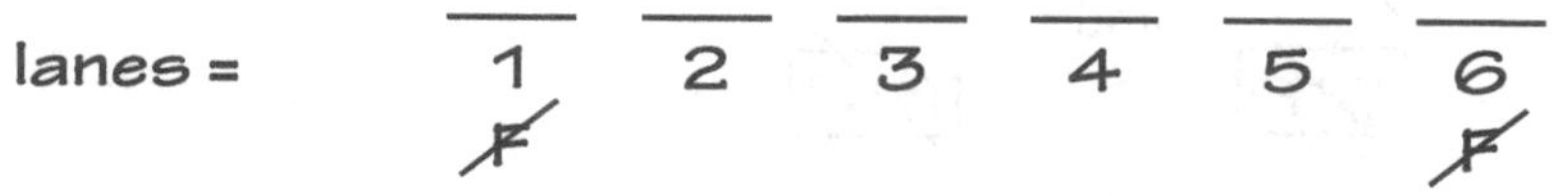

lanes =

1	2	3	4	5	6
~~F~~					~~F~~

This rule establishes that F runs in the lane between J and N, however since we do not know the relationship between J and N directly we must make two blocks, one for each possible lane assignment. Since in either instance F has at least one person running on either side of her, F can never be in the first or last lanes, and Not Laws are shown to represent this.

Question Stem Classification Drill Answer Key—page 33

1. If L is the third car sold, then which one of the following could be true?

> **Classification:** Local, Could Be True
> **Four Incorrect Answers:** Cannot Be True

---

2. Which one of the following could be false?

> **Classification:** Global, Not Necessarily True
> **Four Incorrect Answers:** Must Be True

Remember, "could be false" is the equivalent of "not necessarily true."

---

3. Which one of the following is a list of all the musicians who could be in the band at any particular time?

> **Classification:** Global, Could Be True, List
> **Four Incorrect Answers:** Cannot Be True

The question asks for a list of musicians; remember to apply proper List question technique.

---

4. If more green shoes than yellow shoes are selected, then which one of the following cannot be true?

> **Classification:** Local, Cannot Be True
> **Four Incorrect Answers:** Could Be True

---

5. If K is displayed fifth, then each of the following could be true EXCEPT:

> **Classification:** Local, Cannot Be True
> **Four Incorrect Answers:** Could Be True

Remember, "Except" turns the question around.

Question Stem Classification Drill Answer Key—page 33

6. If T and R each received a rating of "excellent," then which one of the following cannot be false?

   Classification: Local, Must Be True
   Four Incorrect Answers: Not Necessarily True

Remember, "cannot be false" is the equivalent of "must be true."

---

7. Each of the following must be false EXCEPT:

   Classification: Global, Could Be True
   Four Incorrect Answers: Cannot Be True

Remember, "must be false" is the equivalent to "cannot be true," and then "Except" turns the question around.

---

8. What is the minimum number of animals that could be in the barn at any given time?

   Classification: Global, Must Be True, Minimum
   Four Incorrect Answers: Not Necessarily True

The classification here is not a mistake. This is a Must Be True question, not a Could Be True question even though the question stem uses the word "could." In asking for the "minimum number of animals," the question seeks a number that Must Be True, that is, the minimum is a global certainty that is always constant and therefore must be true.

---

9. Suppose that the condition requiring W to perform earlier than Y is replaced by a new condition requiring that Y performs earlier than W. If all of the other original conditions remain in effect, which one of the following cannot occur?

   Classification: Local, Cannot Be True, Suspension
   Four Incorrect Answers: Could Be True

This is a Suspension question because it asks you to suspend one of the original rules of the game. When questions such as this one appear, they always appear at the end of the game. Be wary of Suspension questions if time is low because they force you to re-setup the game and can be time-consuming.

Question Stem Classification Drill Answer Key—page 33

10. There is only one acceptable group of five speakers that can be selected if which one of the following pairs of speakers is selected?

Classification: Global, Must Be True, Justify
Four Incorrect Answers: Not Necessarily True

This is actually a Justify question. The question stem asks you to select the answer choice that will, when added to the existing rules, force only one outcome. The question has been classified as "Must Be True, Justify" because the correct answer must justify (or produce) the desired solution and the four incorrect answers do not necessarily justify the desired outcome.

---

11. Which one of the following could be a list of the homes in the order of their scheduled inspections, from day 1 through day 7?

Classification: Global, Could Be True
Four Incorrect Answers: Cannot Be True

This is a standard List question, so remember to apply the proper technique, by working from the rules to quickly eliminate the answer choices that are precluded by them.

---

12. If the fifth stone is a sapphire, then each of the following must be true EXCEPT:

Classification: Local, Not Necessarily True
Four Incorrect Answers: Must Be True

This question adds a new constraint, making it Local, and since all of the answer choice except for one must be true, the right answer choice will be the one that it not necessarily true.

---

13. Which one of the following must be false?

Classification: Global, Cannot Be True
Four Incorrect Answers: Could Be True

This is a standard Global question; if exactly one of the answer choice must be false, that means that the four incorrect answer choices are not necessarily false; in other words, the four incorrect answer choices are the ones that could be true.

Question Stem Classification Drill Answer Key—page 33

14. Each of the following is a day that must include an advanced session EXCEPT:

Classification: Global, Not Necessarily True
Four Incorrect Answers: Must Be True

Since this is an "Except" question, the correct answer choice will present the only day on which an advanced session is not dictated.

---

15. Tennis can be scheduled for any day EXCEPT:

Classification: Global, Cannot Be True
Four Incorrect Answers: Could Be True

Again, "Except" turns the question around, requiring you find the answer choice for which tennis cannot be scheduled.

---

16. If T lives on the fifth floor and O lives on the first floor, then which one of the following can be true?

Classification: Local, Could Be True
Four Incorrect Answers: Cannot Be True

Since the question tells you that only one of the answer choices can be true, that means that the four incorrect answer choices will the ones that cannot be true.

---

17. If P performs immediately before R, then each of the following must be true EXCEPT:

Classification: Local, Not Necessarily True
Four Incorrect Answers: Must Be True

This local question imposes a new rule (creating the PR block), and provides that all of the answer choices but one are dictated to be true, which means that the right answer will be the only one that is not necessarily true.

Question Stem Classification Drill Answer Key—page 33

18. If Felicia does not visit the same store on any two consecutive days, then which one of the following cannot be false?

Classification: Local, Must Be True
Four Incorrect Answers: Not Necessarily True

"Cannot be false" is the equivalent of "Must be True," so the right answer will be the choice that is dictated to be true when the new local rule (no two consecutive days) is considered.

---

19. Each of the following could be false EXCEPT:

Classification: Global, Must be True
Four Incorrect Answers: Not Necessarily True

If all four answer choices could be false except for one, then the right answer choice is the one that could not be false; the right answer is the one that must be true.

---

20. Which one of the following CANNOT be the complete list of records sold at Daulton's?

Classification: Global, Cannot Be True
Four Incorrect Answers: Could Be True

---

21. If three of the trucks are red, then each of the following could be the truck that arrives fourth EXCEPT:

Classification: Local, Cannot Be True
Four Incorrect Answers: Could Be True

---

22. Which one of the following CANNOT be the songs scheduled for the second, third, and fourth performances, listed in that order?

Classification: Global, Cannot Be True
Four Incorrect Answers: Could Be True

Question Stem Classification Drill Answer Key—page 33

23. If T is not paired with L, then exactly how many sessions are there any one of which could be last?

Classification: Local, Must Be True
Four Incorrect Answers: Not Necessarily True

Note that while the logical opposite of "must be true" is "not necessarily true," in this case the correct answer choice will present the exact number of sessions that could be last, while the four other answer choices will present choices that are inaccurate (that is, beyond "not necessarily true").

---

24. The question of which judges will be chosen to preside over the competition and in what order they will vote can be completely resolved if which one of the following is true?

Classification: Global, Must Be True, Justify
Four Incorrect Answers: Not Necessarily True (Not Justify)

This justify question stem asks you to select the answer choice that will resolve the question of judges selected and their order. It is classified as a "Must Be True, Justify" question because the correct answer must justify the desired solution, while the four incorrect answers do not necessarily produce the desired outcome.

---

25. Which one of the following, if substituted for the condition that Raul cannot be selected third, would have the same effect in determining the order of the selections?

Classification: Local, Rule Substitution
Four Incorrect Answers: Improper Substitution

This Local Rule Substitution question requires you to find the choice which, when applied to the scenario presented, produces the same outcome as the condition that "Raul cannot be selected third." The correct answer choice will have the same impact on the determination of the order as the rule that is to be substituted, while none of the four incorrect answer choice will have the same exact ramifications.

Basic Linear Setup Practice Drill Answer Key—page 38

Note: Most of the problems in this drill are diagrammed with horizontal setups. In many cases these problems could be diagrammed with vertical setups, although some games should be shown horizontally, such as one about houses on a street. Also, if you encounter a Not Law in the answer key that appears incorrectly placed, put that variable into that position and observe the consequences. This will allow you to better understand the interaction taking place between the variables and the rules.

1. A manager must schedule six employees—Kwame, Lars, Marina, Noriko, Oliver, and Paulo—to work during a single workweek, Monday through Saturday. Each employee must work on exactly one day, and no two employees can work on the same day. The schedule must observe the following constraints:

    If Noriko works on Tuesday, then Marina works on Saturday.

    Either Oliver or Paulo works on Wednesday.

    Kwame works on Monday or else on Saturday.

Whenever a game introduces the days of the week as a variable sct, always use the days of the week as the base. As the two variable sets both contain six members, and each member is either used or filled, the two variable sets are in a one-to-one relationship (1-1-1-1-1-1).

The base diagram appears as follows:

K L M N O P[6]
  *

K/		O/P			/K
M	Tu	W	Th	F	S

$N_{Tu} \longrightarrow M_S$

$W \longrightarrow O/P$

$K \longrightarrow M/S$

The relationships can be linked by connecting the two rules that reference Saturday:

If Noriko works on Tuesday, then Marina works on Saturday, and Kwame must work Monday. This can be diagrammed as:

$$N_{Tu} \longrightarrow M_S \longrightarrow K_M$$

PRACTICE DRILL EXPLANATIONS

Basic Linear Setup Practice Drill Answer Key—page 38

If Kwame works on Saturday, then Marina cannot work on Saturday, and Noriko cannot work on Tuesday. This can be diagrammed as:

$K_S \longrightarrow \not{M}_S \longrightarrow \not{N}_{Tu}$

Either relationship reduces to:

$N_{Tu} \longleftrightarrow\!\!\!\!\!\!\!+\;\; K_S$

---

2. Five birds—a parrot, a quail, a raven, a sparrow, and a thrush—are being held in five different cages, numbered 1 through 5. Each cage holds exactly one bird in accordance with the following conditions:

   The raven is held in the second cage.

   There is exactly one cage between the cage holding the parrot and the cage holding the quail.

There are two variable sets in this problem: the five birds and the five cages holding the birds. Since the cage numbers have an inherent sense of order, they are chosen as the base. Again, the two variable sets are in a one-to-one relationship (1-1-1-1-1).

PQRST^5
  * *

R ⟶ 2

[P/Q ___ Q/P]

___	R	___	___	___
1	2	3	4	5

The split-block has only two spacing options: 1-3 and 3-5. The following diagram shows each option drawn out:

Option #2—Block in 3-5:	___	R	P/Q	___	Q/P
Option #1—Block in 1-3:	P/Q	R	Q/P	___	___
	1	2	3	4	5

Basic Linear Setup Practice Drill Answer Key—page 38

Of course, in each instance only two spaces are open, and only two variables are unaccounted for: S and T. Thus, S and T form a dual-option in the open spaces in each scenario:

	1	2	3	4	5
Option #2—Block in 3-5:	S/T	R	P/Q	T/S	Q/P
Option #1—Block in 1-3:	P/Q	R	Q/P	S/T	T/S

The two templates contain four solutions each, and thus there are only eight solutions in this game.

Although this problem is too simple to appear as an entire Logic Game, it is indicative of the type of "endgame" situations that occur after several variables have already been placed in a question.

Question 2.1. Which one of the following must be true?

(A) Either P or Q is held in the first cage.
(B) Either S or T is held in the first cage.
(C) Either S or T is held in the fourth cage.
(D) Either P or Q is held in the fifth cage.
(E) Either S or T is held in the fifth cage.

Question 2.1. The correct answer is (C). As shown by the two templates above, S or T is always fourth.

Answer choice (A) is incorrect because S or T could be held in the first cage.

Answer choice (B) is incorrect because P or Q could be held in the first cage.

Answer choice (D) is incorrect because S or T could be held in the fifth cage.

Answer choice (E) is incorrect because P or Q could be held in the fifth cage.

3. Six speakers—B, C, D, F, G, and H—are scheduled to speak at a political rally. Each speaker will speak exactly once, and no two speakers will speak at the same time. The schedule must satisfy the following requirements:
   C speaks immediately after B.
   F must be the second speaker.
   B speaks at some time before D.

In this problem the speaking order should be chosen as the base, and the variables are in a one-to-one relationship (1-1-1-1-1-1).

BCDFGH [6]

[BC] —— D

G/H	F		B/C	D/	/D
1	2	3	4	5	6
~~D~~		~~D~~	~~D~~	~~B~~	~~B~~
~~B~~		~~C~~			~~C~~
~~C~~					

The first point of interest in this problem is in the representation of F. Since F must speak second, it automatically follows that F cannot speak first, third, fourth, fifth, or sixth. An argument could thus be made that F Not Laws should be shown on those slots. This representation would be correct, but since F is already placed, this would be redundant. However, if you find yourself continually missing these types of inferences, you can certainly show the F Not Laws.

The second point of interest is in the placement of the BC block. Because of the space requirements for the block, and the fact that D speaks later than the block, the block must be placed in positions 3-4 or 4-5. Accordingly, either B or C must always speak fourth and therefore no other student can speak fourth. This dual-option is represented by B/C in the fourth slot.

The next piece of relevant information concerns D. Because D must speak later than the block, D must speak fifth or sixth, and this is represented on the diagram with a split-option.

Last, check to see if any of the spaces are burdened with an unusually high number of Not Laws. The first space is a case in point: out of the six variables, only G or H can speak first. This inference is critical and should be represented with a G/H dual option.

Basic Linear Setup Practice Drill Answer Key—page 38

4. An opening act is selecting the songs for an evening's concert. Seven songs—G, H, J, K, N, O, and P—will be played one after another, not necessarily in that order. Each song will be played exactly once, according to the following conditions:

    G must be played exactly three songs before K.
    The fourth song played is either N or O.
    H must be played immediately before J.

In this problem the order of song performance is chosen as the base, and the variable sets are in a one-to-one relationship (1-1-1-1-1-1-1).

GHJKNOP[7]
*

G ___ ___ K

HJ

1	2	3	4	5	6	7
			N/O			
~~K~~	~~K~~	~~K~~		~~G~~	~~G~~	~~G~~
~~G~~	~~P~~	~~H~~		~~H~~	~~P~~	~~K~~
~~J~~	~~H~~	~~J~~		~~J~~	~~G~~	~~H~~
	~~N~~				~~N~~	
	~~O~~				~~O~~	

The first rule presents a tricky block that is often mis-diagrammed. If G is played *three songs before* K, then there are actually two songs between G and K. To best understand the rule, start with K and then count three spaces going to the left. G is placed in that third space, producing the block above.

Because the GK block requires so much space, the options for placing that block are limited. In fact, the GK block can only be placed in spaces 2-5 or 3-6:

	1	2	3	4	5	6	7
Option #2—Block in 3-6:			G	N/O		K	
Option #1—Block in 2-5:		G		N/O	K		

Of course, in each option the HJ block is limited in placement as well:

	1	2	3	4	5	6	7
Option #2—Block in 3-6:	H	J	G	N/O		K	
Option #1—Block in 2-5:		G		N/O	K	H	J

The remaining two open spaces in each diagram are then filled by P and the remainder of the N/O dual-option. Thus, we can deduce that spaces 2 and 6 are highly restricted and a number of Not Laws follow for each. For example, P must be in space 1, 3, 5, or 7, and thus can never be placed in space 2 or 6.

---

5. A building manager must assign seven companies—Q, R, S, T, W, X, and Y—to seven different floors of the building—floors 1, 2, 3, 4, 5, 6, and 7. The assignments must comply with the following restrictions:

    Q must be assigned to the floor directly above R.
    S must be assigned to floor 2.
    X must be assigned to the floor directly below W.
    T must be assigned to floor 5.

Of the two variable sets, the floors of the building should be chosen as the base because they have the greatest sense of inherent order. The variable sets are in a one-to-one relationship (1-1-1-1-1-1-1), and in this case the best representation is vertical since that is the way the floors of buildings exist in the real world.

QRSTWXY[7]
*

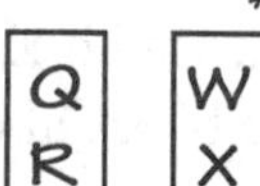

7 ___
6 ___
5 T
4 ___
3 ___
2 S
1 ___

The diagram above shows the basic rule representations. A quick glance at the diagram reveals that the two blocks must be assigned to floors 3-4 and 6-7:

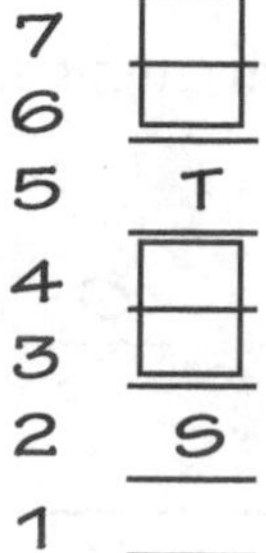

Accordingly, Y, the only remaining variable, must be assigned to floor 1.

Question 5.1. Each one of the following cannot be true EXCEPT:

(A) R is assigned to the floor directly below T.
(B) S is assigned to the floor directly below Q.
(C) R is assigned to the floor directly above W.
(D) T is assigned to the floor directly below R.
(E) Y is assigned to the floor directly above S.

Question 5.1. The correct answer is (D). If the QR block is assigned to the top two floors, T would be assigned to the floor directly below R. Each of the remaining answer choices puts a fixed variable on the "wrong" side of the block, or attempts to place the two blocks consecutively.

---

6. Each of six tennis players—Gemma, Hiroko, Jun, Kurt, Lenisha, and Mahita—is assigned to exactly one of seven tennis courts in preparation for a tournament. The courts are consecutively numbered 1 through 7, and each court is assigned no more than one player. Court assignments must meet the following requirements:
   Kurt is assigned to a lower-numbered court than the court to which Hiroko is assigned.
   Courts 1, 2, and 3 must each be assigned exactly one player.
   Lenisha and Mahita must be assigned to higher-numbered courts than the court to which Hiroko is assigned.
   Jun cannot be assigned to court 1, 3, or 5.

Of the two variable sets, the courts should be chosen as the base since they are numbered and stand consecutively. The game is Underfunded with only six players for the seven courts (6 into 7). However, this shortage can be alleviated by representing the "missing" player with an "E" variable for empty. Whenever there is a shortage of variables (in this case, the players) available to fill a set number of spaces (in this case, the courts), you can always combat this problem by representing the missing variable with an E (or if the given variables already include E, use another letter, such as X). With the shortage of variables eliminated, the variable set relationship can be seen as a one-to-one (1-1-1-1-1-1-1).

Basic Linear Setup Practice Drill Answer Key—page 38

GHJKLM E⁷
*

K —— H < L, M

G/K						
1	2	3	4	5	6	7
~~E~~	~~E~~	~~E~~	~~K~~	~~K~~	~~K~~	~~K~~
~~L~~	~~L~~	~~J~~		~~J~~	~~H~~	~~H~~
~~M~~	~~M~~					
~~H~~						
~~J~~						

In all game types, one of the basic methods for identifying inferences is to examine the points of restriction in the game. In games with Not Laws, that involves looking closely at the slots with the greatest number of Not Laws. In this case, it becomes apparent that court 1 is the most restricted court in the problem. In fact, since five of the seven variables cannot be assigned to court 1 (E is counted as a variable for this purpose), only two players—G and K—are available to play at court 1. This inference would most likely be tested in a game by a question such as, "If K is assigned to court 4, which one of the following must be true?" The correct answer would be "G must be assigned to court 1." In one-to-one Linear games, always examine any space that has a large number of Not Laws, and do not forget that any variable that is already placed is automatically eliminated from all other slots!

In addition, the "K" Not Law on court 4 is correct because placing K on 4 causes a violation of the second rule:

> When K is assigned to court 4, then courts 5, 6, and 7 must be occupied by players H, L, and M (not necessarily in that order). This forces the Empty court (variable "E") to be assigned to court 1, 2, or 3. Unfortunately, that assignment is a violation of the second rule that states that courts 1, 2, and 3 cannot be empty.

7. There are exactly seven houses on a street, numbered 1 through 7. Each house is occupied by exactly one of seven families: the Pearsons, the Quarles, the Rodriguezes, the Sesays, the Tangs, the Valerios, and the Zolkins. All the houses are on the same side of the street, which runs from west to east. House 1 is the westernmost house. The following restrictions apply:

   Either the Quarles or the Rodriguezes live in House 4.

   The Rodriguezes and the Tangs do not live in consecutively numbered houses.

   The Quarles live to the west of the Tangs.

The houses should be chosen as the base since they are numbered and stand on the same side of the street. The two variable sets are in a one-to-one relationship (1-1-1-1-1-1-1), and the game should be set up horizontally.

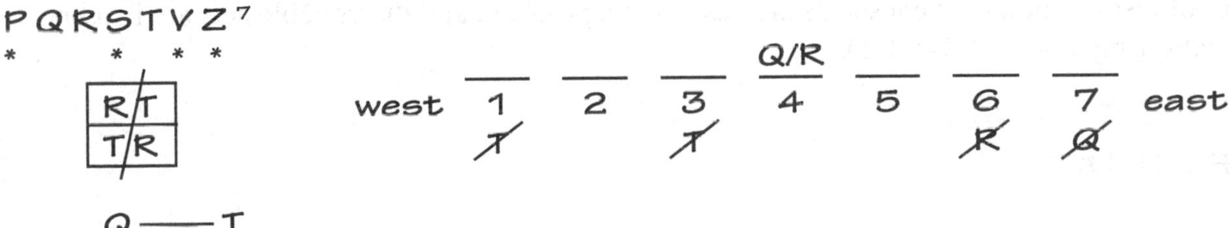

Initially this seems like a fairly simple setup. The rules are easy to represent, and two quick Not Laws follow from the Q —— T relationship. In a real game, at this point most students would stop and move to the questions. However, always make sure to examine the linkages in a game before moving to the questions. In this drill, the rules link together on several counts: the first two rules are linked through R, and the third rule is linked to both of the first two rules. When this type of multiple link situation arises, you can expect there will either be some immediate inferences, or that the connections will play a significant role in the game.

The inferences involving T not occupying house 3 and R not occupying house 6 are quite challenging. Let us review each:

T cannot occupy house 3

If T occupies house 3, then Q must live to the west of T in house 1 or 2. From the first rule, R must then occupy house 4, creating a violation as R and T occupy consecutively numbered houses.

R cannot occupy house 6

If R occupies house 6, then from the first rule Q must occupy house 4. From the third rule, T must then live east of house 4 in houses 5 or 7. As either house is consecutively numbered with R in house 6, a violation of the second rule occurs.

---

8. A researcher must test exactly eight products—B, C, D, F, G, H, J, and K—one product at a time, not necessarily in that order. The tests must be made in accordance with the following conditions:
   K is tested exactly two products before F is tested.
   Either J or K must be tested fourth.
   Either F or G must be tested sixth.
   Only if D is tested first is J tested fourth.

The order of testing should be chosen as the base in this problem, and the variable sets are in a one-to-one relationship (1-1-1-1-1-1-1-1).

BCDFGHJK[8]

K ___ F

$J_4 \longrightarrow D_1$

1	2	3	4	5	6	7	8
			J/K		F/G		
~~F~~	~~F~~	~~F~~				~~K~~	~~K~~
~~K~~	~~K~~						~~F~~

All of the Not Laws above follow from the KF block. Note that because the fourth and sixth tests are already assigned, these affect the block as well.

The interaction of the first, second, and third rules establishes that there are only two possibilities for the fourth and sixth tests: K in four and F in six, or J in four and G in six. Using this information the best attack is to Identify the Templates:

Basic Linear Setup Practice Drill Answer Key—page 38

K in 4:

1	2	3	4	5	6	7	8
			K		F		

	1	2	3	4	5	6	7	8
J in 4, K in 5:	D			J	K	G	F	
J in 4, K in 3:	D		K	J	F	G		

In the first template, there are no restrictions on the placement of any variable (D can be tested first, even if J is not tested fourth; do not make a Mistaken Reversal!).

In the second set of templates, when J is tested fourth, then D must be tested first. This limits the placement of the KF block to 3-5 or 5-7. The remaining spaces are then taken by B, C, and H.

Note also that the fourth rule is conditional, and uses the necessary condition indicator "only if." We did not show the contrapositive because over time you should begin to understand that the contrapositive inherently follows from any conditional relationship. The rule of thumb is to write out the contrapositive when you feel that doing so will make the game easier for you.

Advanced Linear Rule Diagramming Drill Answer Key—page 43

Each item shows the appropriate rule representation, and then any relevant inferences or representations on the diagram.

1. Both green vehicles are inspected before the Ford car.

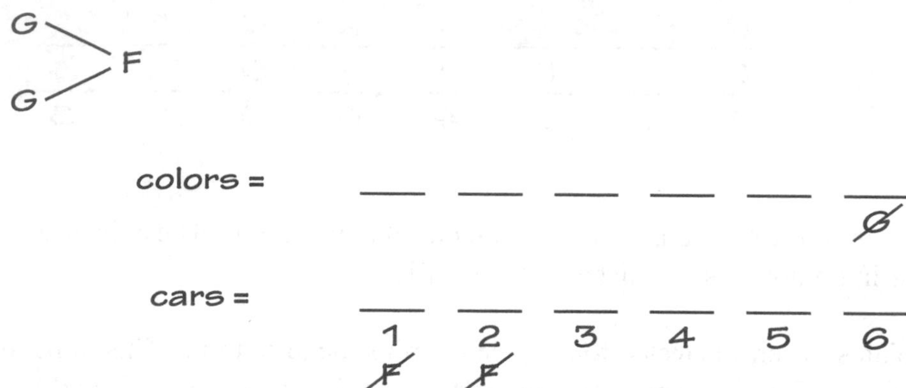

Because both green vehicles are inspected prior to the Ford car, the Ford cannot be inspected first or second, and the green cars cannot be inspected last. The Not Laws are shown on the appropriate stack for each variable set. Note that if the rule said "*Two* green cars are inspected before the Ford car," then there would be no "G" Not Law on the color row because perhaps there are more than two green cars, and as long as two are inspected before F, one or more would be inspected after F (that would then create extra F Not Laws on the car row, however).

---

2. Martina reviews the Thai restaurant, which is reviewed immediately after the French restaurant.

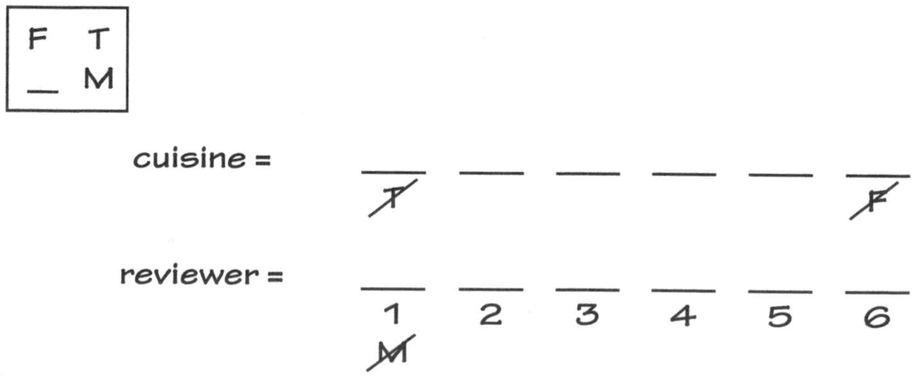

F T
_ M

cuisine =

reviewer =

1 2 3 4 5 6

As is often the case in Advanced Linear games, the rule connects two variable sets. Martina and the Thai restaurant create a vertical block, and the French and Thai restaurants create a horizontal block. Combining the two creates the representation above.As the French restaurant is reviewed before the Thai restaurant, the French restaurant cannot be reviewed last, and the Thai restaurant cannot be reviewed first. And, since Marina is the one who reviews the Thai restaurant, we can conclude that she cannot be the first reviewer.

Advanced Linear Rule Diagramming Drill Answer Key—page 43

3. An activity is assigned to each time period, and the activity selected for the afternoon of day 3 must be the same as the activity selected for the morning of day 4.

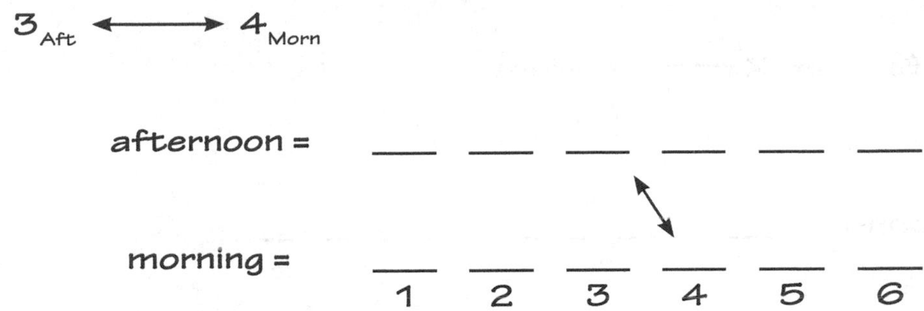

Most students will represent the rule as $4_{Morn} \longrightarrow 3_{Aft}$. There is nothing incorrect about this representation, but it does not capture the full meaning of the rule. Because an activity must always be assigned to the morning of day 4, whatever that activity is will also be the activity assigned to the afternoon of day 3. Thus, if we establish what activity is assigned to the afternoon of day 3, then that *must* also be the activity assigned to the morning of day 4. For example, let us say that one of the activities is Skiing. If Skiing is assigned to the morning of day 4, then Skiing must also be assigned to the afternoon of day 3, and this matches the wording of the rule. However, consider what occurs if Skiing is first assigned to the afternoon of day 3. What options are available for the morning day 4? Could another activity be assigned, such as Painting or Climbing? No, because if one of those activities were assigned, then that activity would also have to be assigned to the afternoon of day 3. Thus, because the activity assigned to the afternoon of day 3 is Skiing, the activity assigned to the morning of day 4 must also be Skiing. Therefore, the proper representation of the rule is with a double-arrow.

The double-arrow should also be represented on the diagram itself. By doing so, you make it less likely that you would forget the operational effects of the rule during the game.

4. Kim cannot compete in the morning sessions, and Rosen cannot compete in the afternoon sessions.

K ⟶ ~~Morn~~ *or* K ⟶ Aft

R ⟶ ~~Aft~~ *or* R ⟶ Morn

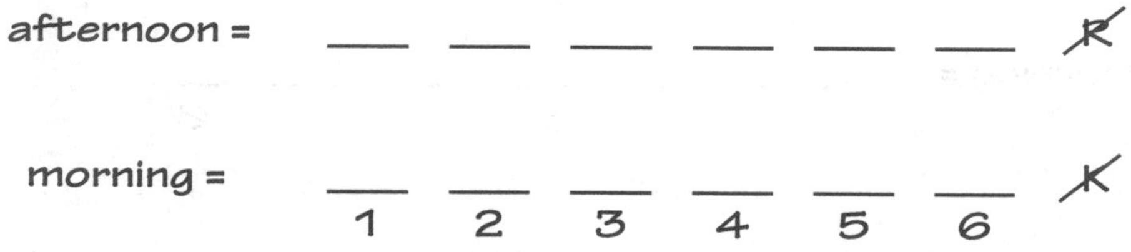

afternoon = ___ ___ ___ ___ ___ ___ ~~R~~

morning = ___ ___ ___ ___ ___ ___ ~~K~~

1 2 3 4 5 6

The K portion of the rule can be diagrammed in two ways, as K cannot compete in the morning, or alternately that K must compete in the afternoon. The same holds true for the R portion of the rule, with the times reversed. The choice is yours, although we have a slight preference for the "K ⟶ Aft" and "R ⟶ Morn" representations, especially when combined with Side Not Laws on the main diagram (which should be shown regardless of which representation you choose).

---

5. The Great Dane dog is shown before the Siamese cat, which is shown before the Calico cat.

G_D — S_C — C_C

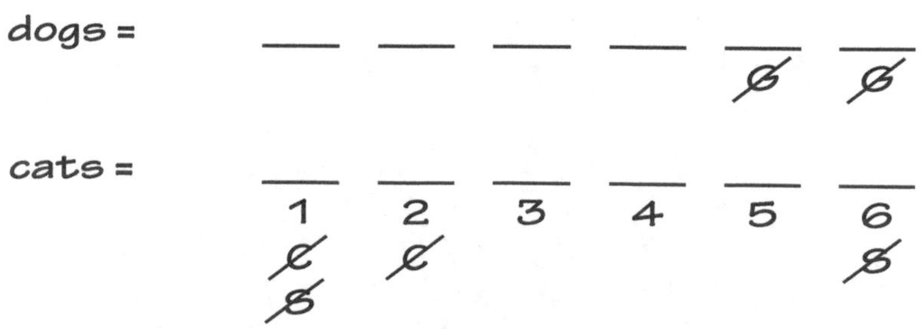

dogs = ___ ___ ___ ___ ___ ___

(5: ~~G~~; 6: ~~G~~)

cats = ___ ___ ___ ___ ___ ___

1 2 3 4 5 6

(1: ~~C~~, ~~S~~; 2: ~~C~~; 6: ~~S~~)

The rules link the two variable sets, creating a sequence that spans both rows. Use subscripts for cat and dog to easily identify the animal type, and then place the appropriate Not Laws under each row.

Advanced Linear Setup Practice Drill Answer Key—page 45

1. A bicycle manufacturer produces six bike models—T, U, W, X, Y, and Z—in three different colors—black, red, and silver. Each bike is produced at a different time, and each bike is exactly one color. The production adheres to the following conditions:
   The only silver bike is produced immediately before the only red bike.
   The fourth bike produced is X or Y.
   Model W is silver.
   The second and fourth bikes are black.

There are three variable sets in this problem: the six production positions, the six bike models, and the colors. Because the production positions have the greatest sense of inherent order, they should be chosen as the base. Consequently, the base diagram should appear as follows:

Colors: B R S [3]
Bikes: T U W X Y Z [6]

Colors:	___	___	___	___	___	___
Bikes:	___	___	___	___	___	___
	1	2	3	4	5	6

The first rule forms an SR block and indicates that only one silver bike and only one red bike are produced, meaning the other four bikes must be black. The third rule adds in that W is the silver bike, producing an advanced stacked block:

S	R
W	___

The last rule stipulates that the second and fourth bikes are black, meaning that the block can only be produced fifth and sixth (and thus the first and third bikes are black), leading to the following complete setup:

Colors: B B B B [S R] [6]
Bikes: T U W X Y Z [6]
(* * under T, U and under Z)

Colors:	B	B	B	B	S	R
Bikes:	___	___	___	X/Y	W	___
	1	2	3	4	5	6

Advanced Linear Setup Practice Drill Answer Key—page 45

2. K, L, N, O, P, R, and S are the only runners in a race. Four of the runners are male, and three are female. Each runner finishes the race, and no two runners finish at the same time. The following restrictions apply:
   - P finishes immediately ahead of S.
   - Either L or N finishes fourth.
   - S is female.
   - No two male runners finish in consecutive positions.

There are three variable sets in this problem: the seven finishing positions, the seven runners, and the male/female designation. The finishing positions have an inherent order, and they should be chosen as the base, leading to the following base setup:

Sex: M M M M F F F [7]
Runner: K L N O P R S [7]

M/F:	___	___	___	___	___	___	___
Runner:	___	___	___	___	___	___	___
	1	2	3	4	5	6	7

The last rule is the most powerful. Because there are four males and no two males can finish consecutively (and thus each male must be next to a female), the Separation Principle applies and the males must finish 1-3-5-7. The three females then finish 2-4-6:

M/F:	M	F	M	F	M	F	M
Runner:	___	___	___	___	___	___	___
	1	2	3	4	5	6	7

With this information in place, the movement of the runners is considerably restricted, and the remaining rules can be diagrammed as follows:

___ F
P S

M/F:	M	F	M	F	M	F	M
Runner:	P/	S/	___	L/N	/P	/S	___
	1	2	3	4	5	6	7

4 ⟶ L/N

Advanced Linear Setup Practice Drill Answer Key—page 45

3. A lawyer schedules the depositions of ten individuals—A, B, C, D, F, G, H, J, K, and L—over the course of five consecutive weekdays, Monday through Friday. There are exactly two depositions each day—one in the morning, and one in the afternoon. Each individual is deposed exactly once in accordance with the following conditions:

   Neither A nor B can be deposed in the afternoon.
   H must be deposed before K is deposed.
   D cannot be deposed on Monday afternoon.
   K and L must be deposed on consecutive mornings, with K deposed before L.
   H is deposed on the afternoon of the day immediately following G's morning deposition.

There are four variable sets in this problem: the days of the week, the morning depositions, the afternoon depositions, and the ten individuals being deposed. Because the days of the week have the greatest sense of inherent order, they should be chosen as the base. Consequently, the base diagram should appear as follows:

Depositions: A B C D F G H J K L [10]

Afternoon: ___ ___ ___ ___ ___

Morning: ___ ___ ___ ___ ___
M Tu W Th F

The first and third rules establish the following Not Laws:

Afternoon: ___ ___ ___ ___ ___ ~~A~~ ~~B~~
~~D~~

Morning: ___ ___ ___ ___ ___
M Tu W Th F

The second, fourth, and fifth rules create a powerful block sequence:

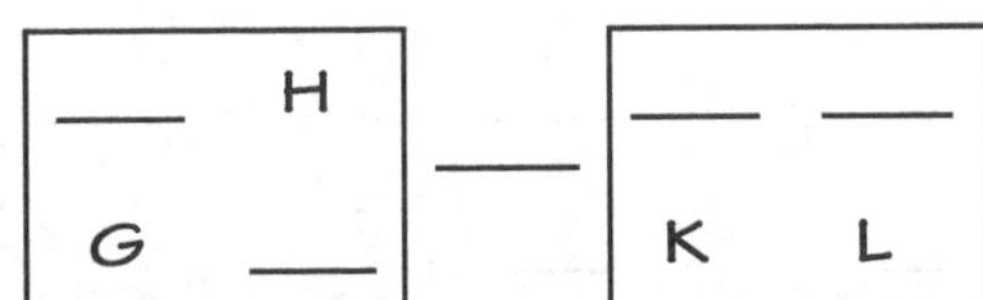

Although you could show the Not Laws that follow from this configuration, doing so is time-consuming, and the visual power of the block is enough so that showing the Not Laws is probably unnecessary. There are, of course, powerful inferences that follow from the limited options available for the blocks. For example, the Thursday morning deposition must be K or L.

At this point, many students stop working, but there is one final set of inferences that can be drawn. Because the blocks establish that G, K, and L are all deposed in the morning, and A and B cannot be deposed in the afternoon and thus must be deposed in the morning, we can conclude that A, B, G, K, and L are the morning depositions, and the remaining five individuals—C, D, F, H, and J—are the afternoon depositions.

---

4. A design company displays artworks in two office buildings—A and B, each of which has six floors, numbered 1 through 6. Each artwork is made of glass, plaster, or steel, and each floor is used to display exactly one artwork. The following conditions govern the display:

   No two artworks made of the same type of material as each other can be displayed on identically numbered floors.

   The artwork displayed on Floor 3 of Building A is made of the same kind of material as the artwork displayed on Floor 4 of Building B.

   The artwork displayed on Floor 6 of Building A is not made of plaster.

   No artwork made of steel can be displayed on a floor immediately above, or immediately below, a floor on which an artwork made of glass is displayed.

There are three variable sets to consider: the two office buildings, the six floors, and the three types of material used to make each artwork. The six floors have an inherent sense of order and should therefore be used to represent the base. Since the floors of a building are stacked vertically in the real world, it would be wise not to deviate from this arrangement in your diagram:

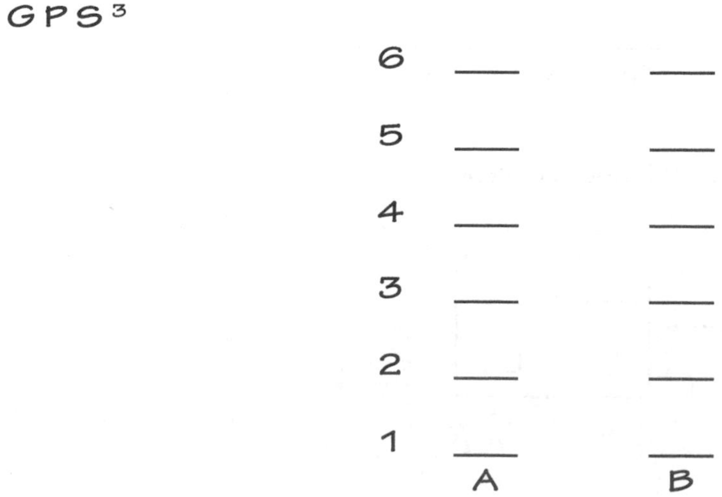

GPS^3

6	___	___
5	___	___
4	___	___
3	___	___
2	___	___
1	___	___
	A	B

Advanced Linear Setup Practice Drill Answer Key—page 45

The three types of material used to make each artwork represent a repeating variable set. However, the scenario does not stipulate either a minimum or a maximum number of times that each of these variables can (or must) repeat. Consequently, you should not assume that all three of them must appear in your setup.

The first rule establishes a horizontal not-block, with "T" designating "type:"

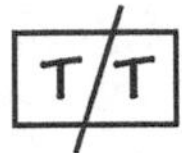

The second rule creates a block on Floor 3 of Building A and Floor 4 of Building B. Because showing this can be difficult, use a double arrow to represent the rule (and also place the double arrow on the diagram):

3A ⟷ 4B

The third rule can be diagrammed as a Not Law on Floor 6 of Building A, creating a G/S dual-option on that space.

The last rule establishes a rotating vertical not-block:

When combined, the rules create the following diagram:

GPS³

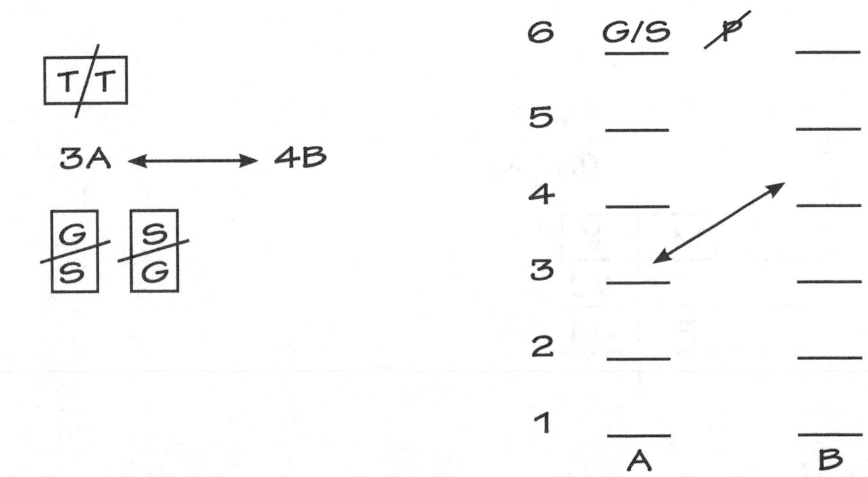

Advanced Linear Setup Practice Drill Answer Key—page 45

5. A total of nine books occupies three shelves, with three books on each shelf. Three of the books are anthologies—M, N, and O. Three others are biographies—I, J, and K. The remaining three are children's books—F, G, and H. The books' arrangement is consistent with the following:
   No two biographies are on the same shelf.
   M and K are both on the same shelf.
   K is two shelves above F.

Since bookshelves are stacked vertically in real life, a vertical diagram of three stacks would be appropriate. Three books occupy each shelf, which means that each stack must have three spaces, as shown below:

Top:	___	___	___
Middle:	___	___	___
Bottom:	___	___	___

Since there are a total of three biographies, no two of which can be on the same shelf, there must be exactly one biography on each shelf. Even if the exact biography on each shelf is not yet known, make sure to reserve a space on each shelf for that biography. This is the Hurdle the Uncertainty principle in action.

Putting together the last two rules, if M and K are both on the same shelf, and K is two shelves above F, it follows that the MK block must be placed on the top shelf, and F on the bottom shelf. Clearly, then, K is the biography on the top shelf:

Anthologies: M N O
Biographies: I J K
Children's Books: F G H

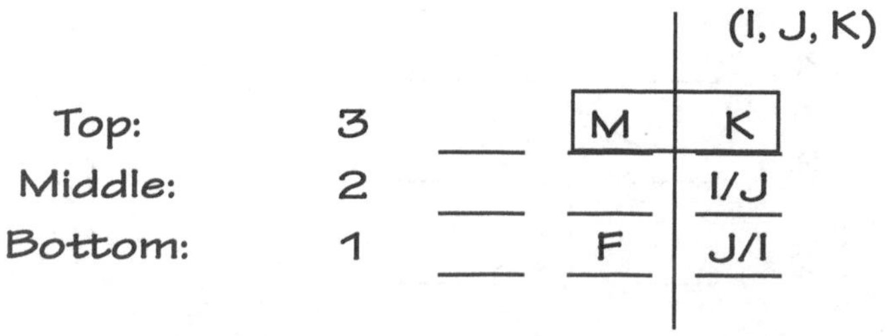

				(I, J, K)
Top:	3	___	M	K
Middle:	2	___	___	I/J
Bottom:	1	___	F	J/I

Advanced Linear Setup Practice Drill Answer Key—page 45

6. Four athletes—Don, Eddie, Frank, and George—compete in three separate events—Hammer Throw, Ice Ballet, and Javelin. The athletes are ranked from first through fourth based on the results. The following information is all that is known about the rankings:

   Don's rank in Javelin is lower than his rank in Ice Ballet.

   Frank ranks third in the Hammer Throw.

   Eddie ranks higher than George in all three events.

There are three variable sets in this game: the rankings, the athletes, and the events. Since the greatest sense of order is present, of course, in the rankings, they should be chosen as the base, with three spaces above each to accommodate the athletes who are ranked accordingly:

D_I —— D_J

E —— G

	1	2	3	4
J:	E/F			
(not)	G, D			E
I:				F/G
(not)	G			E, D
H:	D/E		F	D/G
(not)	G			E

7. During one week, from Monday through Thursday, a health inspector must inspect exactly eight restaurants—Q, R, S, T, U, V, W, and X. An inspection requires either an entire morning or an entire afternoon. No more than two restaurants can be inspected in a single day. The inspections for the week are scheduled in accordance with the following conditions:

   Q must be inspected in the morning, on the same day that X is inspected.

   S must be inspected in the afternoon.

   T must be inspected in the morning.

There are three variable sets in this problem, the days of the week, the morning and afternoon inspections, and the eight restaurants to be inspected. Since the days of the week have an inherent sense of order, they should be chosen as the base. Inspections take place on either the morning or the afternoon of a given day, requiring the creation of two stacks for each day:

Advanced Linear Setup Practice Drill Answer Key—page 45

QRSTUVWX[8]

X
Q

Afternoon:	___	___	___	___	~~T~~
Morning:	___	___	___	___	~~S~~
	M	T	W	Th	

---

8. A movie Cineplex with four theaters—1, 2, 3, and 4—must screen eight films—O, P, Q, R, S, T, U, and V. Each theater screens exactly two films, and each film is screened in exactly one theater. The following conditions apply:

    Q is screened in Theater 2.

    O and P are screened in the same theater as each other.

    S is screened in a higher-numbered theater than T.

This game creates a diagram with four spaces across, one for each of the four consecutively numbered theaters. Since no stipulation is made as to the order in which each theater must screen the two films, the resulting pair of stacks are functionally identical (i.e. the film in the top stack is not necessarily screened before or after the film in the bottom stack).

OPQRSTUV[8]

T —— S

1	2	3	4
___	___	___	___
___	Q	___	___
~~S~~	~~O~~ ~~P~~		~~T~~

Advanced Linear Setup Practice Drill Answer Key—page 45

9. An auto magazine ranks five cars—A, B, C, D, and E—from first to fifth in three categories—mileage, overall quality, and performance. The cars are ranked in accordance with the following conditions:
   All five cars are ranked in each category.
   In mileage, A is ranked third and B is ranked fourth.
   In performance, D is ranked second and E is ranked fifth.
   In overall quality, B is ranked higher than A.

The ranks of the cars create the best base, given their inherent sense of order, and each of the five ranks requires three spaces above it, for the three categories: P, O, and M. Each of the five variables will appear three times within the diagram, for a total of fifteen spaces to be filled:

ABCDE[5]

	1	2	3	4	5
P	___	D	___	___	E
O	___	___	___	___	___
	not A				not B
M	___	___	A	B	___

B —— A

10. Each of six passengers—Q, R, S, T, U, and V—will be assigned to exactly one of six airplane seats in two rows, O and P. There are three seats, numbered from 1 through 3, in each row. Only seats in the same row as each other are immediately beside each other, and consecutively numbered seats within each row are adjacent. Seat assignments must meet the following conditions:
    Q's seat is P3.
    R's seat is O2.
    S's seat is either directly in front of, or directly behind, T's seat.

There are three variable sets in this game: The rows, the passengers, and the seat numbers, which form the base with a nice inherent sense of order. Basically, this setup calls for two rows with three seats each.

QRSTUV[6]

[S over T] or [T over S]

	1	2	3
P	S/T	___	Q
O	T/S	R	___

Grouping Games—Unified Grouping Theory Classification Drill Answer Key—page 50

1. A student must select college courses from a group of nine possible courses.

Classification: Undefined

Since the number of courses to be selected is unknown, the game is Undefined. Since the game is Undefined there is no Moving/Fixed element, nor is there a Balance element.

---

2. Nine research grants are allocated to three different universities—university H, university S, and university Y. Each university receives exactly three grants, and each grant is given to only one university.

Classification: Defined-Fixed, Balanced

Because each university receives exactly three grants, the game is Defined-Fixed. Because there are nine grants for exactly nine positions, the game is Balanced.

---

3. Eight scientists attending a conference are assigned to two panels—the Policy Panel and the Research Panel. Each panel includes at least three members, and no scientist is assigned to more than one panel.

Classification: Defined-Moving, Balanced

Since each panel contains at least three scientists, but the total number of assigned scientists is eight, the game is Defined-Moving (there are three fixed numerical distributions: 5-3, 4-4, and 3-5). Since there are eight scientists for exactly eight positions, the game is Balanced.

Grouping Games—Unified Grouping Theory Classification Drill Answer Key—page 50

4. The members of four committees will be selected from among seven candidates. Each committee must select exactly two members, and each candidate must be selected for membership on at least one committee.

Classification: Defined-Fixed, Unbalanced: Underfunded

Since each committee contains exactly two members, the game is Defined-Fixed. Since there are only seven candidates for the eight positions, the game is Unbalanced: Underfunded. The seven-into-eight scenario creates a numerical distribution of 2-1-1-1-1-1-1. Remember, each of the seven candidates must be assigned to at least one committee. That means that seven of the eight committee spaces are automatically filled. The remaining space goes to a candidate who is assigned to two committees, and hence the 2-1-1-1-1-1-1 distribution.

---

5. Exactly six of nine reviewers are selected to review four restaurants. Each selected reviewer must review exactly one restaurant, and each restaurant must be reviewed by at least one reviewer.

Classification: Defined-Moving, Unbalanced: Overloaded

Since exactly six reviewers will be assigned to the four restaurants, but it is unknown how many reviewers will review each restaurant (it is either a 3-1-1-1 numerical distribution or a 2-2-1-1 numerical distribution), the game is Defined-Moving. Since there are nine reviewers for the six positions, the game is Unbalanced: Overloaded.

---

6. A dinner reservation for at least four people will be made at a local restaurant. The diners will be selected from a group of ten people.

Classification: Partially Defined

Since the number of diners is at least four, but it is uncertain exactly how many diners there will be, the game is Partially Defined. Since the game is Partially Defined, there is no Moving/Fixed element, nor is there a Balance element.

Grouping Games—Unified Grouping Theory Classification Drill Answer Key—page 50

7. Exactly six of eight weight lifters are assigned to two weight lifting teams of three weight lifters each.

Classification: Defined-Fixed, Unbalanced: Overloaded

Since each weight lifting team contains exactly three weight lifters, the game is Defined-Fixed. Since there are eight weight lifters for exactly six positions, the game is Unbalanced: Overloaded.

---

8. A traveler must visit at least one of the following seven countries over the course of a year: Australia, Denmark, Guatemala, Kenya, Morocco, Thailand, and Venezuela.

Classification: Undefined

Since the exact number of countries to be visited is unknown, the game is Undefined. Since the game is Undefined there is no Moving/Fixed element, nor is there a Balance element.

---

9. A manager must select exactly five individual employees to attend a skills workshop. The employees under consideration are B, D, F, G, H, K, and L.

Classification: Defined-Fixed, Unbalanced: Overloaded

Since the number of employees attending the skills workshop is set at exactly five, the game is Defined-Fixed. Since there are seven employees for exactly five spots, the game is Unbalanced: Overloaded.

---

10. Antonio and Jun each take at least two art classes at a local art museum that offers only five types of art classes: contemporary, impressionism, modern, neoclassic, and realism.

Classification: Partially Defined

Since the number of classes taken is at least two, but it is uncertain exactly how many classes will be taken, the game is Partially Defined. Since the game is Partially Defined, there is no Moving/Fixed element, nor is there a Balance element.

Grouping Games—Unified Grouping Theory Classification Drill Answer Key—page 50

11. A moving company employs eight workers: M, O, P, R, S, T, V, and X. Exactly five of the eight workers are selected to work three different jobs—jobs 1, 2, and 3. Each job is assigned at least one worker, and no worker is assigned to more than one job.

Classification: Defined-Moving, Unbalanced: Overloaded

Since exactly five workers will be assigned to the three jobs, but the exact number of workers per job is unknown (it is either a 3-1-1 or 2-2-1 unfixed numerical distribution), the game is Defined-Moving. Because there are eight workers but only five are selected, the game is Unbalanced: Overloaded.

---

12. Five pilots—Bae, Chisholm, Dayani, Fang, and Gutierrez—are assigned to four separate flights. Each flight must be assigned exactly two pilots, and each pilot must be assigned to at least one flight.

Classification: Defined-Fixed, Unbalanced: Underfunded

Because each flight is assigned exactly two pilots, the game is Defined-Fixed. Because there are only five pilots for the eight positions, the game is Unbalanced: Underfunded. The five pilots-into-eight positions scenario creates multiple unfixed numerical distributions: 4-1-1-1-1, 3-2-1-1-1, and 2-2-2-1-1.

---

13. A dog walker must walk eight dogs—F, G, H, J, K, L, M, and P—in three separate groups. Each group must be assigned at least two dogs.

Classification: Defined-Moving, Balanced

Because each of the eight dogs is assigned to a group, but it is unknown exactly how many dogs are assigned to each group, the game is Defined-Moving (with two unfixed numerical distributions: 4-2-2 and 3-3-2). Because all eight dogs are assigned to the three groups, the game is Balanced.

Grouping Games—Unified Grouping Theory Classification Drill Answer Key—page 50

14. A gardener is planting flowers in three separate flower beds. The gardener will use exactly six types of flowers: asters, daffodils, lilies, pansies, roses, and tulips. Each flower type will be used at least once, and each flower bed will contain at least three different types of flowers.

Classification: Partially Defined

Since the number of flowers used in each bed is at least three, but it is uncertain exactly how many flowers are used in each, the game is Partially Defined. Since the game is Partially Defined, there is no Moving/Fixed element, nor is there a Balance element.

---

15. Four products—M, P, Q, and R—are each featured in a local store over a period of five weeks. Each product is featured on exactly two of the weeks, and each week features at least one, but no more than four, products.

Classification: Defined-Moving, Unbalanced: Underfunded

Because the four products are each assigned exactly two times, but it is unknown exactly how many products are assigned to each week, the game is Defined-Moving (with three unfixed numerical distributions: 4-1-1-1-1, 3-2-1-1-1, and 2-2-2-1-1). Because the four products are assigned into eight spaces, the game is Unbalanced: Underfunded.

---

16. A corporate retreat features confidence-building exercises. Six employees—Fung, Jackson, Narvaez, Patterson, Sandeep, and Williams—complete each exercise either alone or in groups with one another.

Classification: Undefined

Since the number of exercises to be completed is unknown, and the number of participants in each exercise is also unknown, the game is Undefined. Since the game is Undefined there is no Moving/Fixed element, nor is there a Balance element.

Grouping Games—Unified Grouping Theory Classification Drill Answer Key—page 50

17. Ten rowers compete for membership on one of two rowing teams—Team A and Team B. Each team consists of exactly four members, and no rower can be a member of more than one team.

Classification: Defined-Fixed, Unbalanced: Overloaded

Since there are exactly two teams of four rowers each, the game is Defined-Fixed. Since there are ten rowers for exactly eight spots, the game is Unbalanced: Overloaded.

---

18. Each of seven students—Khan, Martin, Paulo, Qadira, Sara, Takeshi, and Uchenna—is assigned exactly one of two speech topics—freedom and liberty. Each speech topic is assigned to at least three students.

Classification: Defined-Moving, Balanced

Because each of the seven students is assigned to a topic, but it is unknown exactly how many students are assigned to each topic, the game is Defined-Moving (with two fixed numerical distributions: 4-3 and 3-4). Because all seven students are assigned to the two topics, the game is Balanced.

Grouping Games Rule Diagramming Drill Answer Key—page 53

1. Of the three applicants W, X, and Y, exactly two are interviewed.

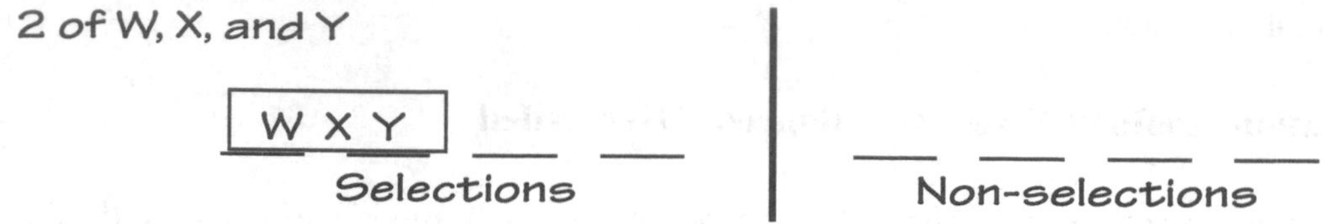

The most efficient representation of this rule is directly in the diagram, with a block taking up two spaces (any two spaces will do, although spaces at the far left or far right of the group seem most intuitive and the least confusing). This representation allows you to visually "reserve" the two spaces for W, X, and Y.

---

2. W and Y cannot be selected together.

The rule is shown with the double not-arrow since there is no vertical element in the setup:

W ←|→ Y

Although we cannot be certain that either of W or Y is always selected, at least one can never be selected, and thus a W/Y dual-option appears on the "out" group.

W ←|→ Y

___ ___ ___ ___ ___ | W/Y ___

Selections | Non-selections

3. K and L cannot be assigned to the same group, and every salesperson is assigned to at least one of the two groups.

Because this game has a vertical component, K and L are represented in a not-block:

Because K and L cannot be in the same group, and every salesperson is assigned to a group, one of K and L must be in group 1, and the other must be in group 2. This can be shown with K/L dual-options on the diagram.

K/L	L/K
1	2

---

4. If D is assigned to group 2, then E is assigned to group 2.

$D_2 \longrightarrow E_2$

$E_1 \longrightarrow D_1$

1	2

Many students diagram this rule as a block, but that is incorrect. While both variables are assigned to group 2 when D is assigned to group 2, and via the contrapositive both variables are assigned to group 1 when E is assigned to group 1, the variables do not always have to be in the same group. For example, D could be assigned to group 1 and E could be assigned to group 2 without violating the rule. Note also the power of a contrapositive in a two-value system game.

Grouping Games Rule Diagramming Drill Answer Key—page 53

5. If R is not selected, then S must be selected.

This is a straight conditional rule and is consequently diagrammed with an arrow:

R̸ ⟶ S

However, as you hopefully recall, the negative on the *sufficient* condition makes this statement very tricky. The meaning of the statement above is that if R is not selected, then S must be selected, and via the contrapositive, if S is not selected then R must be selected. Thus, the two can never both be *not selected.* This can be shown as a double-not arrow statement:

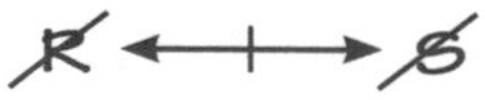

R̸ ⟷ S̸ (double-not arrow)

On the diagram, because both R and S can never be not selected, an R/S dual-option can be placed in the Selection group. Because it is possible for *both* R and S to be selected, no further inferences can be drawn, and an R/S dual-option *cannot* be placed under the Non-selections group.

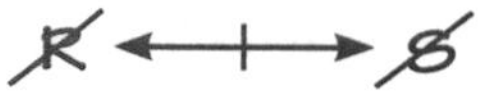

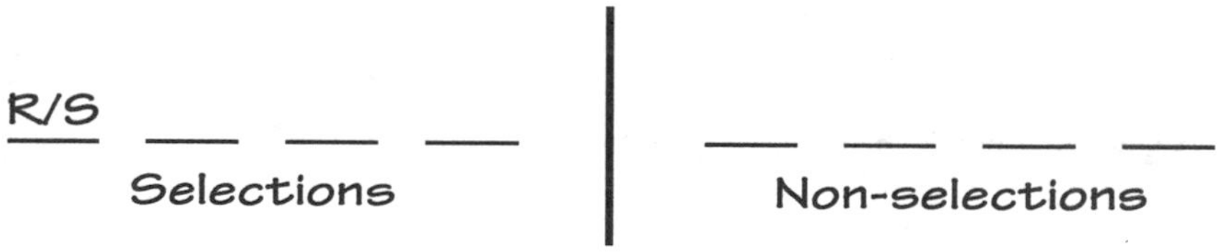

R̸ ⟷ S̸ (double-not arrow)

Selections	Non-selections
R/S ___ ___ ___	___ ___ ___ ___

Grouping Games Rule Diagramming Drill Answer Key—page 53

6. Either P or Q, but not both, must be selected.

This rule is also shown with the double not-arrow since there is no vertical element in the setup:

P ←|→ Q

There could be an additional double-not arrow as well, one with slashes on both variables. Thus, the operating effecting of the rule is that exactly one of P and Q is selected.

Note that this rule can also be represented using a double arrow connecting a positive and a negative variable:

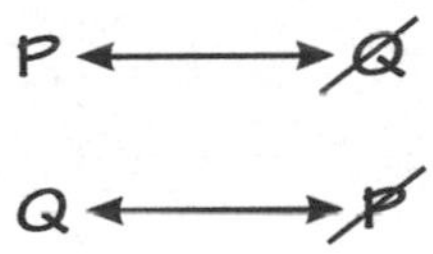

P ←→ ~~Q~~

Q ←→ ~~P~~

This is so because of the bi-conditional relationship between the presence of one of the variables and the absence of the other: If one of them is selected, the other one isn't; but if one of them is *not* selected, the other one is.

Reserve one space in each group for the choice of P or Q since exactly one must be selected, and exactly one cannot be selected.

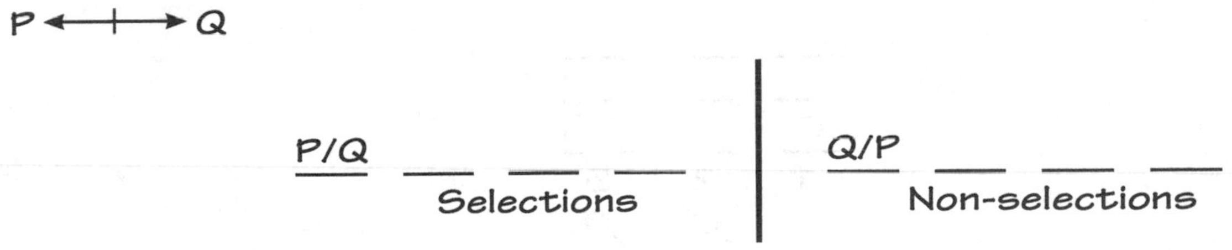

P ←|→ Q

P/Q ___ ___ ___ | Q/P ___ ___ ___

Selections | Non-selections

7. Group 2 and group 3 do not have any members in common.

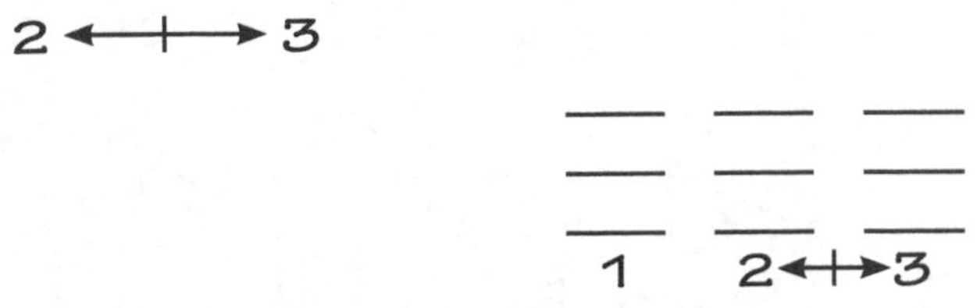

2 ←|→ 3

1   2 ←|→ 3

This rule is best shown internally with a double-not arrow between group 2 and group 3 (or you can place a not-block around 2 and 3 if you prefer).

Grouping Games Rule Diagramming Drill Answer Key—page 53

8. R and S cannot be assigned to the same group as each other.

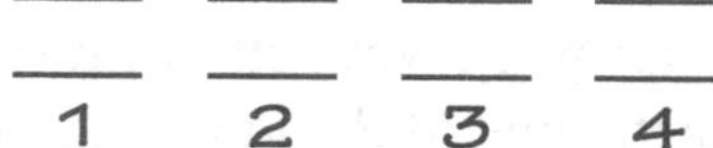

Compare this representation to the representation in item #2. Because there is a vertical component to this diagram, we have chosen a vertical not-block.

---

9. O is not assigned to group 2 or group 3, and every player is assigned to exactly one of the groups.

Because O cannot be assigned to group 2 or group 3, O Not Laws can be drawn under each group. However, the operating effect of this rule is that O *must* be assigned to group 1, so you can simply place O in group 1, and eschew the Not Laws under groups 2 and 3:

1	2	3
O		
	Ø	Ø

If you did not draw the Not Laws, that is not incorrect (and if O hadn't been automatically assigned to group 1 that would have been the correct and only representation).

Grouping Games Rule Diagramming Drill Answer Key—page 53

10. Neither F nor G works in Areas 2 or 3.

Since neither F nor G works in Areas 2 or 3, and all variables must be used, it follows that F and G must work in Areas 1 and 4, not necessarily in that order. This establishes F/G and G/F dual-options.

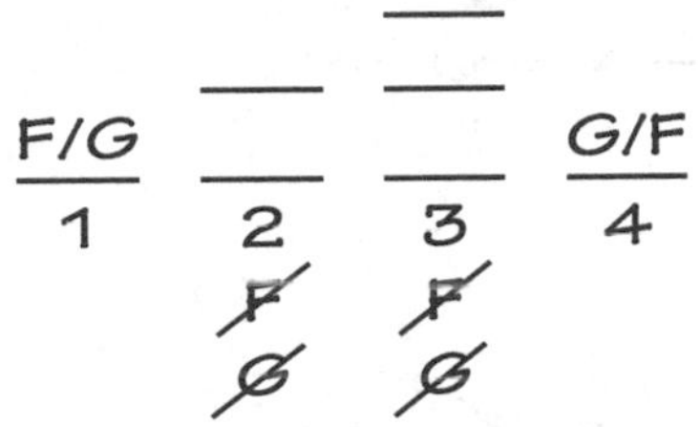

F/G	___	___	G/F
1	2	3	4
	F (crossed out)	F (crossed out)	
	G (crossed out)	G (crossed out)	

11. If M is hired, then O must be hired.

This is a straight conditional rule and is consequently diagrammed with an arrow:

$$M \longrightarrow O$$

The contrapositive also applies, but because the contrapositive is inherently present in all conditional statements, we do not draw out the contrapositive unless the original statement is tricky, or some other benefit might be gained.

In this case, although you wouldn't typically draw out the contrapositive, you should still consider the implications of the relationship. The diagram only allows for one person to not be hired. But, if O is not hired, then via the contrapositive M also cannot be hired. That would create two people not hired, which would violate the setup of the game. Thus, we can determine that O can never be out, and must therefore be hired.

$$M \longrightarrow O$$

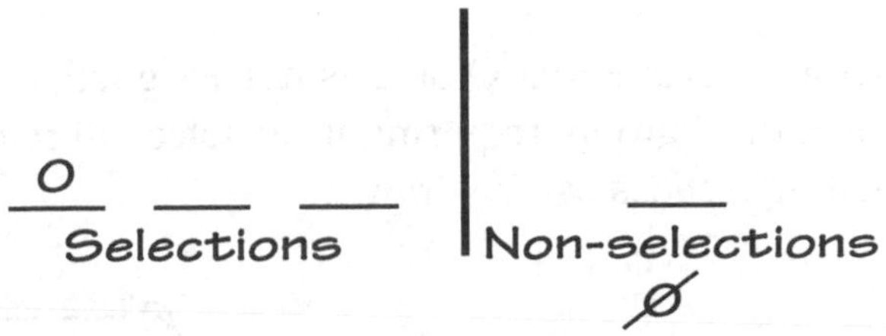

O ___ ___	___
Selections	Non-selections
	O (crossed out)

Grouping Games Rule Diagramming Drill Answer Key—page 53

12. If Z is assigned, then Q and U must be assigned.

The diagram of the rule itself is straightforward:

Diagram: Z ⟶ Q and U

Contrapositive: Q̸ or U̸ ⟶ Z̸

Note that we've shown the contrapositive because the initial rule is not just a simple conditional relationship. The contrapositive also reveals an interesting inference: if either Q or U is *not* assigned, then Z is not assigned. But, because our diagram provides that only two variables are unassigned, when one of Q or U is not assigned, then that variable—along with Z—make up both non-assignments. Thus, we can infer that Q and U cannot both be unassigned, resulting in the inference that at least one of Q and U is always assigned.

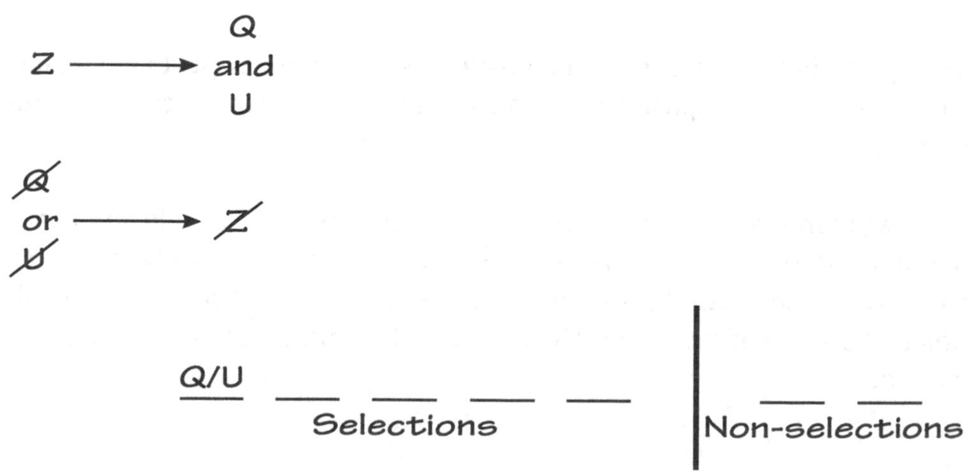

Note that whenever either Q or U is not assigned, Z is also not assigned. This would max out the "non-selections" group, requiring us to select all remaining variables. Accordingly, the following additional inferences can be drawn:

Q̸ ⟶ U

U̸ ⟶ Q

Grouping Setup Practice Drill Answer Key—page 57

1. Six waiters—S, T W, X, Y, and Z—are assigned in pairs to wait on four tables—tables A, B, C, and D. The assignment of the waiters will meet the following conditions:

    Each waiter is assigned to at least one table.
    S is not assigned to table A.
    W is assigned to table B only if Y is assigned to table D.
    S and T are both assigned to the same table.

The scenario states that there are six waiters for four tables, so at first this game appears to be Overloaded. However, the scenario states that the waiters are assigned in pairs, and thus there are eight total positions to fill. With only six waiters, some waiters will have to be assigned to more than one table, and thus the grouping classification of this drill is Defined-Fixed, Unbalanced: Underfunded.

Because each waiter is assigned to a table, and there are eight positions, there are two numerical distributions of assignments-to-waiters in this game:

Three tables assigned to one waiter, one to each of the rest:	3-1-1-1-1-1
Two tables assigned to two waiters, one to each of the rest:	2-2-1-1-1-1

The remainder of the setup is relatively straightforward:

STWXYZ^6

$W_B \longrightarrow Y_D$

[S T] (block)

A B C D

~~S~~ ~~T~~ (under A)

The one inference of note is that if W is assigned to table B, then Y must be assigned to table D, forcing S and T to be assigned to table C (S cannot be assigned to table A):

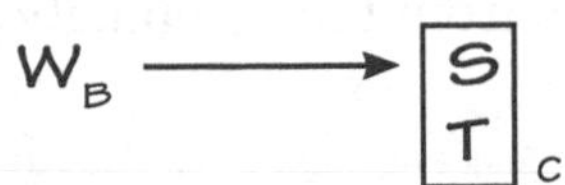

Grouping Setup Practice Drill Answer Key—page 57

2. Seven horses—A, B, C, D, F, G, and H—are in a horse paddock at various times. The horses are in the paddock in a manner consistent with the following conditions:
    If C is in the paddock, then D is not in the paddock.
    Every time F is in the paddock, C is in the paddock.
    D is in the paddock only when G is in the paddock.
    If A is not in the paddock, then B is in the paddock.

This game is classified as Undefined because no specification is made as to how many horses are in the paddock at any given time.

The four rules, as given, can be diagrammed as follows:

1. C ←|→ D

2. F ——→ C

3. D ——→ G

4. ~~A~~ ——→ B

As you diagrammed the rules, you should have been looking for connections. The first and third rules can be combined:

F ——→ C ←|→ D

This relationship yields the following inference:

F ←|→ D

Some students attempt to draw an inference from the combination of the first and second rules:

C ←|→ D ——→ G

However, this relationship does not yield a usable inference for Logic Games (the inference that it does yield, "Some Gs are not Cs" typically is useful only in Logical Reasoning).

The last rule also bears consideration. If A is not in the paddock, then B must be in the paddock. Via the contrapositive, if B is not in the paddock, then A must be in the paddock. Thus, at all times, either A or B must be in the paddock. Of course, the rule also allows for *both* A and B to be in the paddock but at least one of A and B must be there.

---

3. At a music festival, eight bands—Cage, Deadbolt, Fluster, Gravel, Hammer, Irony, Kernel, and Lunar—are assigned to two stages—the Main Stage and the Side Stage. Each band must be assigned to a single stage. The assignments are made in accordance with the following conditions:

   At least four bands are assigned to the Main stage, and at least three bands are assigned to the Side Stage.
   Kernel cannot be assigned to the Side Stage unless Deadbolt is assigned to the Main Stage.
   Fluster and Gravel are not assigned to the same stage.

The scenario states that there are eight bands playing two stages at a music festival. The exact number of bands on each stage is not fixed; the Main Stage must be assigned at least four bands and the Side Stage must be assigned at least three bands. These requirements create two fixed distributions:

	Main Stage	Side Stage
Distribution #1:	5	3
Distribution #2:	4	4

Thus, the selection group is Defined-Moving, and as there are eight bands for the eight spaces, the variable pool is Balanced.

Grouping Setup Practice Drill Answer Key—page 57

The initial scenario appears as follows:

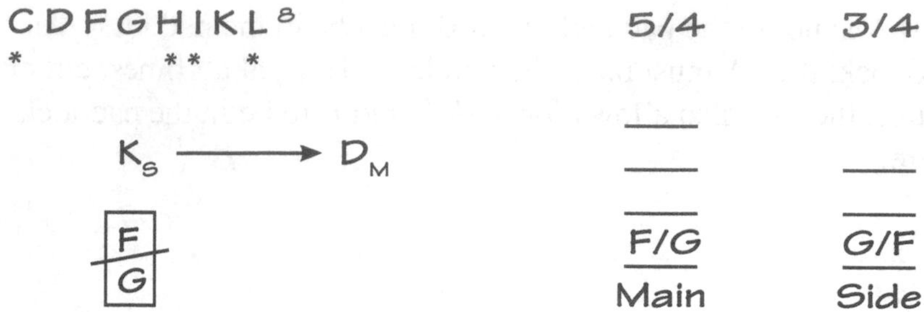

The second rule bears further examination. At first, this appears to be a standard conditional grouping rule. Thus, the contrapositive of this rule would be:

$$\not{D}_M \longrightarrow \not{K}_S$$

But, because there are only two stages, and each band must be assigned to one of the two stages, this is actually a two-value system game. Thus, if a band is not assigned to the Main Stage it must be assigned to the Side Stage, and if a band is not assigned to the side stage it must be assigned to the Main Stage. This allows us to restate the contrapositive as follows:

$$D_S \longrightarrow K_M$$

Although D and K do not have to perform on different stages (they could both perform on the Main Stage), should one of them perform on the Side Stage the first rule will come into play and the other band will occupy a space on the Main Stage.

Grouping Setup Practice Drill Answer Key—page 57

4. Eight senators—J, K, L, M, O, P, Q, and R—serve on three subcommittees—Defense, Finance, and Policy. Each subcommittee has three members, except for the Finance subcommittee, which has two members. The following is known about the three subcommittees:

    P serves on the Defense subcommittee.

    Q serves on the Finance subcommittee.

    K and L serve on the same subcommittee.

    J serves on a subcommittee if and only if M serves on that subcommittee.

The scenario states that there are eight senators serving on three subcommittees. This makes the game Defined-Fixed. As there is a space for each senator, the final classification is Defined-Fixed, Balanced.

The initial scenario with the first two rules diagrammed appears as follows:

JKLMOPQR[8]
   *   *

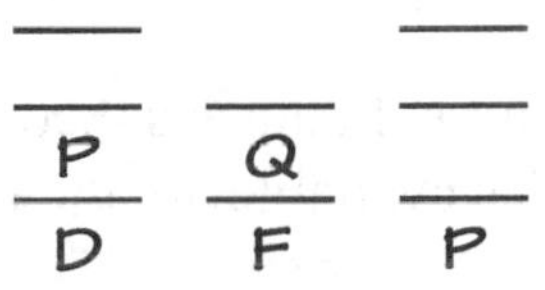

D	F	P
___		___
___	___	___
P	Q	___

The last two rules are fairly easy to diagram as they are both positive grouping rules.

Third rule:

K
L

Fourth rule:

J
M

Grouping Setup Practice Drill Answer Key—page 57

The fourth rule can be a bit more challenging, but remember that "if and only if" introduces a double-arrow. The proper conditional diagram is thus:

J ⟷ M

In a grouping game featuring verticality, we turn this double-arrow into a vertical block.

Applying the last two rules to the diagram, although we cannot ascertain where each block is placed, we do know that neither block can be on the Finance subcommittee due to insufficient space, and thus one of the blocks must serve on the Defense subcommittee and the other block must serve on the Policy subcommittee. These inferences can be shown as:

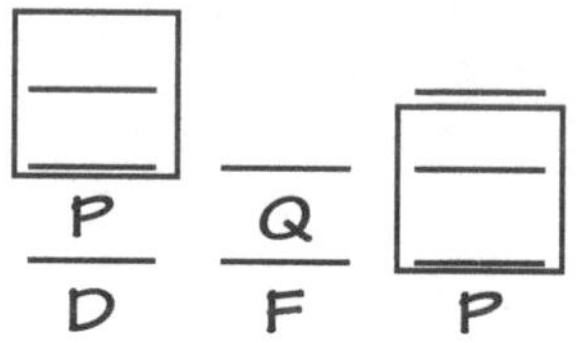

P Q
D F P

Of course, this leaves only one "open" space on the Finance subcommittee and one open space on the Policy subcommittee. The only two variables available are the two randoms—O and R—leading to the final setup for the game:

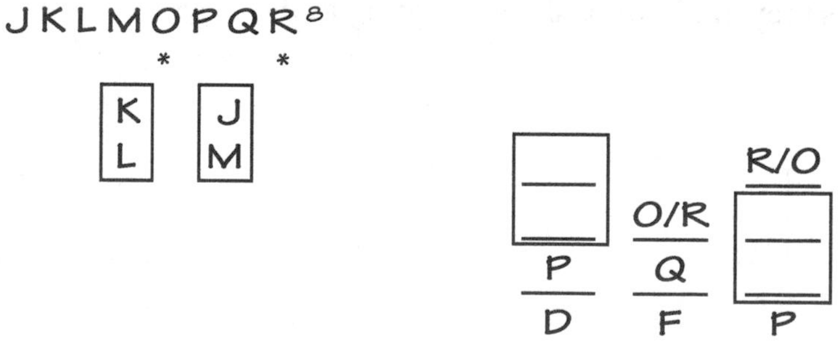

JKLMOPQR[8]
* *

K J
L M

R/O
O/R
P Q
D F P

Grouping Setup Practice Drill Answer Key—page 57

5. A window display consists of exactly three flowerpots. Each flowerpot contains at least three of the following six types of houseplants: forsythia, geranium, hibiscus, iris, jasmine, and kalanchoe. Each houseplant must be planted in at least one flowerpot, and no houseplant can be planted in all three flowerpots. The following conditions hold:
   - Exactly two of the flowerpots contain hibiscuses.
   - If a flowerpot contains geraniums, then that flowerpot contains forsythias.
   - If a flowerpot contains irises, then that flowerpot contains neither jasmines nor kalanchoes.
   - If a flowerpot contains no geraniums, then that flowerpot contains both jasmines and kalanchoes.

This Partially Defined grouping game requires that we select at least three of the six houseplants available for each flowerpot. The game is challenging for two reasons: 1) No maximum number of houseplants per pot is specified; and 2) each houseplant can be planted in more than one flowerpot, so each variable can repeat. The second provision is subject to an important limitation, however: since no houseplant can be planted in all three flowerpots, no variable can repeat three times. The set-up would therefore look like this:

F, G, H, I, J, K [6]

	1	2	3
	__	__	__
Min. 3:	__	__	__
	H	H	__
			~~H~~

G ⟶ F

I ⟷ (not both) J, K

~~G~~ ⟶ J and K

~~J~~ or ~~K~~ ⟶ G

min. 3 plants/pot
max. 2 of each plant

Grouping Setup Practice Drill Answer Key—page 57

Inferences:

Due to the conditional nature of the rules in this game, the first step is to combine them in order to make additive inferences:

~~J~~ ⟶ G ⟶ F

I ⟶ and

~~K~~ ⟶ G ⟶ F

Given the additive inference (I ⟶ G ⟶ F), you should immediately realize that if F is not planted in a given flowerpot, that flowerpot can contain neither G nor I:

J ⟶ ~~I~~

~~F~~ ⟶ ~~G~~ ⟶ and

K ⟶ ~~I~~

Recall, however, that there are only six houseplants available, at least three of which must be planted in each flowerpot. So, if F were not planted in a flowerpot, the only houseplants available to plant in that flowerpot would be H, J, and K, all of which *must* be planted in it in order to reach the minimum of 3 houseplants per flowerpot:

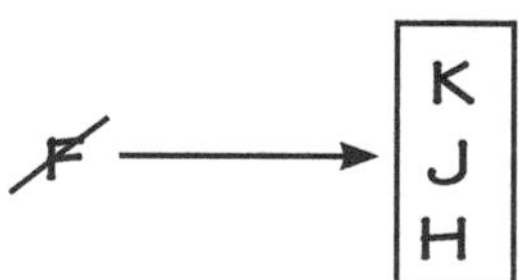

Clearly, any flowerpot that does not contain F must contain H, J, and K. And since no houseplant can be planted in all three flowerpots, at least one of the flowerpots will not contain F. Therefore, that flowerpot *must* contain H, J, and K:

Min. 3:

1	2	3
K	___	___
J	___	___
H	___	___
~~F~~		

Grouping Setup Practice Drill Answer Key—page 57

Next, let's focus on H. According to the first rule of the game, exactly two of the flowerpots contain H. What about the one flowerpot that does *not* contain H? By the contrapositive property of our inference above, that flowerpot must contain F:

~~H~~ ⟶ F

This inference should immediately be represented in your main set-up:

Min. 3:

K		
J		
H	H	F
1	2	3
~~F~~		~~H~~

Finally, recall that each houseplant must be planted in at least one flowerpot. The remaining houseplants to consider are G and I, each of which must be planted in at least one of the two remaining flowerpots. Given the additive inference I ⟶ G ⟶ F, we can create three templates based on which flowerpot(s) contain I:

Template 1:

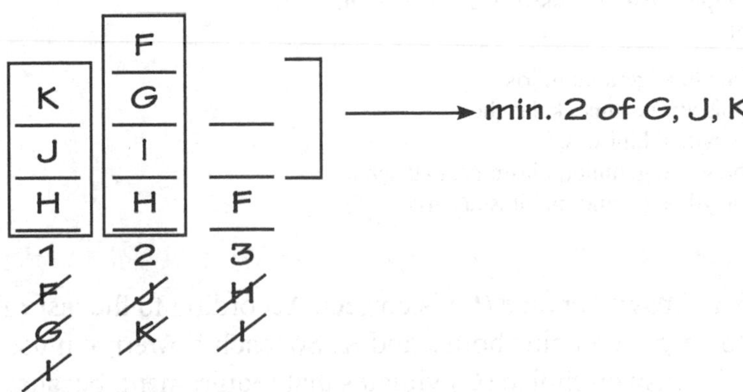

Grouping Setup Practice Drill Answer Key—page 57

Template 2:

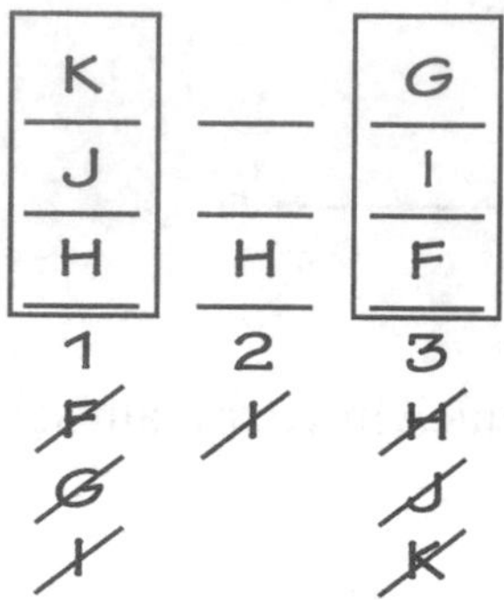

Template 3:

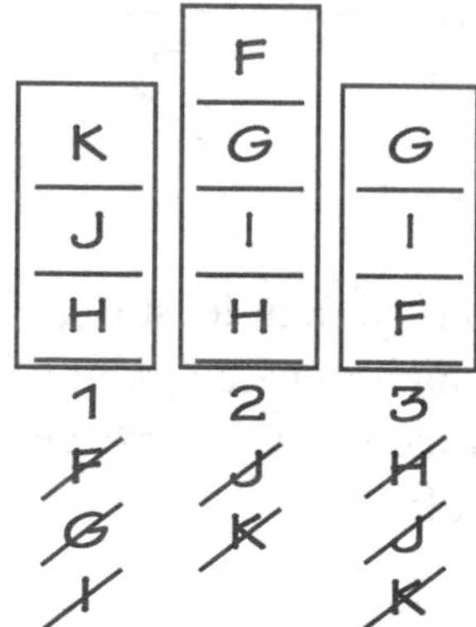

Question 5.1. Which one of the following CANNOT be the complete list of houseplants in one of the flowerpots?

(A) forsythia, geranium, iris
(B) hibiscus, jasmine, kalanchoe
(C) forsythia, hibiscus, iris
(D) forsythia, geranium, jasmine, kalanchoe
(E) forsythia, geranium, hibiscus, iris

Question 5.1. Answer choice (C) is correct. According to the last rule, if a flowerpot contains no G, then that flowerpot contains both J and K. So, each flowerpot must contain G, or else it must contain both J and K. Answer choice (C) violates that requirement, because the list of houseplants in it (F, H, I) includes neither G, nor J and K.

Note, however, that the rule does not prohibit a scenario where G, J, and K are all included in the same flowerpot. See Template 1.

Grouping Setup Practice Drill Answer Key—page 57

Question 5.2. Which one of the following must be the complete list of houseplants in one of the flowerpots?

(A) hibiscus, jasmine, kalanchoe
(B) forsythia, geranium, iris
(C) forsythia, geranium, hibiscus
(D) forsythia, jasmine, kalanchoe
(E) hibiscus, iris, kalanchoe

Question 5.2. Answer choice (A) is correct. This question tests if you made the main inference in this game, namely, that one of the flowerpots must contain exactly three houseplants: H, J, and K.

Question 5.3. If each flowerpot contains exactly three houseplants, then which one of the following must be true?

(A) Exactly one of the flowerpots contains forsythias.
(B) Exactly one of the flowerpots contains geraniums.
(C) Exactly one of the flowerpots contains irises.
(D) Exactly one of the flowerpots contains jasmines.
(E) Exactly one of the flowerpots contains kalanchoes.

Question 5.3. Answer choice (C) is correct. According to Template 2, where each flowerpot contains exactly three houseplants, one of the flowerpots contains I (along with F and G). None of the other answer choices must be true, because flowerpot #2 in Template 2 can contain any number of houseplant combinations.

Question 5.4. Which one of the following lists the minimum and maximum possible numbers, respectively, of different houseplants in one of the flowerpots?

(A) 3, 3
(B) 3, 4
(C) 3, 5
(D) 4, 4
(E) 4, 5

Question 5.4. Answer choice (C) is correct. Answer choices (D) and (E) are incorrect, because the minimum number of houseplants in any given flowerpot is 3. Additionally, there can be as many as 5 houseplants in a given flowerpot, as long as that flowerpot does not contain I (see, e.g. Template 2, where flowerpot #2 is an open group—as many as 5 houseplants can be planted in it). Also, note that the last rule of the game requires each flowerpot to contain G, or else to contain both J and K. As discussed in Question 1, above, this rule does not prohibit a flowerpot from containing all three variables (G, J, and K).

Grouping Setup Practice Drill Answer Key—page 57

Question 5.5. If two of the flowerpots contain exactly the same houseplants as each other, then which one of the following could be false?

(A) Exactly one of the flowerpots contains forsythias.
(B) Exactly one of the flowerpots contains geraniums.
(C) Exactly two of the flowerpots contain irises.
(D) Exactly two of the flowerpots contain jasmines.
(E) Exactly two of the flowerpots contain kalanchoes.

Question 5.5. Answer choice (C) is correct. If two of the flowerpots contain exactly the same houseplants as each other, they must both contain K, J, and H (Template 2). In that scenario, only one of the flowerpots contains I. So, answer choice (C) could be false (in fact, it *must* be false).

Question 5.6. If the complete list of houseplants in one of the flowerpots is forsythias, jasmines, and kalanchoes, then which one of the following houseplants CANNOT be planted in more than one of the flowerpots?

(A) forsythia
(B) geranium
(C) hibiscus
(D) jasmine
(E) kalanchoe

Question 5.6. Answer choice (B) is correct. If the complete list of houseplants in one of the flowerpots is F, J, and K, then that flowerpot must be flowerpot #3 in Template 1. According to that template, neither G nor I can be planted in more than one of the flowerpots.

Grouping/Linear Combination Setup Practice Drill Answer Key—page 61

1. During a five week period, an elementary school teacher will select exactly five students from among a group of eight to do class presentations. Exactly one student will be selected from among two first grade students—Alan and Bobby; two students will be selected from among three second graders—Charlotte, Debra, and Edward; and two students will be selected from among three third graders: Frankie, Greg, and Hank. The presentations are given in accordance with the following conditions:

   The student chosen from the first grade class will be the first to present.
   If Alan is selected, then Debra must also be selected.
   If Debra is selected, then her presentation is scheduled for the third week.
   If Edward is selected, then Frankie and Greg must both be selected, and both must present before Edward.
   Alan is selected only if Frankie is selected.

In this scenario, there are eight choices from which five children are to be chosen to do class presentations. Since there are more children than available spaces for the presentations, this eight-into-five relationship leaves the three children that are not selected in the "Out" group.

The initial scenario can be diagrammed as follows:

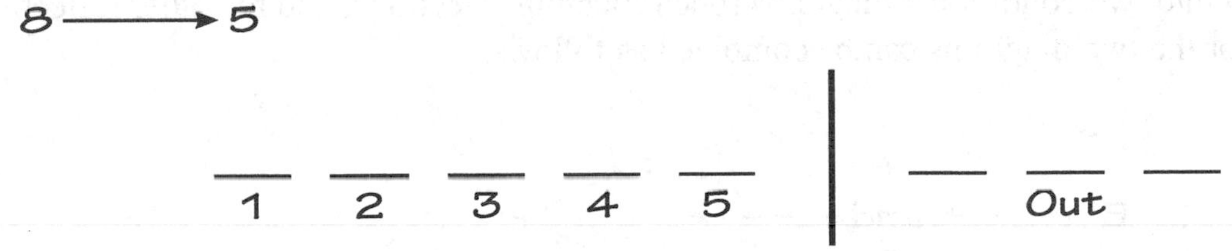

8 ⟶ 5

1	2	3	4	5	Out
__	__	__	__	__	__ __ __

The scenario provides that exactly one first grader is to be selected, meaning that one first grader will be among the presenters, and the other will be part of the "Out" group. On a closely related note, the first rule specifies that the first grader who is selected will give the first presentation. As such, we can be sure that the first space will be inhabited by either A or B:

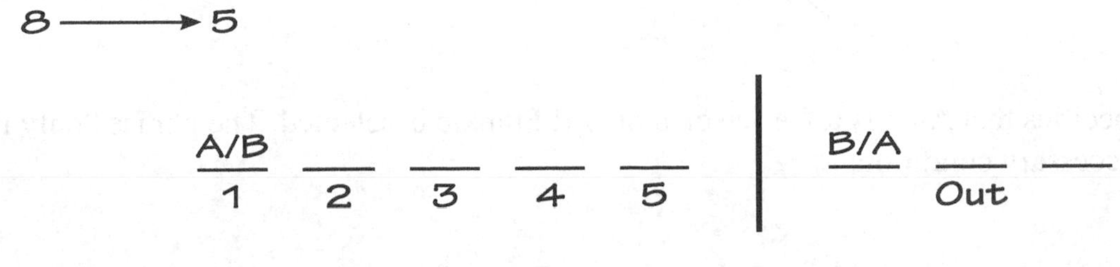

8 ⟶ 5

1	2	3	4	5	Out
A/B	__	__	__	__	B/A __ __

Grouping/Linear Combination Setup Practice Drill Answer Key—page 61

The next rule provides that if Alan is selected, then Debra must also be selected:

A ⟶ D

..and the contrapositive:

~~D~~ ⟶ ~~A~~

The next rule specifies that if Debra is selected, she must present third:

D ⟶ D_3

Clearly, then, D cannot present at any other time, an inference we can represent with Not Laws on our main diagram as shown below.

Combining these two rules: If Alan is selected, D is selected and must go third:

A ⟶ D_3

The next rule provides another conditional statement: If Edward is selected, then Frankie and Greg are also to be selected, further specifying that both must precede Edward in the order. This rule could either be broken into two conditional diagrams (one reflecting selections, and the other reflecting relative order), or the two diagrams can be combined as follows:

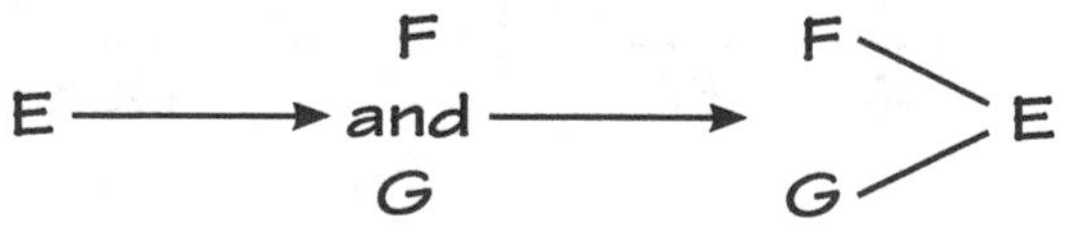

E ⟶ F and G ⟶ F, G > E

...and the contrapositove of the conditional portion of the rule:

~~F~~ or ~~G~~ ⟶ ~~E~~

The final rule specifies that Alan is to be selected only if Frankie is selected. The phrase "only if" introduces the necessary condition:

A ⟶ F

Grouping/Linear Combination Setup Practice Drill Answer Key—page 61

We can combine this with the rule that if Alan is selected Debra will be selected (A ⟶ D), and the rule that requires D's placement to be third when selected (D ⟶ D_3), to create the following diagram:

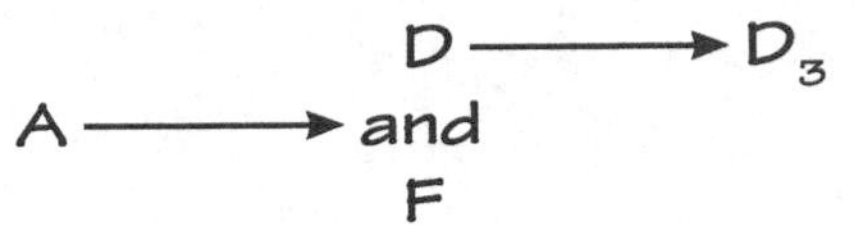

D ⟶ D_3
A ⟶ and
F

This also tells us that if either D or F is absent, A cannot be selected either:

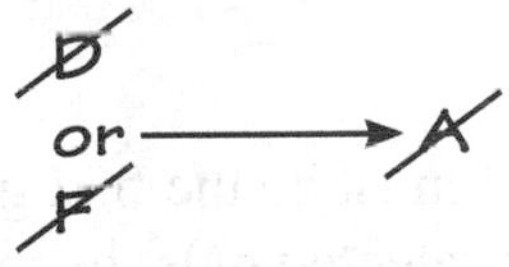

~~D~~
or ⟶ ~~A~~
~~F~~

Together, the rules create the following Global Diagram:

ABCDEFGH* [8]

(Hank is not constrained by any of the rules, so his status as a random is denoted with an asterisk.)

First Grade: A B (exactly one selected)
Second Grade: C D E (exactly two selected)
Third Grade: F G H (exactly two selected)

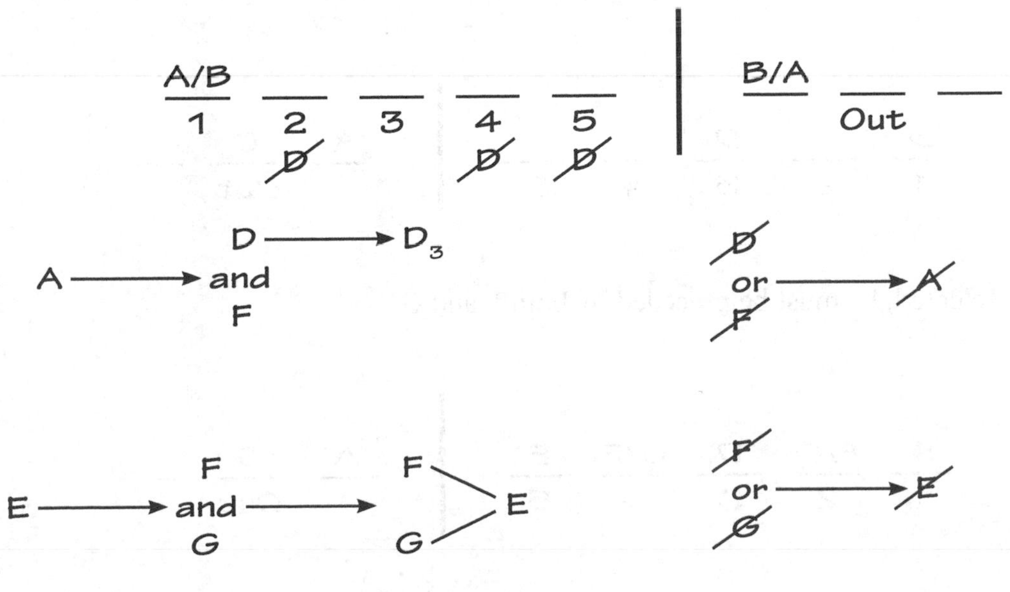

A/B	___	___	___	___		B/A	___	___
1	2	3	4	5		Out		
	~~D~~		~~D~~	~~D~~				

D ⟶ D_3
A ⟶ and
F

~~D~~
or ⟶ ~~A~~
~~F~~

F
E ⟶ and ⟶ F, G > E
G

~~F~~
or ⟶ ~~E~~
~~G~~

Question 1.1. If neither Alan nor Charlotte is selected, which one of the following could be true?

(A) Bobby is not selected to give the first presentation.
(B) Hank is selected to give the second presentation
(C) Debra is not selected to give the third presentation.
(D) Frankie is selected to give the fourth presentation.
(E) Edward is not selected to give the fifth presentation.

Question 1.1. This is a local question specifying that neither A nor C is selected, placing them both in the "Out" group, as reflected above.

Since A is not selected, we can conclude that B must be the first grader selected to present, and the global rules require that the first grader who is selected must be the first to present.

Since C is not selected, and C is in second grade, that dictates that the other two second graders (D and E) must be selected:

C̸ ⟶ D and E

When D is selected, as we know, she must present third...

B	___	D	___	___	A	C	___
1	2	3	4	5		Out	

...and when E is selected, he must be preceded by both F and G

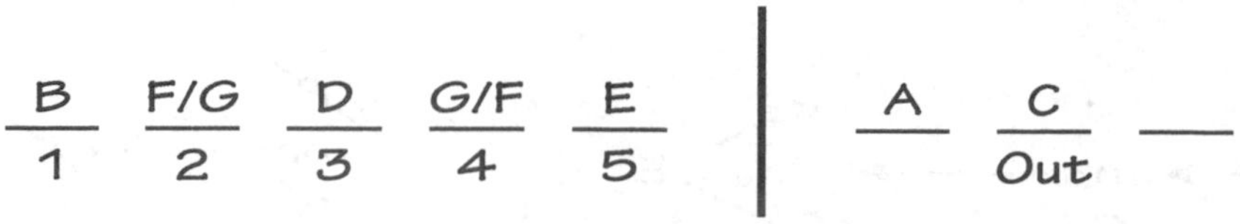

B	F/G	D	G/F	E	A	C	___
1	2	3	4	5		Out	

This leaves only our wild card, H, who must then be in the "Out" group.

B	F/G	D	G/F	E	A	C	H
1	2	3	4	5		Out	

With our local diagram complete, we can move on to the question:

Question 1.1. If neither Alan nor Charlotte is selected, which one of the following could be true?

(A) Bobby is not selected to give the first presentation.
(B) Hank is selected to give the second presentation
(C) Debra is not selected to give the third presentation.
(D) Frankie is selected to give the fourth presentation.
(E) Edward is not selected to give the fifth presentation.

Since Question 1.1 is a Could Be True question, the correct answer choice will be the only answer that presents a viable scenario based on the rules of the game. The four incorrect answer choices with be the ones that Cannot Be True.

Answer choice (A) cannot be true, because Bobby *must* give the first presentation.

Answer choice (B) cannot be true, because the second presentation must be given by either F or G.

Answer choice (C) cannot be true, because Debra is selected and therefore must present third.

Answer choice (D) is the correct answer choice, because it is the only one that could be true; the fourth presentation must be given by either G or F.

Answer choice (E) cannot be true, because Edward must give the fifth presentation.

Question 1.2. If both Frankie and Debra are selected, which one of the following CANNOT be true?

(A) Alan is selected to give the first presentation.
(B) Bobby is selected to give the first presentation.
(C) Neither Charlotte nor Greg is selected to give a presentation.
(D) Alan is not selected to give a presentation.
(E) Neither Hank nor Edward is selected to give a presentation.

Question 1.2. This is another local question, requiring that both Frankie and Debra be selected.

First, F's selection leaves room for only one other third grader (either G or H), relegating exactly one of the two to the Out group.

A/B	___	___	___	___	B/A	H/G	___
1	2	3	4	5		Out	

Further, when Debra is selected, the global rules specify, she must present third...

A/B	___	D	___	___	B/A	H/G	___
1	2	3	4	5		Out	

...and Debra's selection leaves room for only one other second grader (either C or E), while whoever is not selected must be placed into the Out group:

(F, C/E, G/H)	A/B	___	D	___	___	B/A	E/C	H/G
	1	2	3	4	5		Out	

Having completed the local diagram above, we can move on to the question.

Since Question 1.2 is a Cannot Be True question, the correct answer choice will be the one that cannot be true based on the information in the stimulus, and the four incorrect answers will be scenarios that *could* be true.

Answer choice (A) is incorrect, because it is possible that Alan could present first.

Answer choice (B) is incorrect, because Bobby could give the first presentation.

Answer choice (C) is the correct answer choice. If Charlotte is not selected, then the other two second graders must be selected:

C̸ ⟶ D and E

And the global rules specify that if E is selected, that F and G must be selected as well:

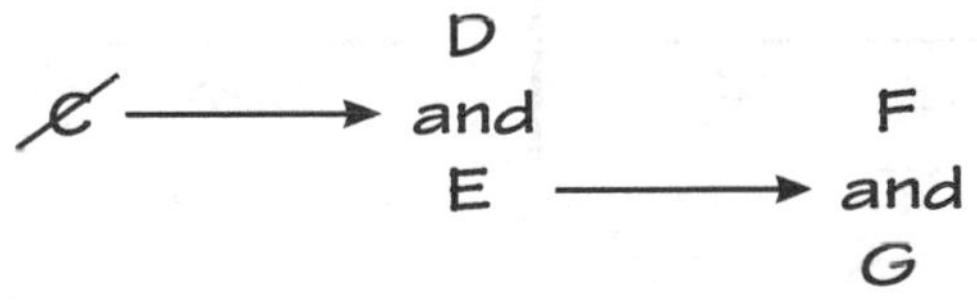

C̸ ⟶ D and E ⟶ F and G

Thus, there is no way that this scenario could come to pass. The diagram above reflects the fact that when C is absent, G must be present.

Since this cannot be true, this is the right answer to this Cannot Be True question.

Answer choice (D): This cannot be the right answer, because this choice could be true; Alan need not present, so long as Bobby presents first.

Answer choice (E): This answer choice could be true: if Hank is in the Out group, Greg must be selected, and if Edward is in the Out group, Charlotte must be selected.

2. In a dance competition, four co-ed teams (each comprised of one man and one woman) will be selected to compete, one team at a time. The players are paired at random, from among six women—I, J, K, L, M, N—and six men—O, P, Q, R, S, and T. The following is known about the day's selections:

   O is part of the team that dances first.
   M is part of the team that dances third.
   N is not selected unless P is selected.
   If R is selected, N and J are also selected, and either N or J, but not both, must precede R.
   S is selected if and only if Q is selected.

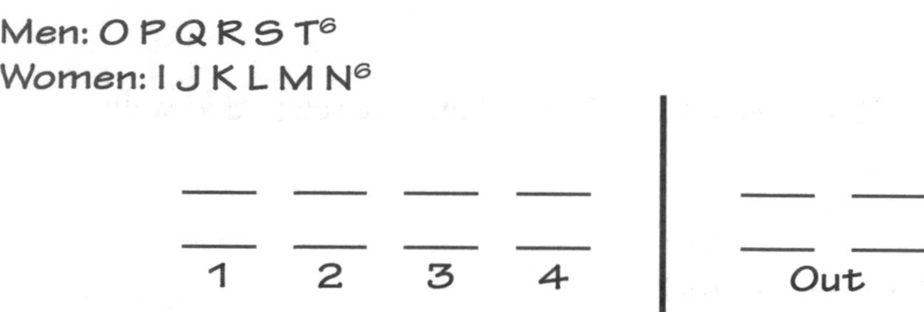

In this example, four couples dance, one at a time, creating a base with a nice sense of inherent order. Since each couple is comprised of two members, a second row is added, and since four of the dancers (two men and two women) will not compete, they must be relegated to the "Out" group.

The first two rules can be reflected directly on the diagram:

	1	2	3	4	Out	
Men:	O					
Women:			M			

The third rule provides a conditional statement with "unless." Applying the Unless Formula, "unless" introduces the necessary condition, and the other condition gets negated to become the sufficient condition.

N is not selected unless P is selected. "Unless" introduces P, the necessary condition, and "N is not selected" gets negated to become the sufficient condition: $N \longrightarrow P$

...and the contrapositive: $\not{P} \longrightarrow \not{N}$

The fourth rule dictates that if R is selected, then N and J are as well...

Rule: R ⟶ N and J

Contrapositive: N̸ or J̸ ⟶ R̸

...the fourth rule further dictates that when R is selected, either N or J, but not both, must precede R. This allows for only two relative configurations for the three variables when R is chosen:

R ⟶ N — R — J or J — R — N

Consequently, if selected, R must dance either second or third. This inference should be represented with an R Not Law in the fourth position (O is the man who dances first, which obviates the need for an R Not Law in the first position).

The last rule specifies that S is selected if and only if Q is selected.

From this rule we know that S and Q will either both be selected: S ⟷ Q

or they will both be in the Out Group: S̸ ⟷ Q̸

Putting together our setup and combining all of the rules, we have our Global Diagram:

Men: O P Q R S T[6]
Women: I J K L M N[6]

	1	2	3	4	Out	
Men:	O					
Women:			M			
				R̸		

R ⟶ N and J; N ⟶ P

P̸ ⟶ N̸; N̸ or J̸ ⟶ R̸

R ⟶ N — R — J or J — R — N

S ⟷ Q

S̸ ⟷ Q̸

Grouping/Linear Combination Setup Practice Drill Answer Key—page 61

Question 2.1. If P and T are both selected to dance in the competition, which one of the following could be true?

(A) R is not selected to dance in the competition.
(B) S is selected to dance in the competition.
(C) J is not selected to dance in the competition.
(D) Q is selected to dance in the competition.
(E) L is not selected to dance in the competition.

Question 2.1 provides that both P and T are selected to dance in the competition. Although their positions are not specified, this rule leaves only one available spot among the male dancers. Since S and Q are either selected together or omitted together, that leaves R to take fill the extra space among the men. The fourth rule dictates that when R is selected, N and J must be selected as well, creating the following local diagram:

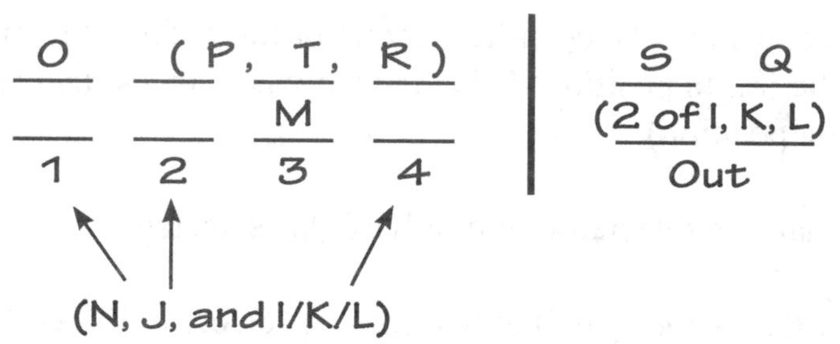

1	2	3	4	Out
O	(P,	T,	R)	S Q
		M		(2 of I, K, L)

(N, J, and I/K/L) → 1, 2, 4

The question asks for the answer choice that could be true. This means that the correct answer choice will be the only one that could be true, while the four incorrect answer choices will all provide scenarios that cannot be true.

Answer choice (A) is incorrect, because R must be selected to dance in the competition.

Answer choice (B) is incorrect, since the SQ pair must be included or excluded together. In this case, since there are not enough spaces for both to be selected, they must both be excluded.

Answer choice (C) is incorrect; based on the fourth rule, J must be selected when R is selected.

Answer choice (D) is incorrect based on the final rule, that Q is selected if and only if S is selected.

Answer choice (E) is the correct answer choice, because it is the only answer presented that could be true; as shown in the local diagram, L may or may not be selected.

Grouping/Linear Combination Setup Practice Drill Answer Key—page 61

Question 2.2. Which one of the following is an acceptable selection and order of the couples chosen to dance in the competition?

(A) O and N; R and I; T and M; S and J
(B) O and J; P and N; R and M; T and K
(C) O and L; S and N; P and M; Q and J
(D) P and J; O and K; R and M; T and N
(E) O and J; R and L, P and N; T and I

Question 2.2 is a List question, so the incorrect answer choices can each be eliminated based on at least one of the rules provided.

Answer choice (A) is incorrect, because of the last rule: the selection of S would also require the selection of Q.

Answer choice (B) is incorrect, because when R is selected, R must be preceded by either J or N, but not both.

Answer choice (C) is the correct answer choice.

Answer choice (D) is incorrect, because O must be part of the first couple to dance.

Answer choice (E) is incorrect, since the second rule dictates that M must be part of the couple that dances third.

3. On Saturday evening, six aircraft must land at Caledonia International Airport. Of the aircraft, two are short-haul, two are medium-haul, and two are long-haul. Each aircraft must use exactly one of two runways for landing: X and Y. Only one aircraft lands at a time.

   No short-haul aircraft lands on the same runway as any long-haul aircraft.

   No two medium-haul aircraft land consecutively on the same runway.

   No short-haul aircraft lands on runway X until at least one medium-haul aircraft lands on runway X.

   No medium-haul aircraft lands on runway Y until at least one long-haul aircraft lands on runway Y.

This Combination Linear/Defined-Moving Grouping Game requires us to divide six aircraft—S, S, M, M, L, L—among two runways (X and Y), and then determine the order in which each aircraft lands.

S, S, M, M, L, L [6]

S ←|→ L

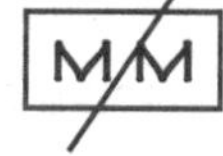

$S_X \longrightarrow (M — S)_X$

$M_Y \longrightarrow (L — M)_Y$

Inferences:

As with all Combination games, the grouping element takes precedence over the linear element, and should be analyzed first.

Since no short-haul aircraft lands on the same runway as any long-haul aircraft, it is clear that both short-haul aircraft must land on the same runway as each other. The same holds true for the two long-haul aircraft:

Template 1: X: (S, S)
Y: (L, L)

Template 2: X: (L, L)
Y: (S, S)

Grouping/Linear Combination Setup Practice Drill Answer Key—page 61

The second rule (Not-Block) is linear in nature, not grouping. Thus, its implication will only become apparent once we have a more solid grasp of the grouping elements that drive the game.

The third rule states:

$$S_X \longrightarrow (M — S)_X$$

That rule does not have a direct impact on Template 2, because in Template 2 both short-haul aircraft land on runway Y, not X. However, the rule requires that at least one medium-haul aircraft arrive before either short-haul aircraft in Template 1:

Template 1: X: M — S — S
Y: L — L

Thus far, Template 1 does not account for the landing of the other medium-haul aircraft. If that aircraft lands on runway Y, it would trigger the fourth rule of the game:

$$M_Y \longrightarrow (L — M)_Y$$

In that scenario, Template 1 must be modified as follows:

Template 1.1: X: M — S — S
Y: L — (M, L)

Alternatively, both medium-haul aircraft can land on runway X. In that case, we need to comply with the prohibition against any two medium-haul aircrafts arriving consecutively (second rule):

Template 1.2: X: M — S — (M, S)
Y: L — L

Finally, let's consider Template 2 in the context of the second and fourth rules:

Template 2: X: (L, L)
Y: (S, S)

The fourth rule affects Template 2 directly: Since both long-haul aircraft land on runway X (not Y), it follows that no medium-haul aircraft can land on runway Y. So, both must land on runway X:

Template 2: X: (M, M, L, L)
Y: (S, S)

Thanks to the second rule of the game, however, no two medium-haul aircraft can arrive consecutively on the same runway. Thus, the sequence in which the aircraft must arrive on runway X must conform to either of the following templates:

Template 2.1: X: M —— L —— (M, L)
Y: S —— S

Template 2.2: X: L —— M —— L —— M
Y: S —— S

<u>Question 3.1</u>. Which one of the following could be a complete and accurate list of aircraft landing on runway X, listed in the order in which they land:

(A) short-haul, short-haul
(B) medium-haul, medium-haul, short-haul, short-haul
(C) medium-haul, long-haul, long-haul
(D) long-haul, medium-haul, long-haul
(E) medium-haul, long-haul, long-haul, medium-haul

Question 3.1. The correct answer choice is (E). See Template 2.1 above.

Question 3.2. Which one of the following must be false?

(A) The number of aircraft landing on runway X is greater than the number of aircraft landing on runway Y.
(B) The number of aircraft landing on runway Y is greater than the number of aircraft landing on runway X.
(C) The number of aircraft landing on runway X is equal to the number of aircraft landing on runway Y.
(D) At least two aircraft land on runway X.
(E) At least two aircraft land on runway Y.

Question 3.2. The correct answer choice is (B), because the number of aircraft landing on runway Y is never greater than the number of aircraft landing on runway X. See templates above.

Question 3.3. If no two medium-haul aircraft land on the same runway, then each one of the following must be true, EXCEPT:

(A) A medium-haul aircraft lands second on runway Y.
(B) A medium-haul aircraft lands first on runway X.
(C) A short-haul aircraft lands second on runway X.
(D) A short-haul aircraft lands third on runway X.
(E) A long-haul aircraft lands first on runway Y.

Question 3.3. The correct answer choice is (A). If no two medium-haul aircraft land on the same runway, we need to look at Template 1.1:

Template 1.1: X: M —— S —— S
Y: L —— (M, L)

Since *at least* one long-haul aircraft must land before the medium-haul aircraft on runway Y, a medium-haul aircraft does not necessarily land second on runway Y: it can also land third.

Question 3.4. If a long-haul aircraft lands first on runway X, then which one of the following could be false?

(A) A short-haul aircraft lands first on runway Y.
(B) A short-haul aircraft lands last on runway Y.
(C) A medium-haul aircraft lands third on runway X.
(D) Exactly four aircraft land on runway X.
(E) Exactly two aircraft land on runway Y.

Question 3.4. The correct answer choice is (C). If a long-haul aircraft lands first on runway X, then both long-haul aircraft land on runway X. The short-haul aircraft land on runway Y. Since no medium-haul aircraft lands on runway Y without at least one long-haul aircraft landing there, we can conclude that both medium-haul aircraft must land on runway X. They cannot, however, land consecutively. Since a long-haul aircraft must land *first* on runway X, it follows that the remaining three aircraft land in the following order: M —— L —— M:

Template 2.2: X: L —— M —— L —— M
Y: S —— S

It is clear from this template that each of the five answer choices must be true, except for answer choice (C), which must be false (and therefore satisfies the "could be false" parameter in the question stem).

Pure Sequencing Diagramming Drill Answer Key—page 64

Note that your diagrams may look different from the ones in the answer key. This is acceptable as long as the relationships are the same.

1. Rules: L is taller than M.
   N is shorter than M.
   L is shorter than J and K.
   O is taller than N.

Diagram:

```
                    O
J \                  \
   > L —— M —————— N
K /
```

Question 1.1. Which one of the following could accurately list the three tallest variables, in order from first to third tallest?

(A) J, L, M
(B) J, L, O
(C) J, K, M
(D) K, O, J
(E) K, L, O

Question 1.1. The correct answer is (D). Although O appears to be a variable that will be short, the only restriction on O is that O is taller than N. Thus, O can be among the three tallest variables. J and K must also be among the three tallest variables, and thus the order K, O, J is viable. Several of the other answers (answers A, B, and E) fail to include J or K, both of which must be among the three tallest. Answer choice (C) is incorrect because M cannot be among the three tallest variables.

Pure Sequencing Diagramming Drill Answer Key—page 64

2. Rules: T is larger than W.
W is smaller than V.
T is not larger than S.
X is larger than W.
X is larger than Y.

A. Which variables in the chain could be largest?

S, T, V, X (T could only tie for the largest)

B. Which variables in the chain could be smallest?

W, Y

Diagram:

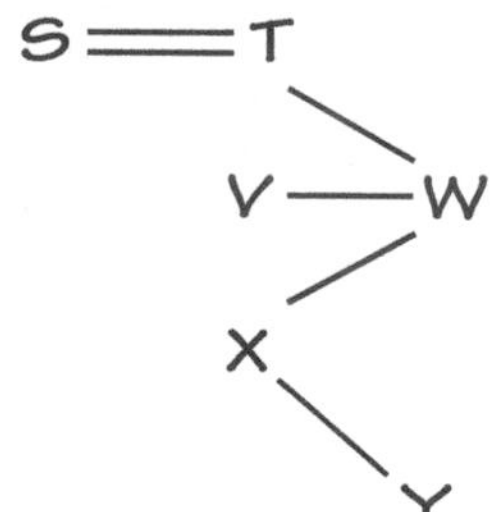

---

3. Rules: B and D are heavier than E.
J is lighter than B.
C is heavier than D.
B is lighter than A.
E is heavier than F and H.
K is heavier than H.
G is lighter than F.

A. Which variables in the chain could be heaviest?

A, C, K

B. Which variables in the chain could be lightest?

G, H, J

Diagram:

Pure Sequencing Diagramming Drill Answer Key—page 64

4. Rules: C is shorter than A and B.
B and D are taller than E.
F is taller than A.

Diagram:

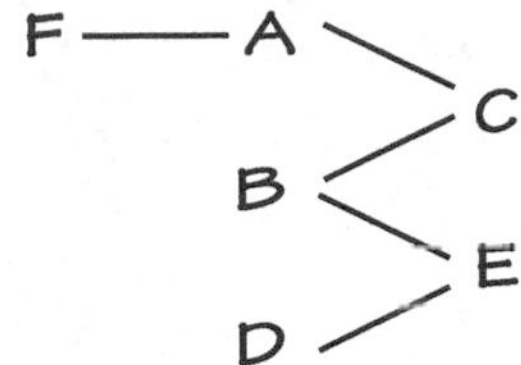

Question 4.1 Which one of the following could be an accurate list of the two shortest variables in a lineup of all six variables?

(A) A, E
(B) B, C
(C) B, E
(D) C, D
(E) D, E

Question 4.1. The correct answer is (E). Answer choice (A) can be eliminated because A is taller than C, so A can only be among the two shortest when the other variable is C.

Variable B cannot be a part of the correct answer because B is always taller than both C and E. Thus, answer choices (B) and (C) can be eliminated.

Similar to (A), answer choice (D) can be eliminated because D is taller than E, so D can only be among the two shortest when the other variable is E.

Pure Sequencing Diagramming Drill Answer Key—page 64

5. Rules: R is faster than S.
U is slower than T.
Q is faster than R and T.
W is faster than R.
T is slower than X.
P is faster than Q.

Diagram:

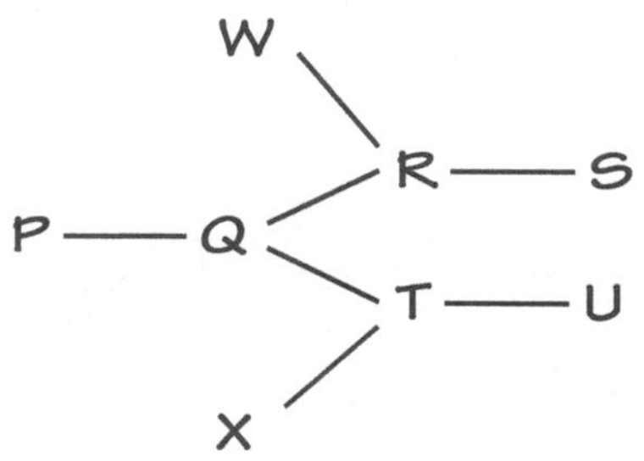

W
R — S
P — Q
T — U
X

Question 5.1 Which one of the following must be false?

(A) S is sixth fastest.
(B) W is sixth fastest.
(C) X is sixth fastest.
(D) Q is fifth fastest.
(E) P is third fastest.

Question 5.1. The correct answer is (D). The question stem asks for an answer that Cannot Be True (remember, convert "false" to "true"), and so any answer choice that Could Be True can be eliminated.

One key to this question is understanding the range of possibilities for W and X. Either W or X could be fastest, but they can also be relatively slow: W must only be faster than R and S, and X must only be faster than T and U. Thus, W or X could be sixth fastest, and both answer choices (B) and (C) can be eliminated. P could also be slower than both W and X, so P could be third fastest, and answer choice (E) can be eliminated.

Answer choice (A) can also be eliminated because S could be faster than both T and U, leaving S sixth fastest.

Answer choice (D) is correct; Q must always be faster than R, S, T, and U, and so Q could only be fourth fastest at worst.

Pure Sequencing Diagramming Drill Answer Key—page 64

6. Rules: P and Q are both lower-rated than M.
Z is higher-rated than Y.
X is lower-rated than W.
Y is higher-rated than X.

A. Which of the variables could be the highest-rated?

M, W, Z

B. Which of the variables could be the lowest-rated?

P, Q, X

C. What is the highest-rated position that Y could occupy? What is the lowest-rated position that Y could occupy?

Highest-rated position that Y could occupy: Second
Lowest-rated position that Y could occupy: Sixth

Diagrams:

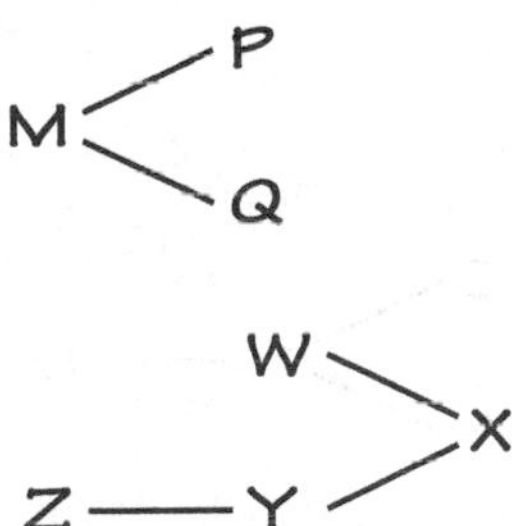

---

7. Rules: J is more popular than L, and L is more popular than P.
E and O are both less popular than D.
J is less popular than E and O.

A. Which of the variables in the chain could be most popular?

D

B. Which of the variables in the chain could be least popular?

P

C. How many solutions exist to this game if no ties occur?

Two: D-E-O-J-L-P and D-O-E-J-L-P.

Diagram:

E
D J — L — P
O

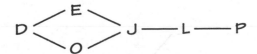

Pure Sequencing Diagramming Drill Answer Key—page 64

8. Rules: B arrives earlier than C.
F arrives later than C and E.
D arrives earlier than E.
F arrives earlier than G.
A arrives earlier than B and D.

A. Which of the variables in the chain could arrive earliest?

A

B. Which of the variables in the chain could arrive latest?

G

C. Assuming no ties are possible, if B arrives second, what is the earliest that D could arrive?

Third. There are only two solutions possible when B arrives second and D arrives as early as possible: A-B-D-C-E-F-G or A-B-D-E-C-F-G. In both instances, D arrives third.

Diagram:

B — C
A F — G
D — E

---

9. Rules: J is delivered after E.
K is delivered before O.
J is delivered before K.
K is delivered after L.

A. Which of the variables in the chain could be delivered first?

E, L

B. Which of the variables in the chain could be delivered last?

O

C. If E is delivered first, how many solutions exist to this game if no ties occur?

Two: E-L-J-K-O and E-J-L-K-O. Do not assume that L must be delivered second just because E and L are the only two variables that could be delivered first.

Diagram:

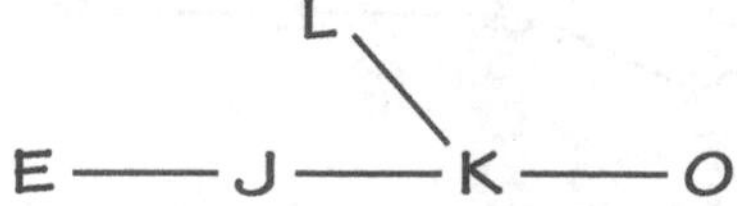

Pure Sequencing Diagramming Drill Answer Key—page 64

10. Rules: T and W sit in the same row.
R sits in a row closer to the stage than T.
Y does not sit in a row closer to the stage than W.
W sits in a row further from the stage than S.
Z can sit in any row.

A. Which of the variables in the chain could sit in the first row?

R, S, Z

B. Which of the variables in the chain could sit in the last row?

T, W, Y, Z. If T and W sit in the last row, they must sit with Y.

C. What is the minimum number of rows that must exist in the game?

Two: R and S could occupy one row, and T, W, and Y could occupy another row. Z could then sit in either row.

Diagram:

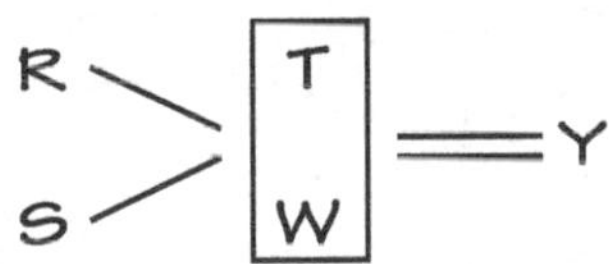

Z?

---

11. Rules: P is taller than F and G.
C is taller than K.
M is shorter than C but taller than P.

A. Which of the variables in the chain could be tallest?

C

B. Which of the variables in the chain could be shortest?

F, G, K

C. If G is taller than F, how many solutions exist to this game if no ties occur?

Five, all of which are triggered by the position of K: C-K-M-P-F-G, C-M-K-P-F-G, C-M-P-K-F-G, C-M-P-F-K-G, and C-M-P-F-G-K.

Diagram:

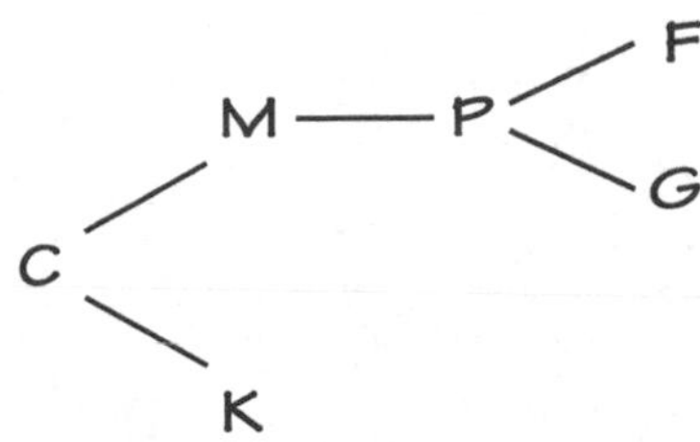

PRACTICE DRILL EXPLANATIONS

Pure Sequencing Diagramming Drill Answer Key—page 64

12. Rules: B and L are both lighter than G.
L and Y are both lighter than R.

A. Which of the variables in the chain could be heaviest?

G, R

B. Which of the variables in the chain could be lightest?

B, L, Y

C. What is the heaviest that Y could rank?

Second. Only R must be ahead of Y, thus Y could be second heaviest among the five variables.

Diagram:

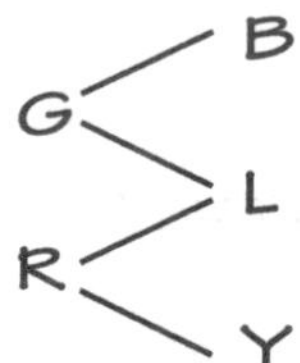

---

13. Rules: F is higher-rated than D, L, and J.
N is higher-rated than D.
G is lower-rated than B and higher-rated than F.

A. Which of the variables in the chain could be the highest-rated?

B, N

B. Which of the variables in the chain could be the lowest-rated?

D, L, J

C. If N is the third lowest-rated variable, how many solutions exist to this game if no ties occur?

Four: B-G-F-J-N-D-L, B-G-F-J-N-L-D, B-G-F-L-N-D-J, and B-G-F-L-N-J-D.

Pure Sequencing Diagramming Drill Answer Key—page 64

Diagram:

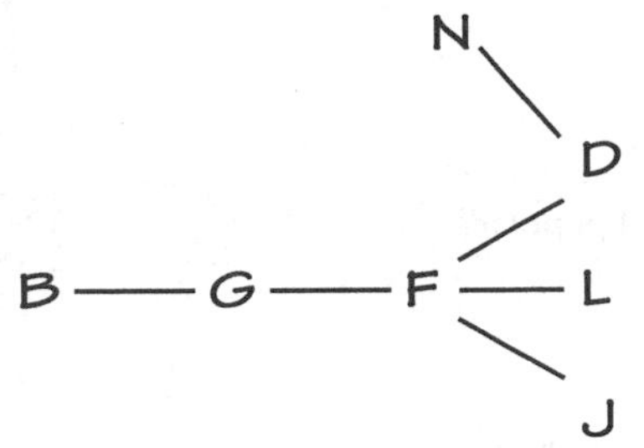

14. Rules: N and S are both smaller than O.
H is larger than R.
L and O are both smaller than R.
E and V are both larger than H.

A. Which of the variables in the chain could be largest?

A. Which of the variables in the chain could be largest? E, V

B. Which of the variables in the chain could be smallest?

B. Which of the variables in the chain could be smallest? L, N, S

C. If L is larger than O, how many of the variables are then limited to a single position in the chain?

Four: H, R, L, and O. H and R must always be third and fourth, respectively (this is true despite any ties, as ties would still count as two positions). When L —— O, then L must be fifth, and O must be sixth, in order to allow sufficient room for N and S (which are seventh and eighth, in some order).

Diagram:

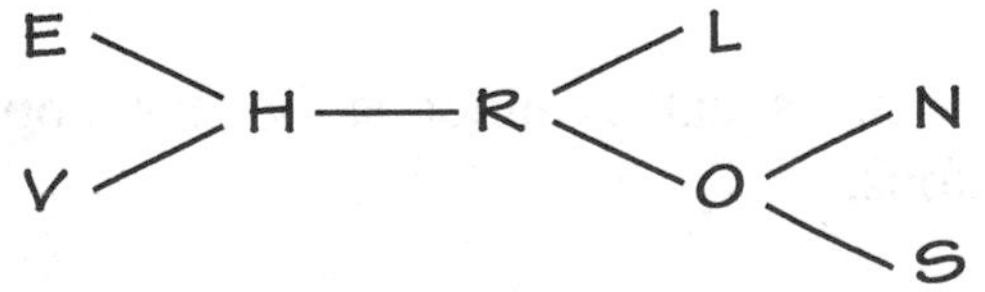

Pure Sequencing Diagramming Drill Answer Key—page 64

15. Rules: T is less popular than X, and W is less popular than Z.
X and Z are both more popular than V.
Y is less popular than W.
Y cannot be the least popular.

A. Which of the variables in the chain could be most popular?

X, Z

B. Which of the variables in the chain could be least popular?

T, V

C. If T and Z have the same level of popularity, then what is the highest popularity rank that V can achieve?

Last (which is the same as sixth). If T and Z are identical, then X must have the highest popularity rank. Because Y cannot have the least popularity, and W is more popular than Y, only V then remains to be least popular. As there are only six positions , the ranks are:

First = X
Second = T and Z (who count as two, tied places)
Fourth = W
Fifth = Y
Sixth = V

Diagram:

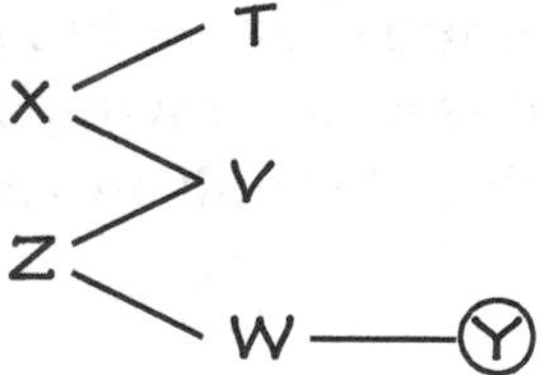

Y is circled because the last rule states that it cannot be the least popular, a fact that would be easy to forget after a few questions.

Pure Sequencing Diagramming Drill Answer Key—page 64

16. Rules: W is delivered after V but before T.
O and X are both delivered before V.
R is delivered before T.
S is delivered before T.
No two deliveries occur at the same time.

A. Which of the variables in the chain could be delivered first?

O, X, R, S

B. Which of the variables in the chain could be delivered last?

T

C. If S is delivered second and V is delivered fourth, how many solutions exist to this game?

Four: if S is second, V is delivered fourth, and T must always be delivered last, then the template appears as follows:

O/X	S	X/O	V	R/W	W/R	T
1	2	3	4	5	6	7

Accordingly, there are four solutions to the game.

Diagram:

R
O
V — W — T
X
S

PRACTICE DRILL EXPLANATIONS

Pure Sequencing Diagramming Drill Answer Key—page 64

17. Rules: H arrives earlier than N.
D, O, and V arrive earlier than H.
V and R arrive earlier than L.
J arrives earlier than N.

A. Which of the variables in the chain could arrive earliest?

D, O, V, R, J

B. Which of the variables in the chain could arrive latest?

N, L

C. If L arrives earlier than H, what is the earliest position that H could arrive, assuming no ties occur?

Sixth: from the second rule D, O, and V must arrive earlier than H, and from the third rule R must arrive earlier than L, meaning that both R and L must arrive earlier than H in this question. Thus, D, O, V, R, and L must—in some order—arrive earlier than H, and the earliest H can arrive is sixth.

Diagram:

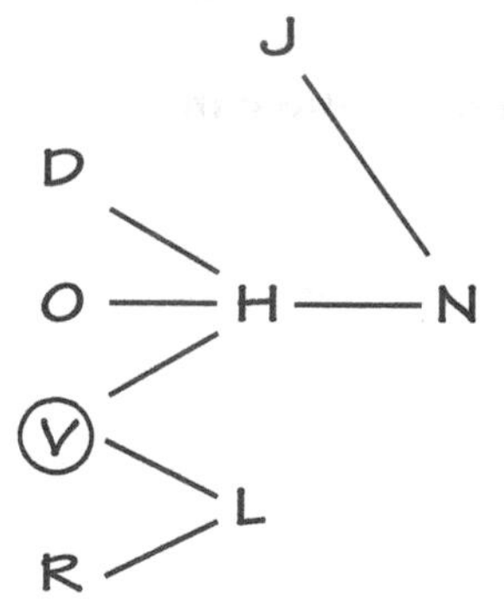

V is circled because it is the only variable that must arrive earlier than both H and L. R arrives earlier than only L, and D and O arrive earlier than only H (and indirectly N).

Pure Sequencing Diagramming Drill Answer Key—page 64

18. Rules: X is taller than J and Q.
N is taller than D.
X is shorter than A.
D is shorter than Q.

A. Which of the variables in the chain could be tallest?

A, N

B. Which of the variables in the chain could be shortest?

J, D

C. If N is shorter than J, how many solutions exist to this game if no ties occur?

Three: **A-X-J-N-Q-D**
A-X-J-Q-N-D
A-X-Q-J-N-D

Diagram:

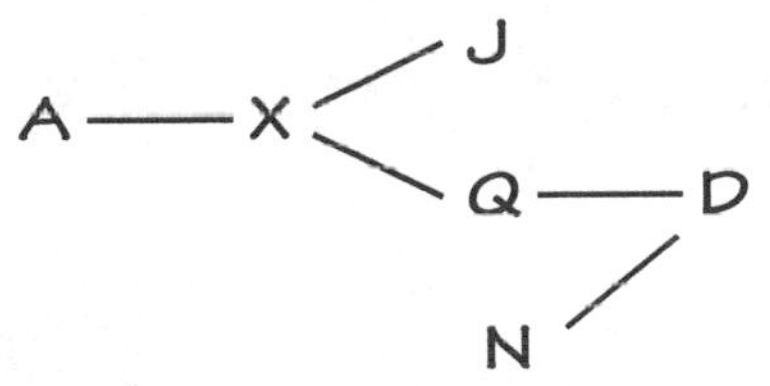

Conditional Sequencing Diagramming Drill Answer Key—page 75

1. Rule: If the N train arrives earlier than the Q train, then the R train does not arrive earlier than the Q train.

Diagram: (N — Q) ⟶ (N — Q — R)

Contrapositive: (R — Q) ⟶ (R — Q — N)

Note: This rule does *not* establish only two possible chains for N, Q, and R. Granted, if either one of N or R arrives earlier than Q, the other one must arrive later than Q. This rule only prevents us from placing both N and R *before* Q, but leaves open the possibility that they are both *after* Q: indeed, Q could arrive earlier than both N and R without violating any rules. There are therefore three possible sequences for N, Q, and R:

N — Q — R

or

R — Q — N

or

Q < N, R

---

2. Rule: If Viva is more popular than Splash, then neither Wonk nor Therapy is more popular than Viva.

Diagram: (V — S) ⟶ V < W, T, S

Contrapositive: W — V or T — V ⟶ (S — V)

PRACTICE DRILL EXPLANATIONS

Conditional Sequencing Diagramming Drill Answer Key—page 75

Note: The logical opposite of V —— (W and T) requires breaking only one part of the chain. This is the essence of logical negation. It is sufficient to show either that W —— V or that T —— V to enact the contrapositive function. In the contrapositive, there are *at least* two variables that are more popular than V (either W or T, along with S), but it is possible that all three variables (W, T, and S) are more popular than V.

---

3. Rule: G is assembled later than both H and I if and only if H and I are both assembled later than J.

Diagram:

```
H \                 / H
   > G <------> J <
I /                 \ I
```

Contrapositive:

```
H                        H
or —— J <------> G —— or
I                        I
```

Note: The logical opposite of J —— (H and I) requires breaking only one part of the chain. It is sufficient to show either that H —— J or that I —— J to enact the contrapositive function.

Also note that the phrase "if and only if" consists of two separate but equally important indicators: "if" (a sufficient condition indicator) and "only if" (a necessary condition indicator). As a result, "if and only if" refers to a condition that is both sufficient and necessary for the other.

Conditional Sequencing Diagramming Drill Answer Key—page 75

4. Rule: If neither Ngu nor Miuccia receives a higher score than Lilly, then both Giacomo and Jordan receive a higher score than Lilly.

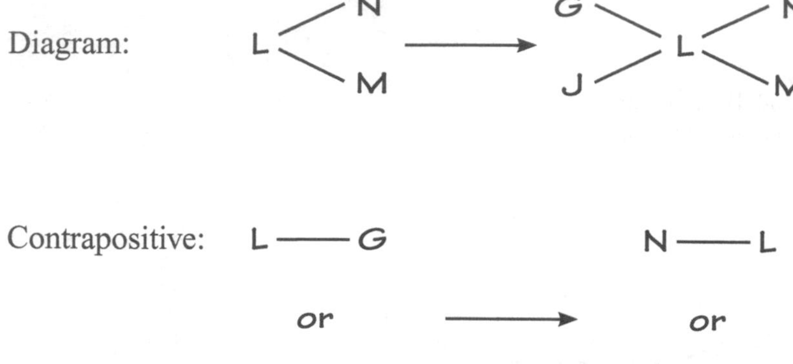

Note: The logical opposite of (G and J) —— L requires breaking only one part of the chain. It is sufficient to show either that L —— G or that L —— J to enact the contrapositive function. Likewise, the necessary condition in the contrapositive requires that at least one of N or M (or both) receive a higher score than L.

Ultimately, at least one person must receive a higher score than Lilly, who cannot receive the highest possible score.

---

5. Rule: Either the Klausen exhibit closes earlier than the Milo exhibit, or the Milo exhibit closes earlier than the Leonardo exhibit, but not both.

The statement contains two separate rules:

1. Either the Klausen exhibit closes earlier than the Milo exhibit, or the Milo exhibit closes earlier than the Leonardo exhibit:

   K —— M   or   M —— L

2. … but not both:

   (K —— M) ——→ K, L —— M

contrapositive: (M — L) ⟶ M < L, K

Taken together, these rules establish only two possible sequences in which K, M, and L can be exhibited:

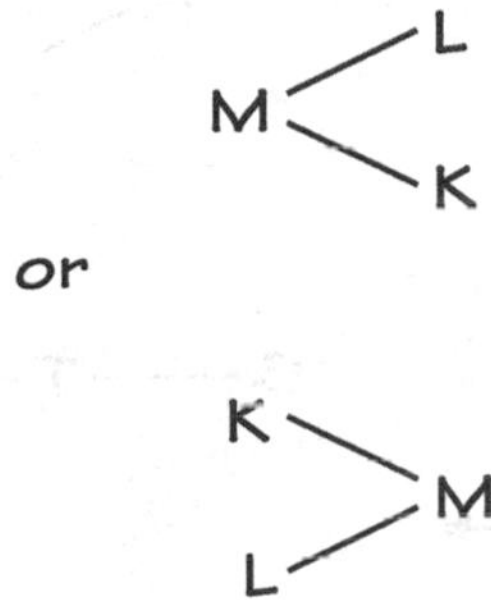

---

6. Rule: Both Cadaques and Girona are visited later than Barcelona, or else Barcelona is visited later than both Cadaques and Girona.

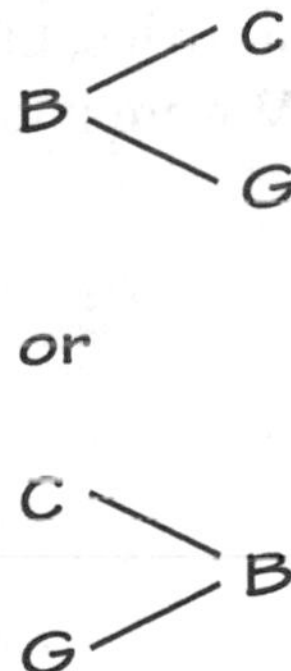

7. Rule: Rodriguez is interviewed earlier than Thompson only if both Sinclair and Velasquez are interviewed later than Thompson.

Diagram:

(R —— T) ——→ R —— T < S, V

Contrapositive:

S —— T or V —— T ——→ S —— T —— R / V —— T —— R

Note: The logical opposite of T —— (S and V) requires breaking only one part of the chain. It is sufficient to show either that S —— T or that V —— T to enact the contrapositive function.

While the contrapositive establishes only two possible chains, the rule as a whole does *not* prohibit T from being interviewed first. Indeed, if both S and V were interviewed later than T, it could be possible that R is also interviewed later than T.

---

8. Rule: J cannot be delivered later than K, unless either L or M is delivered later than J.

Diagram:

(K —— J) ——→ (K —— J —— L or M)

Contrapositive:

L, M > J ——→ L, M > J —— K

Note: the rule only prohibits J from being delivered last; it is possible that J is first.

Conditional Sequencing Diagramming Drill Answer Key—page 75

9\. Rule: M is written earlier than each of L and P, or else M is written later than each of L and P.

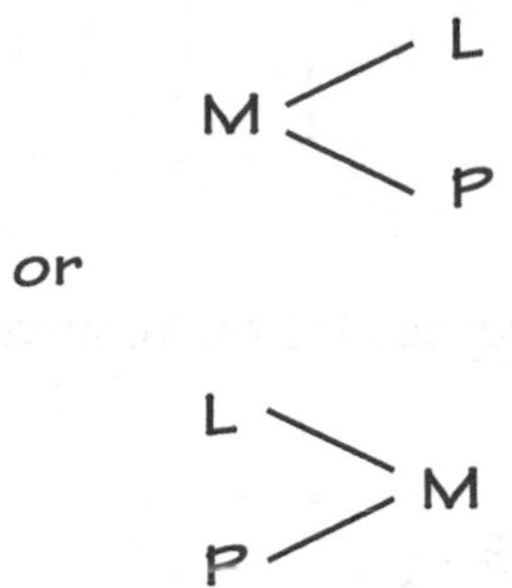

10\. Rule: If J is lower in cost than K, then R is lower in cost than each of S and T; otherwise, R is higher in cost than each of S and T.

The statement contains two separate rules:

1. If J is lower in cost than K, then R is lower in cost than each of S and T:

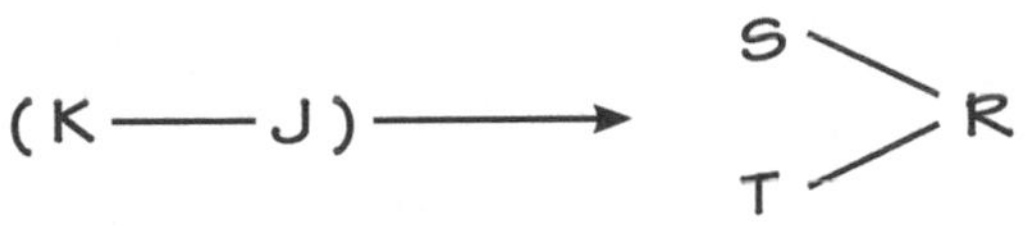

(K—J) ⟶ S, T > R

contrapositive: R—S or R—T ⟶ (J—K)

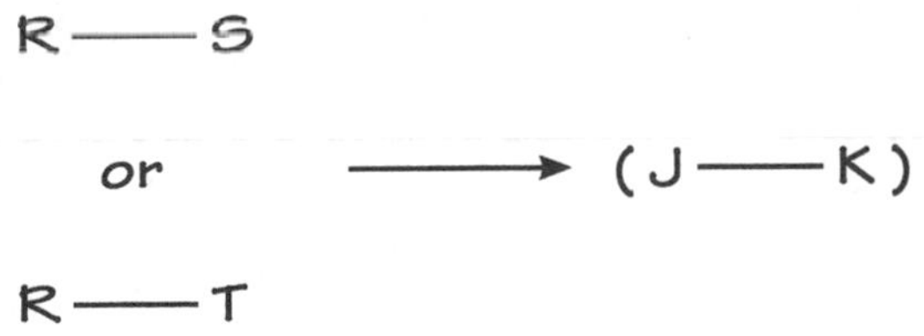

2. … otherwise, R is higher in cost than each of S and T:

(J—K) ⟶ R < S, T

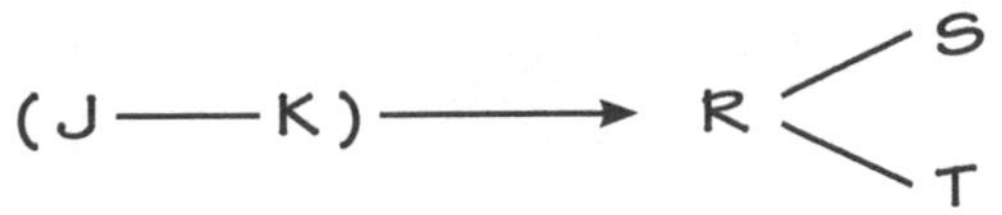

Conditional Sequencing Diagramming Drill Answer Key—page 75

S —— R

contrapositive: or ——→ (K —— J)

T —— R

Taken together, these rules establish only two possible sequences for the relative costs of R, S, and T:

Numerical Distribution Identification Drill Answer Key—page 78

1. Eight books are assigned to three students.

   Eight distributed to three:

   Unfixed: 4-2-2
   3-3-2

---

2. Ten drinks are served to two bar patrons.

   Ten distributed to two:

   Unfixed: 7-3
   6-4
   5-5

---

3. Six bones are given to three dogs—a Greyhound, a Mastiff, and a Terrier.

   Six distributed to three:

   Fixed:

G	M	T
3	2	1
1	3	2

---

4. Eleven cookies are placed in four jars.

   Eleven distributed to four:

   Unfixed: 5-4-1-1
   5-3-2-1
   5-2-2-2
   4-4-2-1
   4-3-3-1
   4-3-2-2
   3-3-3-2

Numerical Distribution Identification Drill Answer Key—page 78

5. Eight tables are assigned to four different servers—servers A, B, C, and D.

Eight distributed to four:

Fixed:	A	B	C	D
	4	2	1	1
	2	1	4	1
	2	1	1	4
	2	1	3	2
	2	1	2	3

6. Twelve students are assigned to five different floors in a dormitory.

Twelve distributed to five:

Unfixed: 4-2-2-2-2
3-3-2-2-2

7. Seven animals are placed into three cages.

Seven distributed to three:

Unfixed: 5-2-0
5-1-1
4-3-0
4-2-1
3-3-1
3-2-2

Careful, the rules do not stipulate that a cage must contain a minimum number of animals, just a maximum.

Numerical Distribution Identification Drill Answer Key—page 78

8. Thirteen toys are given to four children—W, X, Y, and Z.

Thirteen distributed to four:

Fixed:

W	X	Y	Z
2	3	6	2
2	2	6	3

---

9. Twenty-one pills are placed into six bottles.

Unfixed: 6-3-3-3-3-3
5-4-3-3-3-3
4-4-4-3-3-3

---

10. Seven appointments with a doctor are scheduled over four days—Monday, Tuesday, Wednesday, and Thursday.

Fixed:

M	Tu	W	Th
1	1	3	2
3	1	2	1
2	2	2	1
1	3	2	1

---

11. Each of seven lawyers is assigned to represent exactly one of four criminal defendants. Each defendant must be represented by at least one but no more than three of the lawyers.

Seven lawyers distributed to four defendants:

Unfixed: 3-2-1-1
2-2-2-1

PRACTICE DRILL EXPLANATIONS

Numerical Distribution Identification Drill Answer Key—page 78

12. Each of four horses is treated by exactly one of three veterinarians. No veterinarian treats more than three horses.

Four horses distributed to three vets:

Unfixed: 3-1-0
2-2-0
2-1-1

---

13. At a historically preserved home with seven rooms, there is exactly one computer terminal in each room. To avoid circuit overload, at most twice as many terminals can be turned on as can be turned off at any given time. At least two terminals must be turned on at any given time.

Seven computer terminals distributed to two positions (on/off).

Fixed: On - Off
2 - 5
3 - 4
4 - 3

---

14. A movie reviewer screens five new releases in a given week, Sunday through Thursday, to prepare for her live radio interview. The reviewer screens at most two new releases on any given day.

Five releases distributed to five days:

Unfixed: 2-2-1-0-0
2-1-1-1-0
1-1-1-1-1

Numerical Distribution Identification Drill Answer Key—page 78

15. A baseball card collector is adding fourteen new cards to his collection. Each card features exactly one of four baseball players—Jeter, Lasorda, Mantle, and Robinson, and each player is featured on exactly two, four or six cards. The number of Jeter cards is no less than twice the number of Lasorda cards.

Fourteen cards distributed to four players:

<u>Lasorda-Jeter-Mantle-Robinson</u>

Fixed:
2-6-4-2
2-6-2-4
2-4-6-2
2-4-2-6
2-4-4-4

---

16. A company contracts with homeowners to pave exactly thirteen driveways in a given week, Monday through Sunday. The company must pave at least one but no more than four driveways each day.

Thirteen driveways distributed to seven days.

Unfixed:
4-4-1-1-1-1-1
4-3-2-1-1-1-1
4-2-2-2-1-1-1
3-3-3-1-1-1-1
3-3-2-2-1-1-1
3-2-2-2-2-1-1
2-2-2-2-2-2-1

---

17. Each of eight students receives tutoring from a single instructor during a given week, Monday through Friday. The instructor tutors at least one but no more than three students per day.

Eight students distributed to five days.

Unfixed:
3-2-1-1-1
2-2-2-1-1

Numerical Distribution Identification Drill Answer Key—page 78

18. A tennis instructor gives nine balls to two children. Each child is given at least two balls.

Nine tennis balls distributed to two children.

Unfixed: 7-2
6-3
5-4

---

19. A jeweler will use exactly five birthstones to create three rings. Each ring will contain exactly three different birthstones, and each birthstone will be used in at least one ring.

Nine birthstones used distributed to five birthstones available.

Note: Since each of the three rings must contain exactly three different birthstones, no birthstone can be used more than three times (using the same birthstone four times will inevitably result in that birthstone being used at least twice in one of the rings).

Unfixed: 4-2-1-1-1
3-3-1-1-1
3-2-2-1-1
2-2-2-2-1

---

20. Each of four fashion designers, Q, R, S and V, will attend at least one of six fashion shows. S attends exactly one show.

Six fashion shows distributed to four designers.

Fixed: **Q - R - V- S**
3 - 1 - 1 - 1
1 - 3 - 1 -1
1 - 1 - 3 - 1
2 - 2 -1 - 1
2 - 1 - 2 - 1
1 - 2 - 2 - 1

2

Chapter Two: Individual Logic Games

2

Chapter Two: Individual Logic Games

Chapter Notes

This section contains eight individual Logic Games drawn from actual LSATs. You can use these games in a variety of ways, but perhaps the best approach is to complete each game as a time trial, and then check your work against the complete setup and explanation provided at the end of this section. We do *not* recommend that you do all eight games in a row as this will defeat the purpose of learning from your mistakes and improving your performance.

To properly time yourself on these individual games, keep in mind the timing guidelines dictated by the 35-minute format of each LSAT section. The following table displays the amount of time that should be allotted to each game, depending on how many you plan to attempt in a section:

# Games Attempted in a Section	Time per Game Attempted
2	17 minutes and 30 seconds
3	11 minutes and 40 seconds
4	8 minutes and 45 seconds

Thus, if your overall goal in the Logic Games section is to complete all four games, then you should look to complete each individual game in this section in 8 minutes and 45 seconds. If you only expect to complete three games per test, then you should look to finish each individual game in this section in 11 minutes and 40 seconds (although, of course, you should always look to go faster—part of the goal with this book is to give you practice with our methods and techniques in an effort to help you work more quickly and efficiently).

Stay focused, be positive, and good luck!

<u>Game #1: December 2006 Questions 16-22</u>

A courier delivers exactly eight parcels—G, H, J, K, L, M, N, and O. No two parcels are delivered at the same time, nor is any parcel delivered more than once. The following conditions must apply:

L is delivered later than H.
K is delivered earlier than O.
H is delivered earlier than M.
O is delivered later than G.
M is delivered earlier than G.
Both N and J are delivered earlier than M.

16. Which one of the following could be the order of deliveries from first to last?

(A) N, H, K, M, J, G, O, L
(B) H, N, J, K, G, O, L, M
(C) J, H, N, M, K, O, G, L
(D) N, J, H, L, M, K, G, O
(E) K, N, J, M, G, H, O, L

GO ON TO THE NEXT PAGE.

INDIVIDUAL LOGIC GAMES

17. Which one of the following must be true?

(A) At least one parcel is delivered earlier than K is delivered.
(B) At least two parcels are delivered later than G is delivered.
(C) At least four parcels are delivered later than H is delivered.
(D) At least four parcels are delivered later than J is delivered.
(E) At least four parcels are delivered earlier than M is delivered.

18. If M is the fourth parcel delivered, then which one of the following must be true?

(A) G is the fifth parcel delivered.
(B) O is the seventh parcel delivered.
(C) J is delivered later than H.
(D) K is delivered later than N.
(E) G is delivered later than L.

19. If H is the fourth parcel delivered, then each of the following could be true EXCEPT:

(A) K is the fifth parcel delivered.
(B) L is the sixth parcel delivered.
(C) M is the sixth parcel delivered.
(D) G is the seventh parcel delivered.
(E) O is the seventh parcel delivered.

20. Each of the following could be true EXCEPT:

(A) H is delivered later than K.
(B) J is delivered later than G.
(C) L is delivered later than O.
(D) M is delivered later than L.
(E) N is delivered later than H.

21. If K is the seventh parcel delivered, then each of the following could be true EXCEPT:

(A) G is the fifth parcel delivered.
(B) M is the fifth parcel delivered.
(C) H is the fourth parcel delivered.
(D) L is the fourth parcel delivered.
(E) J is the third parcel delivered.

22. If L is delivered earlier than K, then which one of the following must be false?

(A) N is the second parcel delivered.
(B) L is the third parcel delivered.
(C) H is the fourth parcel delivered.
(D) K is the fifth parcel delivered.
(E) M is the sixth parcel delivered.

GO ON TO THE NEXT PAGE.

Game #2: June 2004 Questions 1-5

There are exactly six groups in this year's Civic Parade: firefighters, gymnasts, jugglers, musicians, puppeteers, and veterans. Each group marches as a unit; the groups are ordered from first, at the front of the parade, to sixth, at the back. The following conditions apply:

At least two groups march behind the puppeteers but ahead of the musicians.

Exactly one group marches behind the firefighters but ahead of the veterans.

The gymnasts are the first, third, or fifth group.

1. Which one of the following could be an accurate list of the groups in the Civic Parade in order from first to last?

(A) firefighters, puppeteers, veterans, musicians, gymnasts, jugglers

(B) gymnasts, puppeteers, jugglers, musicians, firefighters, veterans

(C) veterans, puppeteers, firefighters, gymnasts, jugglers, musicians

(D) jugglers, puppeteers, gymnasts, firefighters, musicians, veterans

(E) musicians, veterans, jugglers, firefighters, gymnasts, puppeteers

GO ON TO THE NEXT PAGE.

2. If the gymnasts march immediately ahead of the veterans, then which one of the following could be the fourth group?

(A) gymnasts
(B) jugglers
(C) musicians
(D) puppeteers
(E) veterans

3. If the veterans march immediately behind the puppeteers, then which one of the following could be the second group?

(A) firefighters
(B) gymnasts
(C) jugglers
(D) musicians
(E) veterans

4. If the jugglers are the fifth group, then which one of the following must be true?

(A) The puppeteers are the first group.
(B) The firefighters are the first group.
(C) The veterans are the second group.
(D) The gymnasts are the third group.
(E) The musicians are the sixth group.

5. Which one of the following groups CANNOT march immediately behind the gymnasts?

(A) firefighters
(B) jugglers
(C) musicians
(D) puppeteers
(E) veterans

GO ON TO THE NEXT PAGE.

Game #3: December 2004 Questions 1-6

On one afternoon, Patterson meets individually with each of exactly five clients—Reilly, Sanchez, Tang, Upton, and Yansky—and also goes to the gym by herself for a workout. Patterson's workout and her five meetings each start at either 1:00, 2:00, 3:00, 4:00, 5:00, or 6:00. The following conditions must apply:

Patterson meets with Sanchez at some time before her workout.

Patterson meets with Tang at some time after her workout. Patterson meets with Yansky either immediately before or immediately after her workout.

Patterson meets with Upton at some time before she meets with Reilly.

1. Which one of the following could be an acceptable schedule of Patterson's workout and meetings, in order from 1:00 to 6:00?

(A) Yansky, workout, Upton, Reilly, Sanchez, Tang
(B) Upton, Tang, Sanchez, Yansky, workout, Reilly
(C) Upton, Reilly, Sanchez, workout, Tang, Yansky
(D) Sanchez, Yansky, workout, Reilly, Tang, Upton
(E) Sanchez, Upton, workout, Yansky, Tang, Reilly

GO ON TO THE NEXT PAGE.

INDIVIDUAL LOGIC GAMES

2. How many of the clients are there, anyone of whom could meet with Patterson at 1:00?

(A) one
(B) two
(C) three
(D) four
(E) five

3. Patterson CANNOT meet with Upton at which one of the following times?

(A) 1:00
(B) 2:00
(C) 3:00
(D) 4:00
(E) 5:00

4. If Patterson meets with Sanchez the hour before she meets with Yansky, then each of the following could be true EXCEPT:

(A) Patterson meets with Reilly at 2:00.
(B) Patterson meets with Yansky at 3:00.
(C) Patterson meets with Tang at 4:00.
(D) Patterson meets with Yansky at 5:00.
(E) Patterson meets with Tang at 6:00.

5. If Patterson meets with Tang at 4:00, then which one of the following must be true?

(A) Patterson meets with Reilly at 5:00.
(B) Patterson meets with Upton at 5:00.
(C) Patterson meets with Yansky at 2:00.
(D) Patterson meets with Yansky at 3:00.
(E) Patterson's workout is at 2:00.

6. Which one of the following could be the order of Patterson's meetings, from earliest to latest?

(A) Upton, Yansky, Sanchez, Reilly, Tang
(B) Upton, Reilly, Sanchez, Tang, Yansky
(C) Sanchez, Yansky, Reilly, Tang, Upton
(D) Sanchez, Upton, Tang, Yansky, Reilly
(E) Sanchez, Upton, Reilly, Yansky, Tang

GO ON TO THE NEXT PAGE.

Game #4: June 2004 Questions 13-17

Exactly six of an artist's paintings, entitled *Quarterion, Redemption, Sipapu, Tesseract, Vale,* and *Zelkova,* are sold at auction. Three of the paintings are sold to a museum, and three are sold to a private collector. Two of the paintings are from the artist's first (earliest) period, two are from her second period, and two are from her third (most recent) period. The private collector and the museum each buy one painting from each period. The following conditions hold:

Sipapu, which is sold to the private collector, is from an earlier period than *Zelkova,* which is sold to the museum.

Quarterion is not from an earlier period than *Tesseract.*

Vale is from the artist's second period.

13. Which one of the following could be an accurate list of the paintings bought by the museum and the private collector, listed in order of the paintings' periods, from first to third?

(A) museum: *Quarterion, Vale, Zelkova*
private collector: *Redemption, Sipapu, Tesseract*

(B) museum: *Redemption, Zelkova, Quarterion*
private collector: *Sipapu, Vale, Tesseract*

(C) museum: *Sipapu, Zelkova, Quarterion*
private collector: *Tesseract, Vale, Redemption*

(D) museum: *Tesseract, Quarterion, Zelkova*
private collector: *Sipapu, Redemption, Vale*

(E) museum: *Zelkova, Tesseract, Redemption*
private collector: *Sipapu, Vale, Quarterion*

GO ON TO THE NEXT PAGE.

INDIVIDUAL LOGIC GAMES

14. If *Sipapu* is from the artist's second period, which one of the following could be two of the three paintings bought by the private collector?

(A) *Quarterion* and *Zelkova*
(B) *Redemption* and *Tesseract*
(C) *Redemption* and *Vale*
(D) *Redemption* and *Zelkova*
(E) *Tesseract* and *Zelkova*

15. Which one of the following is a complete and accurate list of the paintings, any one of which could be the painting from the artist's first period that is sold to the private collector?

(A) *Quarterion, Redemption*
(B) *Redemption, Sipapu*
(C) *Quarterion, Sipapu, Tesseract*
(D) *Quarterion, Redemption, Sipapu, Tesseract*
(E) *Redemption, Sipapu, Tesseract, Zelkova*

16. If *Sipapu* is from the artist's second period, then which one of the following paintings could be from the period immediately preceding *Quarterion's* period and be sold to the same buyer as *Quarterion*?

(A) *Redemption*
(B) *Sipapu*
(C) *Tesseract*
(D) *Vale*
(E) *Zelkova*

17. If *Zelkova* is sold to the same buyer as *Tesseract* and is from the period immediately preceding *Tesseract's* period, then which one of the following must be true?

(A) *Quarterion* is sold to the museum.
(B) *Quarterion* is from the artist's third period.
(C) *Redemption* is sold to the private collector.
(D) *Redemption* is from the artist's third period.
(E) *Redemption* is sold to the same buyer as *Vale*.

GO ON TO THE NEXT PAGE.

Game #5: October 2004 Questions 7-12

During a certain week, an animal shelter places exactly six dogs—a greyhound, a husky, a keeshond, a Labrador retriever, a poodle, and a schnauzer—with new owners. Two are placed on Monday, two on Tuesday, and the remaining two on Wednesday, consistent with the following conditions:

The Labrador retriever is placed on the same day as the poodle.

The greyhound is not placed on the same day as the husky.

If the keeshond is placed on Monday, the greyhound is placed on Tuesday.

If the schnauzer is placed on Wednesday, the husky is placed on Tuesday.

7. Which one of the following could be a complete and accurate matching of dogs to the days on which they are placed?

(A) Monday: greyhound, Labrador retriever
Tuesday: husky, poodle
Wednesday: keeshond, schnauzer

(B) Monday: greyhound, keeshond
Tuesday: Labrador retriever, poodle
Wednesday: husky, schnauzer

(C) Monday: keeshond, schnauzer
Tuesday: greyhound, husky
Wednesday: Labrador retriever, poodle

(D) Monday: Labrador retriever, poodle
Tuesday: greyhound, keeshond
Wednesday: husky, schnauzer

(E) Monday: Labrador retriever, poodle
Tuesday: husky, keeshond
Wednesday: greyhound, schnauzer

GO ON TO THE NEXT PAGE.

8. Which one of the following must be true?

(A) The keeshond is not placed on the same day as the greyhound.
(B) The keeshond is not placed on the same day as the schnauzer.
(C) The schnauzer is not placed on the same day as the husky.
(D) The greyhound is placed on the same day as the schnauzer.
(E) The husky is placed on the same day as the keeshond.

9. If the poodle is placed on Tuesday, then which one of the following could be true?

(A) The greyhound is placed on Monday.
(B) The keeshond is placed on Monday.
(C) The Labrador retriever is placed on Monday.
(D) The husky is placed on Tuesday.
(E) The schnauzer is placed on Wednesday.

10. If the greyhound is placed on the same day as the keeshond, then which one of the following must be true?

(A) The husky is placed on Monday.
(B) The Labrador retriever is placed on Monday.
(C) The keeshond is placed on Tuesday.
(D) The poodle is not placed on Wednesday.
(E) The schnauzer is not placed on Wednesday.

11. If the husky is placed the day before the schnauzer, then which one of the following CANNOT be true?

(A) The husky is placed on Monday.
(B) The keeshond is placed on Monday.
(C) The greyhound is placed on Tuesday.
(D) The poodle is placed on Tuesday.
(E) The poodle is placed on Wednesday.

12. If the greyhound is placed the day before the poodle, then which one of the following CANNOT be placed on Tuesday?

(A) the husky
(B) the keeshond
(C) the Labrador retriever
(D) the poodle
(E) the schnauzer

GO ON TO THE NEXT PAGE.

Game #6: June 2004 Questions 18-22

Each of exactly six lunch trucks sells a different one of six kinds of food: falafel, hot dogs, ice cream, pitas, salad, or tacos. Each truck serves one or more of exactly three office buildings: X, Y, or Z. The following conditions apply:

The falafel truck, the hot dog truck, and exactly one other truck each serve Y.

The falafel truck serves exactly two of the office buildings.

The ice cream truck serves more of the office buildings than the salad truck.

The taco truck does not serve Y.

The falafel truck does not serve any office building that the pita truck serves.

The taco truck serves two office buildings that are also served by the ice cream truck.

18. Which one of the following could be a complete and accurate list of each of the office buildings that the falafel truck serves?

(A) X
(B) X, Z
(C) X, Y, Z
(D) Y, Z
(E) Z

GO ON TO THE NEXT PAGE.

INDIVIDUAL LOGIC GAMES

19. For which one of the following pairs of trucks must it be the case that at least one of the office buildings is served by both of the trucks?

(A) the hot dog truck and the pita truck
(B) the hot dog truck and the taco truck
(C) the ice cream truck and the pita truck
(D) the ice cream truck and the salad truck
(E) the salad truck and the taco truck

20. If the ice cream truck serves fewer of the office buildings than the hot dog truck, then which one of the following is a pair of lunch trucks that must serve exactly the same buildings as each other?

(A) the falafel truck and the hot dog truck
(B) the falafel truck and the salad truck
(C) the ice cream truck and the pita truck
(D) the ice cream truck and the salad truck
(E) the ice cream truck and the taco truck

21. Which one of the following could be a complete and accurate list of the lunch trucks, each of which serves all three of the office buildings?

(A) the hot dog truck, the ice cream truck
(B) the hot dog truck, the salad truck
(C) the ice cream truck, the taco truck
(D) the hot dog truck, the ice cream truck, the pita truck
(E) the ice cream truck, the pita truck, the salad truck

22. Which one of the following lunch trucks CANNOT serve both X and Z?

(A) the hot dog truck
(B) the ice cream truck
(C) the pita truck
(D) the salad truck
(E) the taco truck

GO ON TO THE NEXT PAGE.

Game #7: December 2004 Questions 7-12

Exactly six people—Lulu, Nam, Ofelia, Pachai, Santiago, and Tyrone—are the only contestants in a chess tournament. The tournament consists of four games, played one after the other. Exactly two people play in each game, and each person plays in at least one game. The following conditions must apply:

Tyrone does not play in the first or third game.

Lulu plays in the last game.

Nam plays in only one game and it is not against Pachai.

Santiago plays in exactly two games, one just before and one just after the only game that Ofelia plays in.

7. Which one of the following could be an accurate list of the contestants who play in each of the four games?

(A) first game: Pachai, Santiago; second game:Ofelia, Tyrone; third game: Pachai, Santiago; fourth game: Lulu, Nam

(B) first game: Lulu, Nam; second game: Pachai, Santiago; third game: Ofelia, Tyrone; fourth game: Lulu, Santiago

(C) first game: Pachai, Santiago; second game: Lulu, Tyrone; third game: Nam, Ofelia; fourth game: Lulu, Nam

(D) first game: Nam, Santiago; second game: Nam, Ofelia; third game: Pachai, Santiago; fourth game: Lulu, Tyrone

(E) first game: Lulu, Nam; second game: Santiago, Tyrone; third game: Lulu, Ofelia; fourth game: Pachai, Santiago

GO ON TO THE NEXT PAGE.

INDIVIDUAL LOGIC GAMES

8. Which one of the following contestants could play in two consecutive games?

(A) Lulu
(B) Nam
(C) Ofelia
(D) Santiago
(E) Tyrone

9. If Tyrone plays in the fourth game, then which one of the following could be true?

(A) Nam plays in the second game.
(B) Ofelia plays in the third game.
(C) Santiago plays in the second game.
(D) Nam plays a game against Lulu.
(E) Pachai plays a game against Lulu.

10. Which one of the following could be true?

(A) Pachai plays against Lulu in the first game.
(B) Pachai plays against Nam in the second game.
(C) Santiago plays against Ofelia in the second game.
(D) Pachai plays against Lulu in the third game.
(E) Nam plays against Santiago in the fourth game.

11. Which one of the following is a complete and accurate list of the contestants who CANNOT play against Tyrone in any game?

(A) Lulu, Pachai
(B) Nam, Ofelia
(C) Nam, Pachai
(D) Nam, Santiago
(E) Ofelia, Pachai

12. If Ofelia plays in the third game, which one of the following must be true?

(A) Lulu plays in the third game.
(B) Nam plays in the third game.
(C) Pachai plays in the first game.
(D) Pachai plays in the third game.
(E) Tyrone plays in the second game.

GO ON TO THE NEXT PAGE.

Game #8: June 2003 Questions 18-23

For a behavioral study, a researcher will select exactly six individual animals from among three monkeys—F, G, and H—three pandas—K, L, and N—and three raccoons—T, V, and Z. The selection of animals for the study must meet the following conditions:

F and H are not both selected.
N and T are not both selected.
If H is selected, K is also selected.
If K is selected, N is also selected.

18. Which one of the following is an acceptable selection of animals for the study?

(A) F, G, K, N, T, V
(B) F, H, K, N, V, Z
(C) G, H, K, L, V, Z
(D) G, H, K, N, V, Z
(E) G, H, L, N, V, Z

GO ON TO THE NEXT PAGE.

19. If H and L are among the animals selected, which one of the following could be true?

(A) F is selected.
(B) T is selected.
(C) Z is selected.
(D) Exactly one panda is selected.
(E) Exactly two pandas are selected.

20. Each of the following is a pair of animals that could be selected together EXCEPT

(A) F and G
(B) H and K
(C) K and T
(D) L and N
(E) T and V

21. If all three of the raccoons are selected, which one of the following must be true?

(A) K is selected.
(B) L is selected.
(C) Exactly one monkey is selected.
(D) Exactly two pandas are selected.
(E) All three of the monkeys are selected.

22. If T is selected, which one of the following is a pair of animals that must be among the animals selected?

(A) F and G
(B) G and H
(C) K and L
(D) K and Z
(E) L and N

23. The selection of animals must include

(A) at most two of each kind of animal
(B) at least one of each kind of animal
(C) at least two pandas
(D) exactly two monkeys
(E) exactly two raccoons

GO ON TO THE NEXT PAGE.

Game #1: December 2006 Questions 16-22

16. D 17. C 18. D 19. A 20. B 21. C 22. C

This may be the most difficult game of the section even though it is a Pure Sequencing game. Although sequencing games have traditionally been relatively easy, the rules in this game form an ungainly diagram that requires some skill to create and interpret.

The game scenario establishes that a courier delivers eight packages—G, H, J, K, L, M, N, and O—and no two packages are delivered simultaneously:

G H J K L M N O [8]

Packages: ___ ___ ___ ___ ___ ___ ___ ___
1 2 3 4 5 6 7 8

The rules then establish a pure sequence that controls the placement of every variable. Let's first examine each rule separately, and then link them together afterward:

Rule #1. This rule can be diagrammed as:

H —— L

Rule #2. This rule can be diagrammed as:

K —— O

Rule #3. This rule can be diagrammed as:

H —— M

Rule #4. This rule can be diagrammed as:

G —— O

Rule #5. This rule can be diagrammed as:

M—G

Rule #6. This rule can be diagrammed as:

N
M
J

Individually, none of the rules is daunting. Linking them together into a workable diagram, however, is not easy.

To create a super-sequence, first start with the last three rules, which connect together easily:

N
M—G—O
J

Next, add in the second and third rules, using arrows:

H
K
N
M—G—O
J

Finally, add in the first rule:

L
H
K
N
M—G—O
J

LOGIC GAMES EXPLANATIONS

Note that the method of constructing this diagram worked backwards through the rules, which is another reminder that you must read all of the rules before beginning your diagram.

Now that the main diagram is complete, take a moment to analyze the relationships.

> Which packages can be delivered first? Only H, J, K, and N. Note how easy it is to miss K.
>
> Which packages can be delivered last? Only L and O.
>
> What is the earliest L can be delivered? Second, right after H.
>
> What is the latest H can be delivered? Fourth—H can be delivered after J, K, and N.
>
> What is the latest N can be delivered? Fifth—N can be delivered after H, J, L, and K. The same holds true for J, which can also be delivered fifth, after H, L, N, and K.
>
> What is the earliest M can be delivered? Fourth, after H, J, and N have been delivered.
>
> What is the latest M can be delivered? Sixth, just before G and O are delivered.

Whenever you create a complex diagram (sequencing or otherwise), always take a moment to evaluate the relationships contained within because the test makers will surely question you on any confusing relationship.

Using the setup above and keeping the relationships firmly in mind, move ahead and attack the questions.

Question #16: Global, List. The correct answer choice is (D)

To attack this List question, simply apply the rules in the given order. Although the first two rules do not eliminate any answers, there is no way to know this when you begin attacking this question.

Answer choice (A): This answer choice violates the last rule because J is not delivered earlier than M.

Answer choice (B): This answer choice violates the fifth rule because M is not delivered earlier than G.

Answer choice (C): This answer choice violates the fourth rule because O is not delivered later than G.

Answer choice (D): This is the correct answer choice.

Answer choice (E): This answer choice violates the third rule because H is not delivered earlier than M.

The presentation of answer choices by the test makers is interesting because applying the rules in the given order—which is the accepted protocol in a game where the rules are all basically similar—consumes the maximum amount of time possible. This occurs because the first two rules do not eliminate any answers, then the third rule eliminates answer choice (E), the fourth rule eliminates answer choice (C), the fifth rule eliminates answer choice (B), and the last rule eliminates answer choice (A). This presentation forces you to comb through the answers multiple times in order to eliminate all four incorrect answers. Alas, while this presentation is interesting, there is no way to reliably combat this trick—it is simply a weapon the test makers have at their disposal.

Question #17: Global, Must Be True. The correct answer choice is (C)

The only way to attack a Global question in a Pure Sequencing game is to refer to the super-sequence that controls the game.

Answer choice (A): This answer choice is incorrect because K can be delivered first, and thus it is not true that at least one parcel is delivered before K.

Answer choice (B): This answer choice is incorrect because G can be delivered seventh, and thus it is not true that at least two parcels are delivered later than G.

Answer choice (C): This is the correct answer choice. G, L, M, and O must all be delivered later than H.

Answer choice (D): This answer choice is incorrect because only three parcels must be delivered later than J (those parcels are G, M, and O).
Answer choice (E): This answer choice is incorrect because only three parcels must be delivered earlier than M (those parcels are H, J, and N).

Question #18: Local, Must Be True. The correct answer choice is (D)

The condition in the question stem indicates that M is delivered fourth. For M to be delivered fourth, *only* H, J, and N can be delivered before M (all three must be delivered before M regardless, but to allow M to be delivered fourth those can be the only three parcels delivered before M). A diagram including the new condition would appear as:

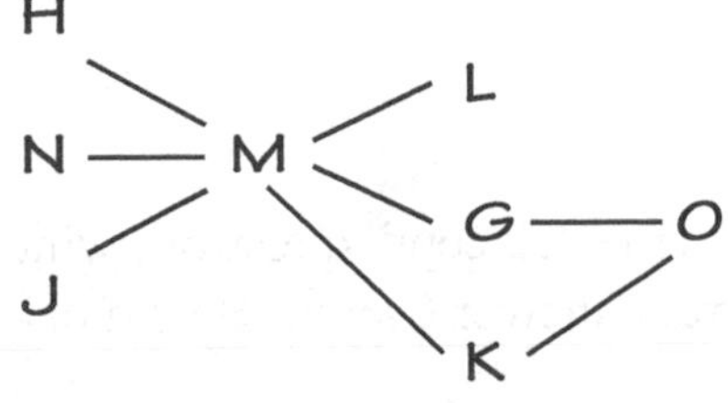

LOGIC GAMES EXPLANATIONS

The arrows "bracketing" K indicate that K is delivered after M but before O. K has no relationship with G or L. Other than the placement of K, the diagram is relatively standard.

From a linear standpoint, this creates the following scenario:

Packages:	(H,	J,	N)	M				L/O
	1	2	3	4	5	6	7	8

Use the above information to attack the answer choices.

Answer choice (A): This answer choice is incorrect because G could be delivered fifth, sixth or seventh.

Answer choice (B): This answer choice is incorrect because O could be the eighth parcel delivered.

Answer choice (C): This answer choice is incorrect because the relationship between J and H is unfixed, and thus H could be delivered later than J.

Answer choice (D): This is the correct answer choice. N must always be one of the first three parcels delivered and K must be delivered fifth, sixth, or seventh.

Answer choice (E): This answer choice is incorrect because G and L do not have a fixed relationship, and therefore L could be delivered later than G.

Question #19: Local, Could Be True, Except. The correct answer choice is (A)

This question is similar to question #18, except that H is specified as the fourth parcel. Because J and N are already delivered before H, in order to deliver H fourth, K must be among the first three parcels delivered (leaving K, J, and N as the first three parcels, not necessarily in that order). The remaining parcels (L, M, G, O) then align behind H. A diagram including the new condition would appear as:

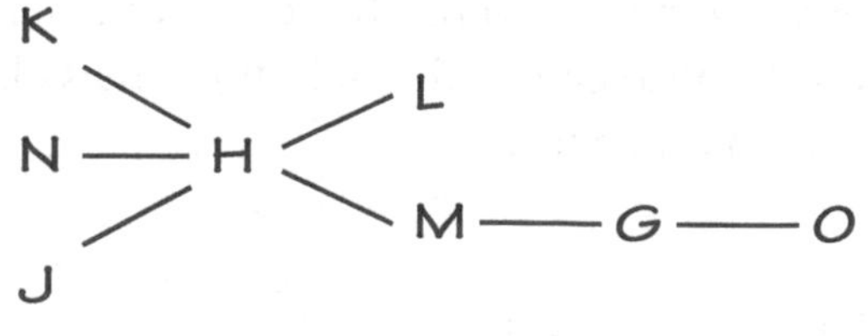

K
N — H — L
J
H — M — G — O

The remainder of the question stem is a Could Be True "Except" question, which means that the four incorrect answers Could Be True, and the one correct answer Cannot Be True.

Answer choice (A): This is the correct answer choice. Because K must be one of the first three parcels delivered, K cannot be delivered fifth. Note how the test makers immediately examine the most difficult variable to place in this question. In this sense, the question becomes a "gut check" on whether you understand the range of possibilities inherent in K's positioning in the game itself.

Answer choice (B): This answer choice could be true, and is therefore incorrect. L could be delivered fifth, sixth, seventh, or eighth.

Answer choice (C): This answer choice could be true, and is therefore incorrect. M could be delivered fifth or sixth.

Answer choice (D): This answer choice could be true, and is therefore incorrect. G could be delivered sixth or seventh.

Answer choice (E): This answer choice could be true, and is therefore incorrect. O could be delivered seventh or eighth.

Question #20: Global, Could Be True, Except. The correct answer choice is (B)

In this Global question, simply use the main diagram to confirm or eliminate answer choices. If an answer choice Could Be True, then it is incorrect. The correct answer choice Cannot Be True.

Answer choice (A): This answer choice is incorrect because H could be delivered later than K. Remember, K could be delivered first, so even though it appears that K is at the "end" of the diagram, K can "move" forward greatly.

Answer choice (B): This is the correct answer choice. J must be delivered earlier than M, and M must be delivered earlier than G, so J can never be delivered later than G.

Answer choice (C): This answer choice is incorrect because L can be delivered last, so L can be delivered later than O.

Answer choice (D): This answer choice is incorrect. The only relationship that L and M have is that they must both be delivered later than H. However, the rules do not specify if L or M is delivered later, so M could be delivered later than L.

Answer choice (E): This answer choice is incorrect because H can be delivered first, so N can be delivered later than H.

Note that the nature of the answer choices in this question makes this a simple diagram interpretation question. If you can create a main diagram that incorporates all of the rules and also understand the relationships inherent in that diagram, then this question is easy.

Question #21: Local, Could Be True, Except. The correct answer choice is (C)

If K is the seventh parcel delivered, then O must be the eighth parcel delivered (because the second rule specifies that K —— O). That leaves the remaining variables to be delivered in the first six spaces:

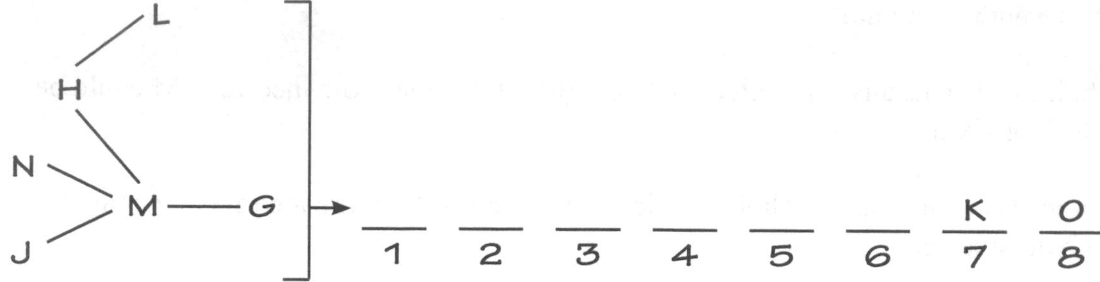

Answer choice (A): This answer choice is incorrect because G could be the fifth parcel delivered. The following hypothetical shows how: N-J-H-M-G-L-K-O.

Answer choice (B): This answer choice is incorrect because M could be the fifth parcel delivered. The following hypothetical shows how: N-J-H-L-M-G-K-O.

Answer choice (C): This is the correct answer choice. Because L, M, and G must all be delivered later than H, the latest that H can be delivered is third (after J and N).

Answer choice (D): This answer choice is incorrect because L could be the fourth parcel delivered. The following hypothetical shows how: N-J-H-L-M-G-K-O.

Answer choice (E): This answer choice is incorrect because J could be the third parcel delivered. The following hypothetical shows how: N-H-J-M-G-L-K-O.

Question #22: Local, False to True, Cannot Be True. The correct answer choice is (C)

When addressing this question stem, first convert the Must Be False statement into its true equivalent, Cannot Be True. Thus, the one correct answer Cannot Be True, and the four incorrect answers Could Be True.

The local condition in the question stem, L —— K, is not easy to handle. The rule adds another layer of complexity to an already complex diagram. The difficulty in the L —— K relationship comes from the fact that L and K are already "floating" because of their relationships with H and O, respectively. To show that the two floating variables have a relationship, and most importantly, to understand the implications of that relationship, is challenging. The diagram would appear as:

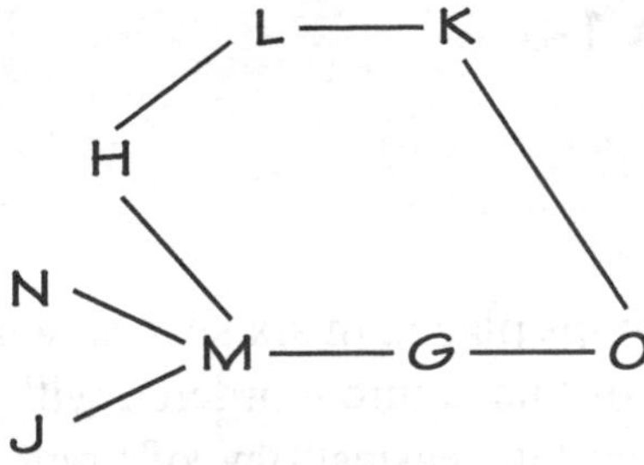

This diagram is deceptive because it makes it appear as though L must be delivered relatively early, and that K must be delivered relatively late. This is not true: L can be delivered as late as sixth (followed by K and O), and K can be delivered as early as third (preceded by H and L). When answering this question—which may be the toughest of the section—be very careful and deliberate.

Answer choice (A): This answer choice is incorrect because N could be the second parcel delivered. The following hypothetical shows how: J-N-H-L-K-M-G-O.

Answer choice (B): This answer choice is incorrect because L could be the third parcel delivered. The following hypothetical shows how: H-N-L-J-M-G-K-O.

Answer choice (C): This is the correct answer choice. Because H must all be delivered earlier than M, G, K, L, and K, the latest that H can be delivered is third (after J and N).

Answer choice (D): This answer choice is incorrect because K could be the fifth parcel delivered. The following hypothetical shows how: N-J-H-L-K-M-G-O.

Answer choice (E): This answer choice is incorrect because M could be the sixth parcel delivered. The following hypothetical shows how: J-N-H-L-K-M-G-O.

LOGIC GAMES EXPLANATIONS

Game #2: June 2004 Questions 1-5

1. D 2. E 3. A 4. E 5. B

This is a basic linear game featuring six groups placed in six spaces, with exactly one group per space (a Defined, Balanced game). Games of this nature—ordered with the exact number of variables for the given spaces—are considered the easiest type of Logic Game, and this is a perfect way to start a Logic Games section. The only drawback is that there are just five questions in this game; it would be preferable to see a greater number of questions attached to such a simple game scenario.

Considering just the game scenario and the rules, you should make the following basic setup for this game:

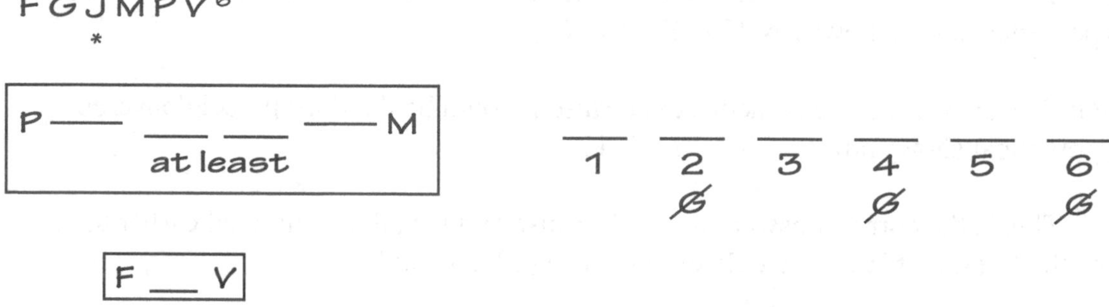

Note that the third rule, which involves G, is represented by Not Laws on groups 2, 4, and 6, and this representation indicates that G can only be in groups 1, 3, or 5.

Although the diagram above captures the basic meaning of each rule, it does not capture the inferences created by the first and second rules (such as Not Laws, etc.). In fact, you have an interesting choice at this juncture of the game: you can either show all the Not Laws that result from the two blocks or you can show templates based on the placement of the blocks. Either approach will work, although the templates approach tends to be faster. Regardless, let's show how each diagramming approach would unfold.

Approach 1: Diagram the Not Laws

Using the diagram above as a base, we can add Not Laws drawn from each of the first two rules.

Rule #1. This rule creates a large, flexible split-block involving P and M. Because there must be at least two groups between P and M, this block takes up a minimum of four spaces (leaving three options if the block is compressed as tightly as possible: groups 1-4, 2-5, or 3-6). Consequently, we can deduce that M can never appear in groups 1, 2, or 3, and we can deduce that P can never appear in groups 4, 5, or 6. Adding these Not Laws to the diagram, we arrive at:

LOGIC GAMES EXPLANATIONS

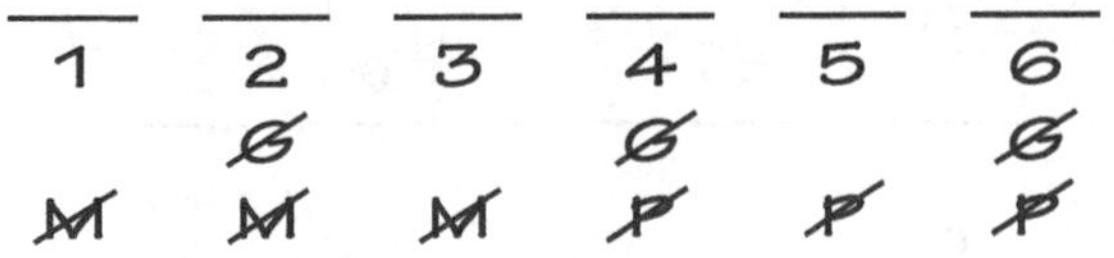

1	2	3	4	5	6
	G̸		G̸		G̸
M̸	M̸	M̸	P̸	P̸	P̸

Rule #2. This rule creates a fixed split block involving F and V. Because V is always two groups behind F, V can never appear in groups 1 or 2; because F is always two groups ahead of V, F can never appear in groups 5 or 6. Adding these Not Laws to the prior diagram, we arrive at:

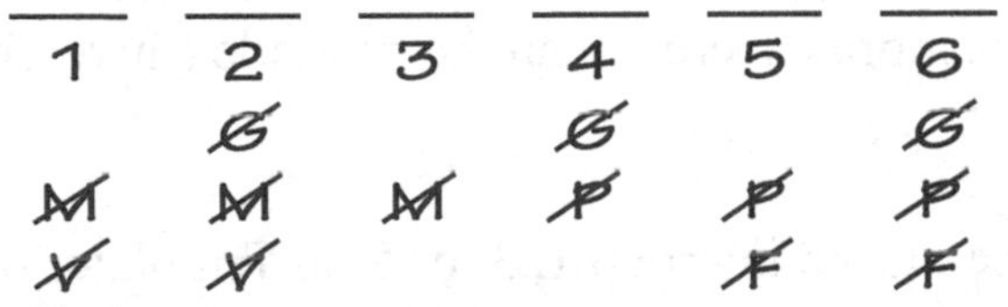

1	2	3	4	5	6
	G̸		G̸		G̸
M̸	M̸	M̸	P̸	P̸	P̸
V̸	V̸			F̸	F̸

What becomes immediately apparent from these Not Laws is that groups 2 and 6 are the most restricted, and each has only three options:

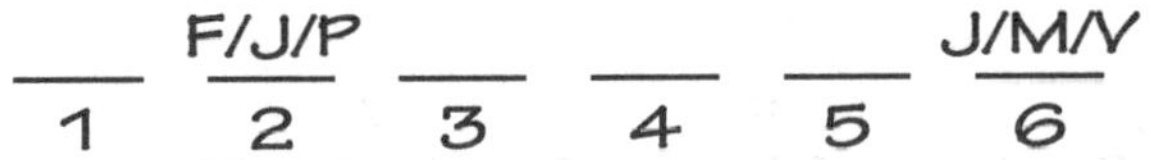

1	2	3	4	5	6
	F/J/P				J/M/V

At this point in the game, you have diagrammed and considered all of the rules, so you should head towards the questions. And, since the meaning of the third rule is completely captured by the Not Laws in the diagram, you will simply need to focus on the first two rules (as an aside, of the first two rules of the game, the first rule is more problematic because it contains a degree of uncertainty—how many other groups are between P and M—that you *must* track throughout the game).

Approach 2: Diagram the Templates

The alternative approach is to diagram the game based on templates created by the blocks. Your first choice is which block to use as the basis for the templates. In this case, the choice should be easy: use the FV block created by the second rule. This block is the better choice because it is fixed, with exactly one group between F and V. Although the PM block is larger and takes up more space, it is an inferior choice because it is flexible, and the number of groups between P and M is not fixed; this flexibility creates more options, and ultimately, more templates.

Using the FV block, we can place the block in four positions: groups 1-3, 2-4, 3-5, and 4-6. The following diagram shows each scenario:

Template #4:				F		V
Template #3:			F		V	
Template #2:		F		V		
Template #1:	F		V			
	1	2	3	4	5	6

Of course, the other rules can also be applied to derive more information about each template. Let's start with the third rule since it is more concrete than the first rule (thereafter, we will consider the first rule).

Rule #3. Since G must always be placed in group 1, 3, or 5, in Template #1 G must be placed in group 5 (groups 1 and 3 are already occupied by F and V). Likewise, in Template #3 G must be placed in group 1 (groups 3 and 5 are already occupied by F and V). Applying these two inferences, we can add G to Templates #1 and #3:

Template #4:				F		V
Template #3:	G		F		V	
Template #2:		F		V		
Template #1:	F		V		G	
	1	2	3	4	5	6

Rule #1. Because the block created by this rule is so large, it has somewhat limited placement options around F and V, especially in the Templates #1 and #3, which are more restricted now that G has been placed in each. Let's examine the effect of the first rule on each template:

Template #1: Because P and M must be separated by at least two groups, in this template P must be placed in group 2 and M must be placed in group 6. The only remaining group is group 4, which must be filled by J, the random. Thus, this template has only one solution:

F	P	V	J	G	M
1	2	3	4	5	6

Template #2: The PM block has several options within Template #2. It can be placed in groups 1-5, 1-6, or 3-6. Consequently, this template will not fill in as completely as Template #1. Aside from the general position of P (group 1 or 3) and M (group 5 or 6), we can deduce that group 6 will be filled by J or M (from the initial Not Laws, group 6 cannot be filled by F, G, or P, and, in this template, group 6 cannot be filled by V, leaving only J or M). Adding all the information together, this template is still only partially complete:

P/	F	/P	V	M/	J/M
1	2	3	4	5	6

Note that if G marches in group 1 or 3, that will create a chain reaction forcing P into the remainder of group 1 or 3. If P is forced into group 3, then M must be in group 6 (and J must be in group 5).

Template #3: As in Template #1, the placement of the PM block is limited in this template. Because P and M must be separated by at least two groups, in this template P must be placed in group 2 and M must be placed in group 6. The only remaining group is group 4, which must be filled by J, the random. Thus, this template has only one solution:

G	P	F	J	V	M
1	2	3	4	5	6

Template #4: At first glance it may appear that not much can be done with this template. However, the size of the PM block again leads to a useful inference. The PM block can only be placed in groups 1-5 or 2-5. Consequently, we can infer that M must always march in group 5 in Template #4, that P can only march in group 1 or 2, and that either G or J must march in group 5:

P/	/P	G/J	F	M	V
1	2	3	4	5	6

Note that if P or G marches in group 1, that will create a chain reaction that, depending on which group is in group 1, either forces P into group 2 or forces G into group 3 (G, from the third rule, can only march in group 1, 3, or 5).

Compiling all four templates, we arrive at the following setup:

Template #4:	P/	/P	G/J	F	M	V
Template #3:	G	P	F	J	V	M
Template #2:	P/	F	/P	V	M/	J/M
Template #1:	F	P	V	J	G	M
	1	2	3	4	5	6

After applying all the rules, we have two very complete and powerful templates, and two other templates that contain a fair amount of information. We are now ready to attack the questions, and we will use the templates as they are more efficient that the Not Law setup.

Question #1: Global, List. The correct answer choice is (D)

As with any List question, simply apply the rules to the answer choices. Remember to apply the rules in order of the easiest to "see" within the answers. In this game, that order would be rule #3, rule #2, and then rule #1.

Answer choice (A): This answer is eliminated by the first rule. In this instance, there is only one group separating P and M.

Answer choice (B): This answer choice is eliminated by the third rule. In this answer there is no group between F and V.

Answer choice (C): This answer is eliminated by the third rule because G marches in group 4.

Answer choice (D): This is the correct answer choice.

Answer choice (E): This answer violates both the first and second rules. Interestingly, if you misdiagram the first two rules by reversing the order of the variables (for example, "V __ F"), this answer would appear correct.

One of the great benefits of this question is that we are given a free hypothetical solution to the game, in this case J-P-G-F-M-V. This could be useful in a later question.

Question #2: Local, Could Be True. The correct answer choice is (E)

This question imposes a local condition that you must address before moving to the answer choices. In this instance, the question stipulates that G and V form a block, and combining this condition with the second rule, we can form a FGV super-block where F, G, and V must appear in consecutive order. Applying our templates, the only place an FGV block can occur is in Template #2, where F is in group 2 and V is in group 4:

Template #2:	P/	F	/P	V	M/	J/M
	1	2	3	4	5	6

Accordingly, G must march in group 3, which forces P to march in group 1. The only remaining uncertainty is the placement of J and M:

Question #2:	P	F	G	V	M/J	J/M
	1	2	3	4	5	6

With the information above, we can quickly determine that (E) is the correct answer choice.

Answer choice (A): Under the condition in this question, G must march in group 3.

Answer choice (B): Under the condition in this question, J must march in group 5 or 6.

Answer choice (C): Under the condition in this question, M must march in group 5 or 6.

Answer choice (D): Under the condition in this question, P must march in group 1.

Answer choice (E): This is the correct answer choice.

Question #3: Local, Could Be True. The correct answer choice is (A)

If V marches immediately behind P, then, by adding the first rule we arrive at the following block:

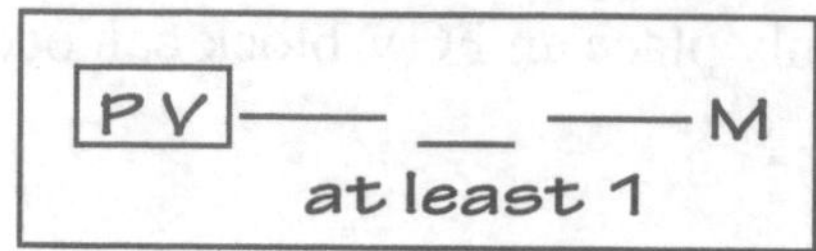

And, after adding the second rule, we arrive at the following super-block:

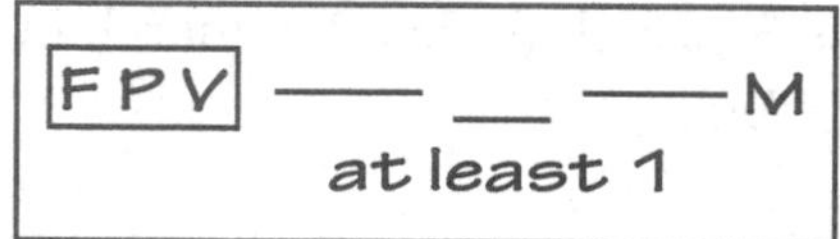

The question asks for which could be the second group, and a quick glance at the templates shows that Template #1 conforms to the block above. However, the group that marches second in Template #1—P—is not one of the answer choices. Hence, we must look at one of the other templates for the answer. Because Templates #3 and #4 cannot conform to the super-block above, the only possible source of the correct answer is Template #2. Because Template #2 features F as the second group, the correct answer to this problem must be F, and answer choice (A) must be correct. However, let's take a moment to examine this further.

In Template #2, F and V are in groups 2 and 4, respectively. Applying the super-block, we can create the following diagram:

Question #3:		F	P	V		M
	1	2	3	4	5	6

At this juncture, the only remaining uncertainty is the placement of G and J, which can be placed in group 1 or 5:

Question #3:	G/J	F	P	V	J/G	M
	1	2	3	4	5	6

As this hypothetical meets the rules of the game and the condition imposed in question #3, it shows that F can be in the second group.

Answer choice (A): This is the correct answer choice.

Answer choice (B): Under the condition in this question, G must march in group 1 or 5.

Answer choice (C): Under the condition in this question, J must march in group 1 or 5.

Answer choice (D): Under the condition in this question, M must march in group 6.

Answer choice (E): Under the condition in this question, V must march in group 4.

Question #4: Local, Must Be True. The correct answer choice is (E)

Within the templates, the only time J can be the fifth group is under Template #2:

Template #2:	P/	F	/P	V	M/	J/M
	1	2	3	4	5	6

If J is in group 5, them M must be in group 6:

Question #4:	P/	F	/P	V	J	M
	1	2	3	4	5	6

The only remaining uncertainty is the placement of G and P, which can rotate between the first and third groups:

Question #4:	G/P	F	P/G	V	J	M
	1	2	3	4	5	6

Because this is Must be true question, you can use the hypothetical above to quickly accelerate through the questions. In this instance, answer choice (E) is quickly proven correct.

Answer choice (A): Although P could be in the first group, P could also be in the third group, and so this answer choice does not have to be true. Note how the test makers immediately attack you on the uncertainty within this question.

Answer choice (B): F must be in the second group, not the first group.

Answer choice (C): V must be in the fourth group, not the second group.

Answer choice (D): Although G could be in the third group, G could also be in the first group, and so this answer choice does not have to be true.

Answer choice (E): This is the correct answer choice.

Question #5: Global, Cannot Be True. The correct answer choice is (B)

This question asks you to identify the group that cannot march immediately behind G. There are two ways to work out the correct answer to this question: either eliminate those variables that *can* march behind G, or find the variable that cannot march behind G. Given the considerable amount of information we have amassed in the templates, and in the hypotheticals in the answer choices, the second approach is likely to be the fastest (unless, of course, you have already deduced which variable cannot march behind G).

First, consider the templates: in Template #1, M marches immediately behind G, and thus we can eliminate M from the answer choices. In Template #3, P marches immediately behind G, and thus we can eliminate P from the answer choices.

Second, and especially important if you did not use the template approach, do not forget to consider the hypotheticals created while you answered the questions. Let's review each hypothetical:

> Question #1: In this question we were given the solution J-P-G-F-M-V. This solution eliminates F from the answer choices.
>
> Question #2: In this question we arrived at the solution P-F-G-V-M/J-J/M. This hypothetical eliminates V from the answer choices.
>
> Question #3: In this question we arrived at the solution G/J-F-P-V-J/G-M. If G marched first, this hypothetical eliminates F from the answer choices; if G marched fifth, this hypothetical eliminates M from the answer choices.

Adding all the information together (some of it redundant), F, M, P, and V can march immediately behind G. Thus, only J cannot march immediately behind G, and therefore answer choice (B) is correct.

Answer choice (A): F can march behind G, as proven by the solution to questions #1 and #3.

Answer choice (B): This is the correct answer choice. If J marches immediately behind G, then there is not enough room to place the other blocks without violating one of the rules (try it: the GJ block would have to be placed in groups 1-2, 3-4, or 5-6; in each instance the MP block can be placed successfully, but doing so leaves no room for the FV block).

Answer choice (C): M can march behind G, as proven by Template #1 and the solution to question #3.

Answer choice (D): P can march behind G, as proven by Template #3.

Answer choice (E): V can march behind G, as proven by the solution to question #2.

Note that a question of this nature reveals that you do not have to have every piece of information about a game in order to successfully complete the game. Students often miss inferences during the setup, only to discover them during the game without negative repercussion. In this case, having the templates makes the game manageable even if you miss an inference or two.

Game #3: December 2004 Questions 1-6

1. E 2. B 3. C 4. D 5. B 6. E

This is a basic Linear game featuring six clients for six time slots (the gym workout can, for the most part, simply be treated as another "client," so the game is balanced as six into six). As mentioned previously, this type of basic linear game is often easy and provides a perfect starting game for an LSAT section.

A diagram of just the game scenario and rules leads to the following basic setup for this game:

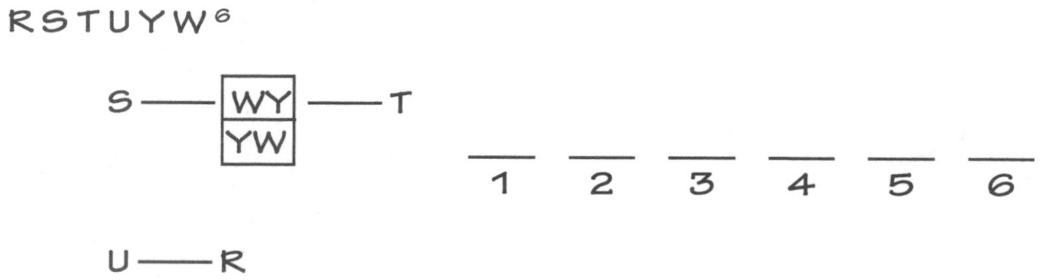

RSTUYW[6]

S —— [WY / YW] —— T

U —— R

___ ___ ___ ___ ___ ___
1 2 3 4 5 6

We have presented the "skeleton" diagram above because this game requires you to make some diagramming choices before moving on to the questions. First, let's review the rules.

Rule #1. This is a basic sequential rule that can be diagrammed as follows:

S —— W

Rule #2. This is another basic sequential rule that can be diagrammed as follows:

W —— T

Rule #3. This is a standard linear rule that places W and Y in an unfixed block:

[WY]

or

[YW]

Note that we prefer to diagram unfixed blocks with both possibilities shown because that minimizes the possibility of making a mistake under the pressure of the actual LSAT.

Of course, the first three rules can be connected together to create the following super-sequence:

S — WY/YW — T

This sequence requires at least four spaces, and we have shown the dual-possibilities of the WY block in the middle so there is no chance of making the false assumption that one of the two is necessarily before the other.

Rule #4. This is another basic sequential rule that can be diagrammed as follows:

U — R

In a typical Linear game, we would diagram the Not Laws that follow from each of the rules above, and indeed there are plenty of Not Laws produced by the rules above. However, given the fact that we have reduced the rules to two sequences (one of which is especially powerful), and because all six variables are contained within the two sequences, the best decision would be to forgo drawing all of the Not Laws and instead to make a basic sequential analysis of which clients could be first or last, and then attack the questions with the two sequences. Using this approach, we will save the time involved in drawing the Not Laws yet not lose any knowledge or ease of attack in the game.

From the sequences, only S or U can be first in this game, and only R or T can be last in the game (more on this in question #2). These facts can be shown on the diagram as dual-options:

S — WY/YW — T

U — R

S/U					R/T
1	2	3	4	5	6

At this point we are ready to attack the game, and we should be somewhat confident since our setup took very little time yet the sequences are easy to use and powerful.

Question #1: Global, List. The correct answer choice is (E)

As with any List question, simply apply the rules to the answer choices. In this game, the easiest approach is to apply the rules in the order given (individually, none of the rules is more complex than any other rule, so there is no reason to apply them out of order).

Answer choice (A): This answer is eliminated by the first rule because the meeting with S is not before the workout.

Answer choice (B): This answer choice is eliminated by the second rule because the meeting with T is not after the workout.

Answer choice (C): This answer violates the third rule because W and Y are not consecutive.

Answer choice (D): This answer violates the fourth rule because the meeting with U is not ahead of the meeting with R.

Answer choice (E): This is the correct answer choice.

Question #2: Global, Must Be True. The correct answer choice is (B)

As briefly mentioned in the game setup, only two of the clients can possibly meet first, at 1:00. Let's take a moment to review this inference further.

As established in the discussion of the third rule, the first three rules can be connected together to create the following chain:

From this chain we can infer that T, W, and Y can never be first since each must come after S (although, for the purposes of this question, W is irrelevant since W is not an actual client).

From the fourth rule, we can infer that R can never be first since R must always meet with Patterson after U meets with Patterson. Consequently, we have eliminated R, T, and Y from meeting with Patterson at 1:00. This leaves only S and U as clients who could possibly meet with Patterson at 1:00, and thus "two" is the correct answer.

Answer choice (A), (C), (D), and (E): As discussed above, these answer choices must be incorrect because they do not state the maximum number of clients that could meet with Patterson at 1:00.

Answer choice (B): This is the correct answer choice.

Question #3: Global, Cannot Be True. The correct answer choice is (C)

This is the most difficult question of the game, and one that is not easy to answer from a quick glance at the rules.

When you encounter a Global question with no obvious answer, remember that one approach is to refer to the hypotheticals created in other questions. For example, question #1 produced a solution that placed U at 2:00. On the strength of that answer, we can eliminate answer choice (B). The discussion in question #2 indicated that U could meet at 1:00, eliminating answer choice (A). However, none of the three remaining answer choices is obviously incorrect so you have a choice: either skip the remaining answer choices and hope that future questions provide more hypotheticals so you can come back and eliminate some answers, or make a few hypotheticals right now to solve the problem.

If you choose to wait until later to answer this question, you will find that the hypothetical from question #5 eliminates answer choice (E). At that point you could simply create a hypothetical to eliminate or confirm answer choice (C) or (D).

If you choose to make hypotheticals to work your way through the final three answer choices, you would be best served by first attacking answer choice (C) or (D), and not by starting with answer choice (E). This is because (E) would seemingly be easily eliminated by the somewhat obvious hypothetical where U and R meet at 5:00 and 6:00, and the four variables in the other sequence fill in the first four hours (as in S-W-Y-T-R-U, for example). In a moment we will create hypotheticals for both answer choices (C) and (D), but before doing so, let's discuss the logic of why U is limited at all in this game.
At first glance, U appears to be a fairly unrestricted variable, with U's only limitation coming from the rule involving R. Obviously, though, 6:00 is not one of the answers to this question, so there must be some further limitation on U that has thus far gone unnoticed. In examining the two chains, the one point of concern is the WY block. The block not only requires two consecutive spaces, but it also affects S and T. Although that may not appear to be of an much issue for U, if U is placed at 3:00, there is not enough room for all the variables:

Step 1. U is placed at 3:00; R must meet at 4:00, 5:00, or 6:00:

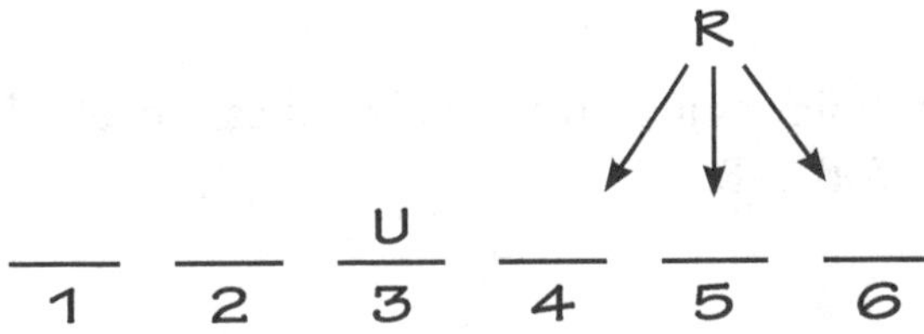

LOGIC GAMES EXPLANATIONS

Step 2. Consider the other sequence:

> Because there are three meetings after Patterson's meeting with S, normally the latest that S could meet is 3:00. But, since U already occupies the 3:00 meeting, S must be somewhere before U. Because this placement leaves only one open time slot before U, it must be that the WY block comes somewhere after U, and, of course, T is somewhere after the WY block. This chain of inferences results in a scenario where R, W, Y, and T must all come somewhere after U, but there are only three spaces for the four variables: 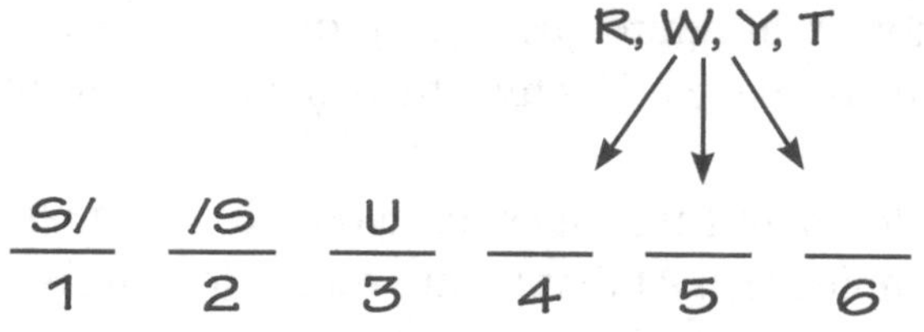
>
> R, W, Y, T
>
> | S/ | /S | U | | | |
> |---|---|---|---|---|---|
> | 1 | 2 | 3 | 4 | 5 | 6 |
>
> Thus, we cannot create a workable solution when U is placed third, and answer choice (C) is correct.
>
> By the way, a similar type of logic holds for R: if R is placed in the fourth position, a workable solution to the game cannot be created.

Answer choice (A): This answer choice is incorrect. Patterson can meet with U at 1:00, as shown by the following hypothetical: U-R-S-W-Y-T.

Answer choice (B): This answer choice is incorrect. Patterson can meet with U at 2:00, as shown by the following hypothetical: S-U-W-Y-T-R.

Answer choice (C): This is the correct answer choice. Although it is proven by the previous discussion, this answer choice is difficult to arrive at without testing a few solutions.

Answer choice (D): This answer choice is incorrect. Patterson can meet with U at 4:00, as shown by the following hypothetical: S-W-Y-U-T-R.

Answer choice (E): This answer choice is incorrect. Patterson can meet with U at 5:00, as shown by the following hypothetical: S-W-Y-T-U-R.

Question #4: Local, Could Be True, Except. The correct answer choice is (D)

The condition in the question stem creates the following block and sequence:

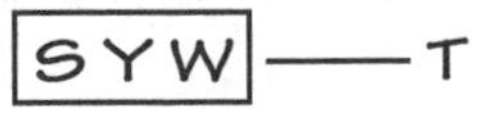

[SYW] —— T

From this sequence, it is obvious that Patterson cannot meet with Y any later than 4:00 because Patterson must meet with W and T later than with Y. Consequently, answer choice (D) is correct.

Answer choice (A): This answer choice is incorrect. Patterson can meet with R at 2:00, as shown by the following hypothetical: U-R-S-Y-W-T.

Answer choice (B): This answer choice is incorrect. Patterson can meet with Y at 3:00, as shown by the following hypothetical: U-S-Y-W-T-R.

Answer choice (C): This answer choice is incorrect. Patterson can meet with T at 4:00, as shown by the following hypothetical: S-Y-W-T-U-R.

Answer choice (D): This is the correct answer choice.

Answer choice (E): This answer choice is incorrect. Patterson can meet with T at 6:00, as shown by the following hypothetical: U-R-S-Y-W-T.

Question #5: Local, Must Be True. The correct answer choice is (B)

When Patterson meets with T at 4:00, then from the super-sequence we know that S, W, and Y must meet with Patterson prior to 4:00, with S at 1:00, and with W and Y rotating between 2:00 and 3:00:

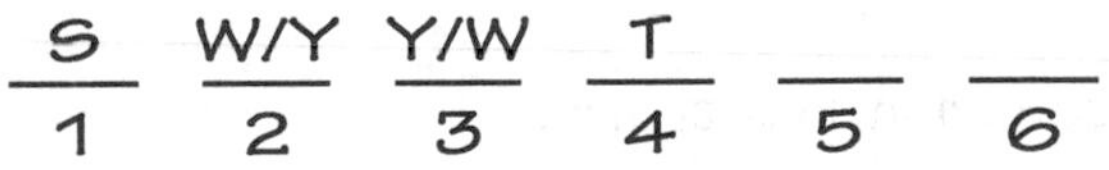

S	W/Y	Y/W	T		
1	2	3	4	5	6

Placing S, T, W, and Y forces U and R into the final two meetings, with U at 5:00 and R at 6:00:

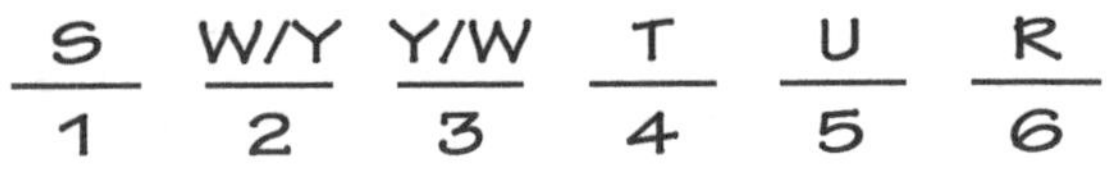

S	W/Y	Y/W	T	U	R
1	2	3	4	5	6

Since this is a Must be true question, you should look for answer choices containing fixed variables (such as S, T, U, and R) and avoid answer choices that contain variables with uncertainty (W and Y).

LOGIC GAMES EXPLANATIONS

Answer choice (A): This answer choice is incorrect because R must meet with Patterson at 6:00.

Answer choice (B): This is the correct answer choice.

Answer choice (C): This answer choice is incorrect because Patterson can meet with Y at 2:00 or 3:00.

Answer choice (D): This answer choice is incorrect because Patterson can meet with Y at 2:00 or 3:00.

Answer choice (E): This answer choice is incorrect because Patterson can workout at 2:00 or 3:00.

Question #6: Global, List. The correct answer choice is (E)

This question is identical to question #1, with the exception that W has been dropped from the ordering (but, of course, the rules involving W are still active). Thus, you should approach this question in the same fashion as any List question.

Answer choice (A): This answer specifies that Patterson meets with Y before S, but, as we know from the combination of the first and second rule, Patterson cannot meet with Y before S, and thus this answer choice is incorrect.

Answer choice (B): This answer specifies that Patterson meets with T before Y, but, as we know from the combination of the second and third rule, Patterson cannot meet with T before Y, and thus this answer choice is incorrect.

Answer choice (C): This answer violates the fourth rule because the meeting with U is not ahead of the meeting with R.

Answer choice (D): Like answer choice (B), this answer specifies that Patterson meets with T before Y, but since Patterson cannot meet with T before Y, this answer choice is incorrect.

Answer choice (E): This is the correct answer choice.

Game #4: June 2004 Questions 13-17

13. B 14. B 15. D 16. B 17. B

This Advanced Linear game is about equal in difficulty to the previous two games. Like the previous two games, this game has only six variables and three rules, and so creating the diagram is not an especially lengthy process.

From the game scenario, we know that there are two purchasers: a private collector and a museum. There are three different periods (periods 1, 2, and 3, from earliest to latest) and that suggests a linear setup with two stacks, one for the private collector and one for the museum:

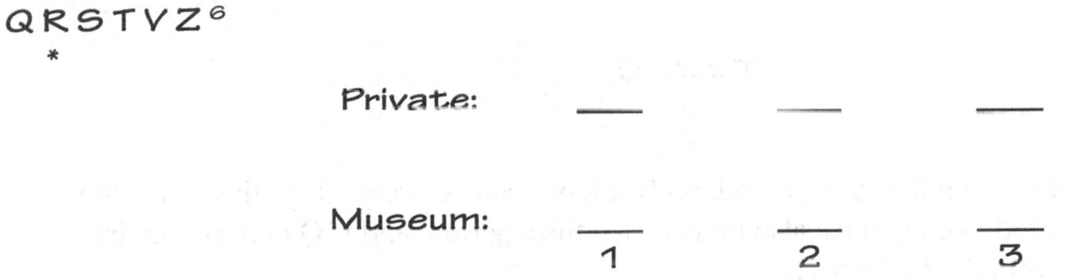

Q R S T V Z [6]
*

Private:	___	___	___
Museum:	___	___	___
	1	2	3

The first rule can be diagrammed as :

S_P —— Z_M

This rule indicates that Z cannot be from the first period (and thus must be from the second or third period), and that S cannot be from the third period (and thus must be from the first or second period). The rule also indicates that S cannot be sold to the museum and that Z cannot be sold to the private collector:

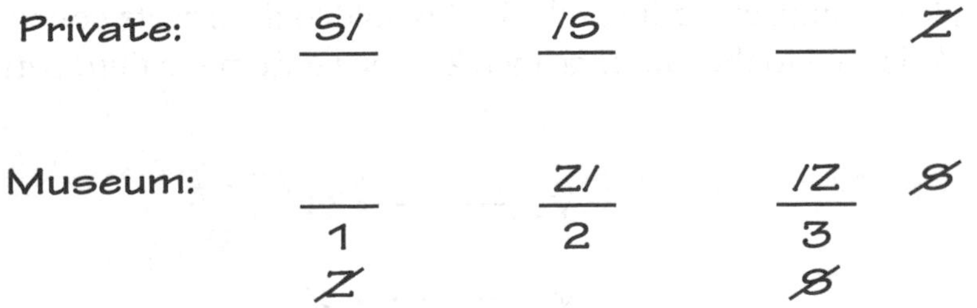

Private:	S/	/S	___	Z̸
Museum:	___	Z/	/Z	S̸
	1	2	3	
	Z̸		S̸	

LOGIC GAMES EXPLANATIONS

Because there are only three periods, if S is from the second period, then Z must be from the third period. Conversely, if Z is from the second period, then S must be from the first period:

$$S_2 \longrightarrow Z_3$$

$$Z_2 \longrightarrow S_1$$

The second rule can be a bit tricky to diagram. The rule states that Q is *not from an earlier period* than T. Many students interpret this rule to mean that T must be from an *earlier* period than Q; that is not correct. Although Q cannot be from an earlier period than T, Q could be from the *same* period as T (remember, always read the rules closely!). Consequently, this rule is best diagrammed as:

T ══ Q

Because T and Q could be from the same period, no Not Laws can be drawn from this rule. However, if T is from the third period, then Q must also be from the third period, and if Q is from the first period, T must also be from the first period.

The third rule indicates that V is from the second period, and that consequently V cannot be from the first or third periods:

Private:	___	V/	___
Museum:	___	/V	___
	1	2	3
	~~V~~		~~V~~

The actions of V clearly impact the first rule. If V is sold to the private collector, then S must be from the first period; if V is sold to the museum, then Z must be from the third period:

$$V_{2P} \longrightarrow S_1$$

$$V_{2M} \longrightarrow Z_3$$

Combining all the rules and inferences together, we arrive at the following diagram for the game:

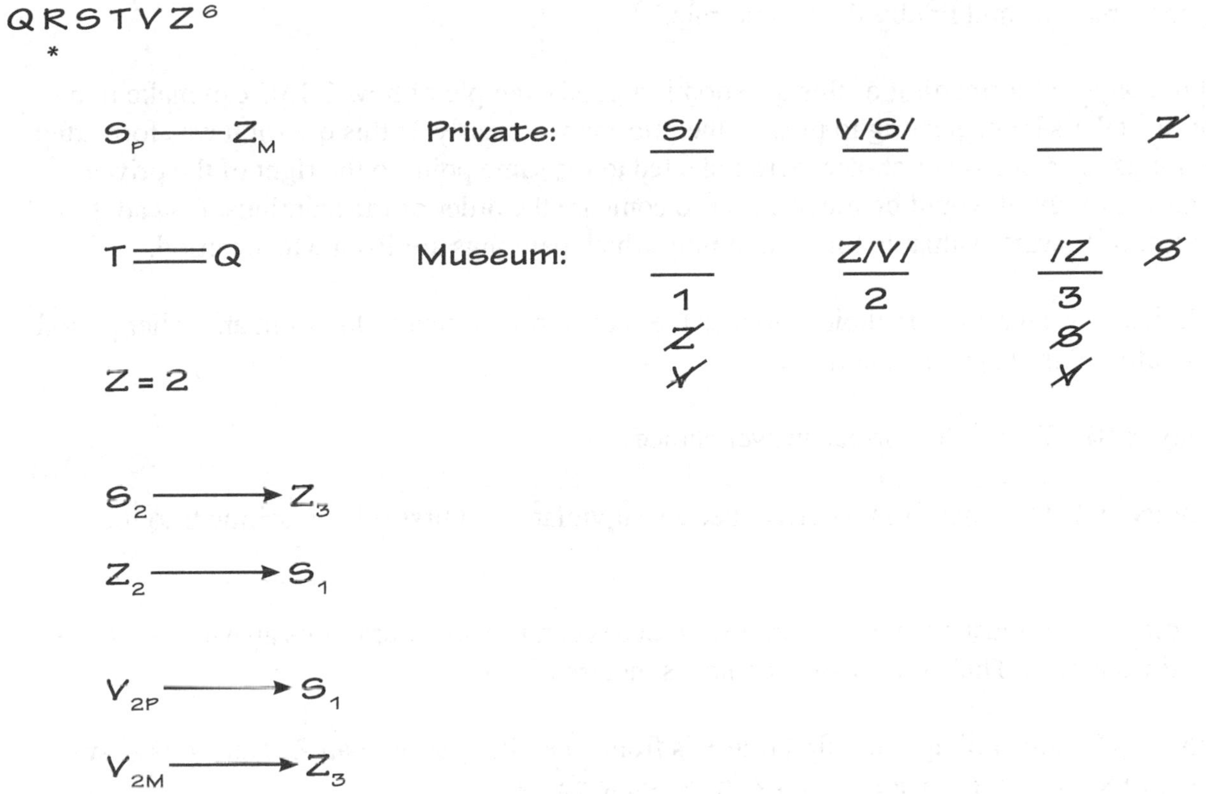

QRSTVZ[6]
*

S_P — Z_M

T ═ Q

Z ≠ 2

$S_2 \longrightarrow Z_3$

$Z_2 \longrightarrow S_1$

$V_{2P} \longrightarrow S_1$

$V_{2M} \longrightarrow Z_3$

	1	2	3
Private:	S/	V/S/	Z̸
Museum:		Z/V/	/Z S̸
	Z̸ V̸		S̸ V̸

Given the amount of information in the diagram, some students ask if it would be wise to make four templates based on the position of S, V, and Z (when V is sold to the private collector, S must be from the first period and Z can be from the second or third period; when V is sold to the museum, Z must be from the third period and S can be from the first or second period). Although at first glance this may seem like a powerful strategy, it only places S, V, and Z in four arrangements, and none of those arrangements definitively place Q, R, or T. Hence, the templates provide little additional insight into the placement of the variables, and it is better to attack the game with a straightforward setup.

LOGIC GAMES EXPLANATIONS

Question #13: Global, List. The correct answer choice is (B)

As usual, use the rules to attack a List question. The best order to apply the rules is to apply the third rule, then the first rule, and finally the second rule.

Note that the physical formatting of this question is a good example of how LSAC can make things harder for test takers by neglecting to present the information clearly. If this question was formatted so the paintings in each answer choice were indented to the same point to the right of the private collector and museum, it would be much easier to compare the order of the paintings. Instead, test takers are forced to waste valuable time examining which paintings are from which period.

Answer choice (A): This answer choice violates the second rule because Q is from an earlier period than T. Therefore this answer is incorrect.

Answer choice (B): This is the correct answer choice.

Answer choice (C): This answer is incorrect because it violates the first rule by selling S to the museum.

Answer choice (D): V must always be from the artist's second period, but in this answer V is from the artist's third period. Thus, this answer choice is incorrect.

Answer choice (E): According to the first rule S is from an earlier period than Z. Thus, this answer choice is incorrect because it places S and Z in the same period.

Question #14: Local, Could Be True. The correct answer choice is (B)

This is an unusually easy question. The first rule of the game establishes that Z must be purchased by the museum. Thus, any answer choice in this question featuring Z must be incorrect. Using that logic, we can eliminate answer choices (A), (D), and (E).

The question stem places S in the artist's second period, which, from our initial discussion of the rules, forces Z into the artist's third period. V, which must also be from the artist's second period, has to be purchased by the museum:

Private:	___	S	___
Museum:	___	V	Z
	1	2	3

At this point, we have established that V must be purchased by the museum, and consequently answer choice (C) can be eliminated.

Answer choice (B): This is the correct answer choice.

Question #15: Global, List. The correct answer choice is (D)

Through the Not Laws we have established that neither V nor Z can be paintings from the artist's first period that are sold to the private collector. Consequently, most students correctly surmise that the remaining four paintings could be the first period paintings sold to the private collector. However, let's systematically prove that assertion.

First, any answer choice containing V or Z can be eliminated. This process removes answer choice (E) from consideration. Second, from question #13, we know that S can be a first period painting sold to the private collector, and since answer choice (A) does not contain S, we can eliminate (A). Third, using the base diagram created in question #14, we can deduce that any of Q, R, and T can be a first period painting sold to the private collector, and thus the correct answer choice must contain those paintings as well.

Answer choice (D): This is the correct answer choice. The deduction above eliminates every answer choice except answer choice (D).

Question #16: Local, Could Be True. The correct answer choice is (B)

From question #14, we know the following diagram is produced when S is from the artist's second period:

Private:	___	S	___
Museum:	___	V	Z
	1	2	3

The wording of the question stem also provides a clue into the placement of Q: by referencing the period "immediately preceding Q's period," it is clear that Q will not be first in this scenario (there is no period that precedes the first period). Consequently, because the second period is already occupied, Q must be from the third period in this question, and since the museum's third period painting is already occupied by Z, Q must be the third period painting of the private collector (and R and T rotate in the first period):

Private:	R/T	S	Q
Museum:	T/R	V	Z
	1	2	3

Answer choices (A), (C), and (E): None of these answer choices contain a painting that can be from a period immediately preceding Q's period. Thus, each of these answer choices is incorrect.
Answer choice (B): This is the correct answer choice. From the diagram, we can determine that S can be the painting from the same buyer in the period immediately preceding Q.

Answer choice (D): Although V can be a painting from the period immediately preceding Q's period, V is sold to a different buyer than Q, and thus this answer choice is incorrect.

Question #17: Local, Must Be True. The correct answer choice is (B)

The conditions in the question stem establish a horizontal ZT block:

[ZT]

Because we have already established that Z can only be sold to the museum as either the second or third period piece, the block *must* be placed so that Z is from the second period and T is from the third period:

	1	2	3
Private:	___	___	___
Museum:	___	Z	T

At this point, we can apply the first rule and third rules, which serve to establish that S is from the first period and that V is sold to the private collector:

	1	2	3
Private:	S	V	___
Museum:	___	Z	T

The only remaining variables yet to be placed are Q and R. From the second rule we know that T ═══ Q, and thus Q must be from the third period (otherwise it would violate the second rule). Consequently, Q must be sold to the private collector, and R, the random, occupies the museum's first period:

Private:	S	V	Q
Museum:	R	Z	T
	1	2	3

Using this analysis, the problem is easy.

Answer choices (A), (C), (D), and (E): Each of these answer choices cannot occur, and therefore each is incorrect.

Answer choice (B): This is the correct answer choice.

Game #5: October 2004 Questions 7-12

7. E 8. B 9. A 10. E 11. D 12. A

This game has a Linear structure paired with four Grouping rules. Because there are two dogs placed each day, our diagram will feature the days as the base, with two spaces per day:

GHKLPS^6

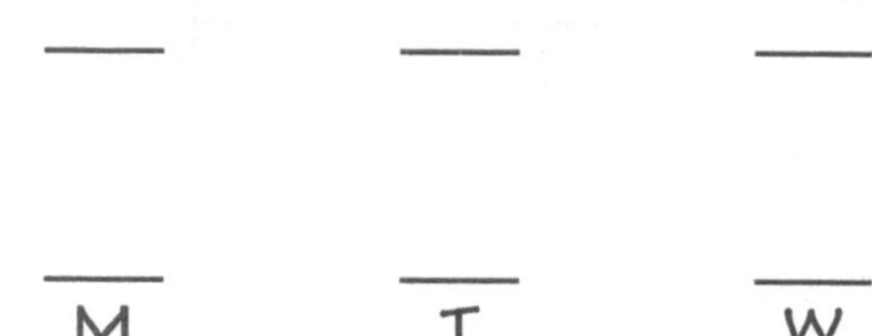

The first two rules include one block and one not-block:

Since these two rules address four of the six dogs in the game, what is the relationship between the two dogs—S and K—not included in these two rules? To determine this relationship, first analyze what happens when the blocks are placed (in this analysis, disregard the linear aspect of the game and just consider the groups).

1. L and P must occupy one entire day:

L

P

Day Day Day

2. G and H cannot be placed on the same day, and since there are only two days open, G and H must form a dual-option that occupies one space on each day:

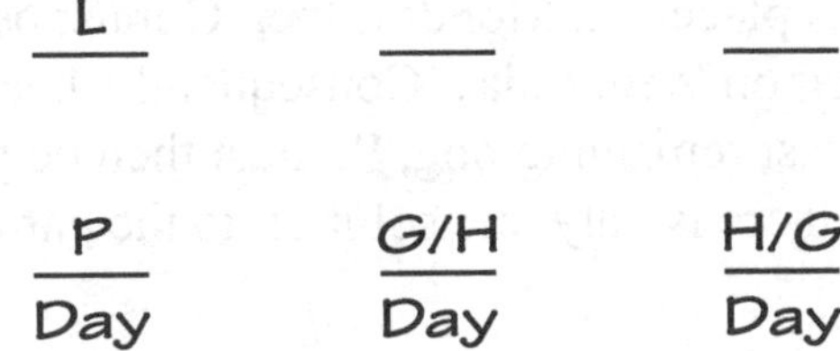

3. By Hurdling the Uncertainty, we can infer that the two remaining variables, K and S, can never be placed on the same day:

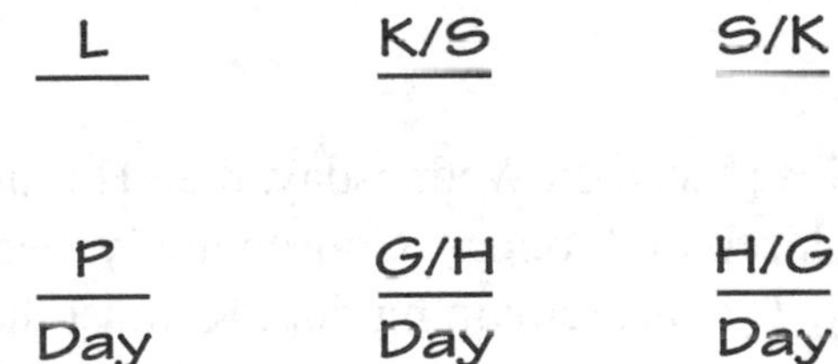

Consequently, we can infer that S and K form a not-block:

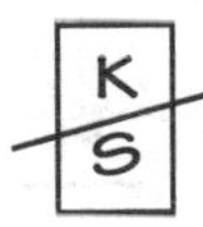

This inference is directly tested in question #8.

There are also two powerful conditional rules in the game:

The third rule: $K_M \longrightarrow G_T$

The fourth rule: $S_W \longrightarrow H_T$

LOGIC GAMES EXPLANATIONS

Because these rules involve two separate days and they both involve the second rule, they ultimately result in a single solution to the game:

The third rule. When K is placed on Monday, then G must be placed on Tuesday. The LP block must then be placed on Wednesday. Consequently, because G is on Tuesday, H must be placed on Monday. The last remaining dog, S, must then be placed on Tuesday. Thus, when K is placed on Monday, there is only one solution to the game:

M	T	W
H	S	L
K	G	P

The fourth rule. When S is placed on Wednesday, then H must be placed on Tuesday. The LP block must then be placed on Monday. Consequently, because H is on Tuesday, G must be placed on Wednesday. The last remaining dog, K, must then be placed on Tuesday. Thus, when S is placed on Wednesday, there is only one solution to the game:

M	T	W
L	K	G
P	H	S

The information above provides more than sufficient information to attack the questions, but a savvy test taker might suspect that given the powerful rules in this game, and the fact that there are no randoms, that there might be a limited number of solutions to this game. In fact, there are only eight solutions to the game, and these eight solutions can be captured using five templates. One option for attacking this game would be to show the templates, and in the interest of absolute clarity we will discuss how to make each template.

The basis for the templates is the placement of the LP block. Since the LP block can go on any of the three days, there are three basic avenues that lead to the templates:

LP on Monday:

When the LP block is placed on Monday, H and G must be split between Tuesday and Wednesday. However, the placement of S and K has an impact on G and H because of the action of the fourth rule. This ultimately creates two templates:

Template #1:
LP on Monday
S on Tuesday, K on Wednesday

L	G/H	H/G
P	S	K
M	T	W

Template #2:
LP on Monday
K on Tuesday, S on Wednesday

L	H	G
P	K	S
M	T	W

Template #1 contains two solutions; template #2 contains only one solution.

LP on Tuesday:

When the LP block is placed on Tuesday, both the third and fourth rules are affected: K cannot be placed on Monday, and S cannot be placed on Wednesday. Consequently, K must be placed on Wednesday and S must be placed on Monday. G and H form a dual-option that rotates between Monday and Wednesday:

Template #3:
LP on Tuesday

G/H	L	H/G
S	P	K
M	T	W

This template contains two solutions.

LOGIC GAMES EXPLANATIONS

LP on Wednesday:

When the LP block is placed on Wednesday, H and G must be split between Monday and Tuesday. However, the placement of S and K has an impact on G and H because of the action of the third rule. This ultimately creates two templates:

Template #4:
LP on Wednesday
S on Monday, K on Tuesday

G/H	H/G	L
S	K	P
M	T	W

Template #5:
LP on Wednesday
S on Tuesday, K on Monday

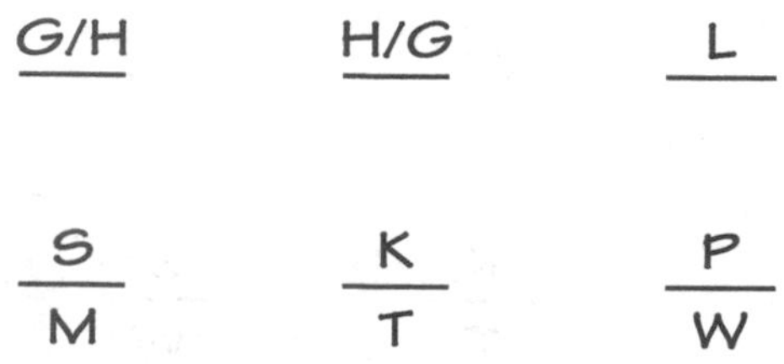

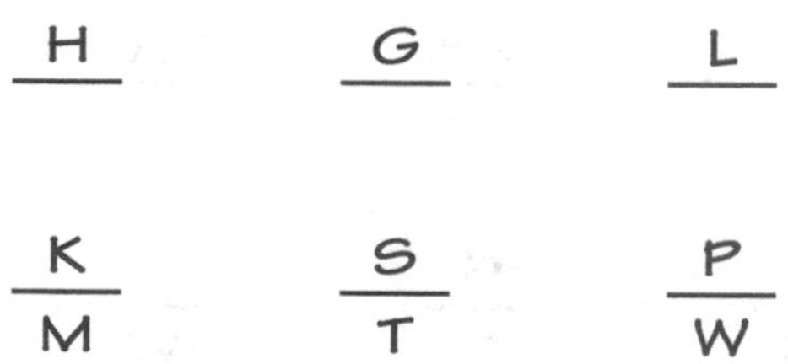

H	G	L
K	S	P
M	T	W

Template #4 contains two solutions; template #5 contains only one solution.

Either a regular setup or the template approach will effectively solve this game. In our explanations of the questions we will use the regular setup because more people attack the game using that method, and the template method still leaves several possible solutions undefined.

Question #7: Global, List. The correct answer choice is (E)

As with any List question, simply apply the rules to the answer choices. In this game, the best order to apply the rules is: rule #1, rule #2, rule #3, and then rule #4.

Answer choice (A): This answer choice violates the first rule and is therefore incorrect.

Answer choice (B): This answer choice violates the third rule and is therefore incorrect.

Answer choice (C): This answer choice violates the second rule and is therefore incorrect.

Answer choice (D): This answer choice violates the fourth rule and is therefore incorrect.

Answer choice (E): This is the correct answer choice.

Question #8: Global, Must Be True. The correct answer choice is (B)

As discussed in the setup to this game, because of the interaction of the first two rules, we can deduce that K and S can never be placed on the same day. Consequently, answer choice (B) is correct.

Answer choices (A), (C), (D), and (E): Each of these answer choices could be true, but none of them must be true, and therefore each is incorrect.

Answer choice (B): This is the correct answer choice.

Question #9: Local, Could Be True. The correct answer choice is (A)

When the L is placed on Tuesday, then from the first rule we know that P is also placed on Tuesday. With Tuesday occupied, both the third and fourth rules are affected: K cannot be placed on Monday (because G cannot be placed on Tuesday), and S cannot be placed on Wednesday (because H cannot be placed on Tuesday). Consequently, K must be placed on Wednesday and S must be placed on Monday. G and H form a dual-option that rotates between Monday and Wednesday:

G/H	L	H/G
S	P	K
M	T	W

Answer choice (A): This is the correct answer choice.

Answer choice (B): This answer choice violates the third rule. K cannot be placed on Monday because there is no space for G to be placed on Tuesday.

Answer choice (C): The question stem stipulates that P must be placed on Tuesday, and from the first rule L must also be placed on Tuesday. Therefore, this answer choice cannot occur and it is incorrect.

Answer choice (D): Since L and P occupy the two spaces on Tuesday, no other dog can be placed on Tuesday, and thus this answer choice is incorrect.

Answer choice (E): This answer choice violates the fourth rule. S cannot be placed on Wednesday because there is no space for H to be placed on Tuesday.

Question #10: Local, Must Be True. The correct answer choice is (E)

The question stem places G and K in a block:

Since L and P are also aligned in a block, two of three days must be completely filled by those two blocks:

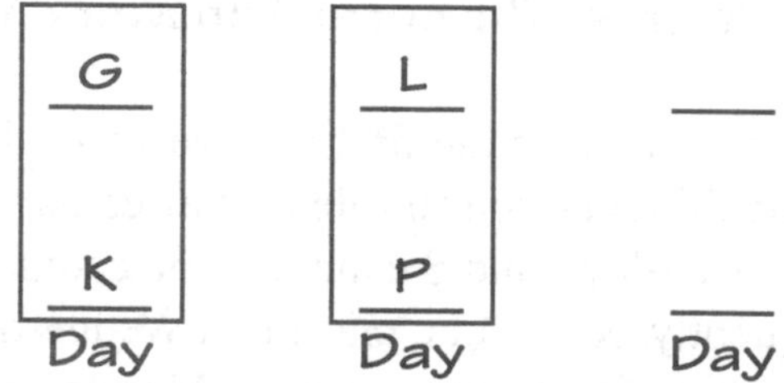

Thus, because the only two remaining spaces are on the same day, the two remaining dogs—H and S—must also be in a block, and the key to this question is to determine the days on which each block can be placed. Let's examine each block in closer detail:

> **__The GK block__**: The only rule applicable to this block is the third rule, which states that if K is placed on Monday then G must be placed on Tuesday. Consequently, we can infer that the GK block cannot be placed on Monday since that placement would violate this rule.
>
> **__The LP block:__** The LP block could be placed on any one of the three days.
>
> **__The HS block:__** The only rule applicable to this block is the fourth rule, which states that if S is placed on Wednesday then H must be placed on Tuesday. Consequently, we can infer that the HS block cannot be placed on Wednesday since that placement would violate this rule.

With the information above, we are ready to attack the answer choices.

Answer choice (A): Although H could be placed on Monday, H does not have to be placed on Monday and so this answer choice is incorrect.

Answer choice (B): Although L could be placed on Monday, L does not have to be placed on Monday and so this answer choice is incorrect.

Answer choice (C): Although K could be placed on Tuesday, K does not have to be placed on Tuesday and so this answer choice is incorrect.

Answer choice (D): This answer choice, like answer choice (E), slips a "not" into the middle of the answer (remember, read carefully!). Because P could be placed on Wednesday, this answer choice is incorrect.

Answer choice (E): This is the correct answer choice. As discussed above, the HS block cannot be placed on Wednesday because doing so would violate the fourth rule.

Question #11: Local, Cannot Be True. The correct answer choice is (D)

The question stem creates a horizontal HS block:

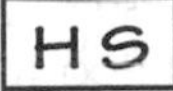

This block must be placed on either Monday and Tuesday, or Tuesday and Wednesday. Consequently, the LP vertical block must be placed on Monday or Wednesday. This deduction is sufficient to show that P cannot be placed on Tuesday, and so answer choice (D) is correct. However, in the interests of fully understanding the relationships at work in this question, let's continue our analysis. So far we have two blocks, and since HS is a horizontal block, we will show the other spaces with H and S:

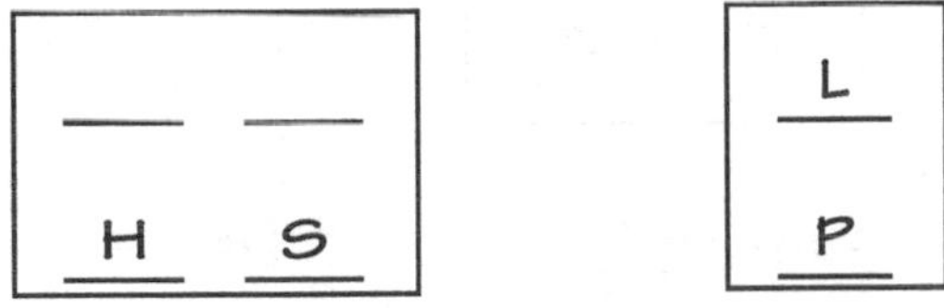

The remaining two variables are G and K. Because the second rule specifies that G and H cannot be placed on the same day, we can infer that G must placed with S. K must then be placed with H:

K G
H S

L
P

Because of the fortuitous arrangement of the variables, the blocks can be placed in any order. Answer choices (A), (B), (C) and (E): Each of these answer choices could be true, as proven by the following hypothetical:

LOGIC GAMES EXPLANATIONS

K	G	L
H	S	P
M	T	W

Answer choice (D): This is the correct answer choice. As discussed above, the LP vertical block must be placed on either Monday or Wednesday.

Question #12: Local, Cannot Be True. The correct answer choice is (A)

One approach to attacking this question is to use the hypotheticals from the previous three questions. Each contains scenarios that match the condition in this question stem, and collectively that information can be used to eliminate every incorrect answer choice. If you do not choose that approach, this question can still be done easily by making hypotheticals.

The condition in the question stem, in combination with the first rule, creates a powerful GLP block:

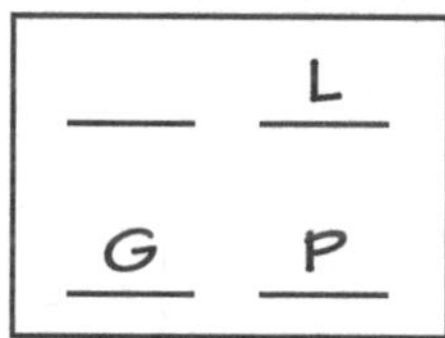

This block can only be placed on Monday-Tuesday or Tuesday-Wednesday:

Hypothetical #1:
GLP on Monday-Tuesday

	L	
G	P	H
M	T	W

Hypothetical #2:
GLP on Tuesday-Wednesday

		L
H	G	P
M	T	W

Of course, due to the second rule, H cannot be placed on the same day as G, so H must be placed on Wednesday in the first hypothetical and on Monday in the second hypothetical.

In addition, because of the fourth rule, in the first hypothetical S must be placed on Monday (otherwise, if it were placed on Wednesday, then H could not be placed on Monday), and therefore K is placed on Monday in the first hypothetical. In the second hypothetical K and S form a dual option:

Hypothetical #1:
GLP on Monday-Tuesday

M	T	W
S	L	K
G	P	H

Hypothetical #2:
GLP on Tuesday-Wednesday

M	T	W
S/K	K/S	L
H	G	P

Answer choice (A): This is the correct answer choice.

Answer choices (B), (C), (D), and (E): As shown in the two hypotheticals, G, K, L, P, and S could be placed on Tuesday. Thus, each of these answer choices is incorrect.

LOGIC GAMES EXPLANATIONS

Game #6: June 2004 Questions 18-22

18. D 19. C 20. E 21. A 22. C

This game was widely considered the most difficult of the June 2004 exam. After three linear-based games, the test makers saved a Partially Defined Grouping game for last, but test takers do get a break because this game has only five questions.

At first, this game appears to be a straight defined Grouping game: six lunch trucks serve three office buildings. However, the game scenario does not specify that each truck serves only one building, and in fact the second rule explicitly indicates that a truck can serve more than one building (by itself, this fact opens up the game to many more possible solutions). If each lunch truck served only one building, the game would be considerably easier because the assignment of a truck to a building would eliminate that truck from further consideration. Thus, one reason test takers felt this game was more difficult was because there is much more to consider within the setup of this game compared to the prior three games (there are also twice as many rules in this game as in any of the other games on this test).

The first decision in this game is what variable set to choose as the base. Either the lunch trucks or the buildings could serve as the base, but we will use the buildings since there are fewer buildings and each of the rules references the trucks going to the buildings. There is also an intuitive element here as it is easier to see the trucks going to the buildings; if the buildings were assigned to the trucks it would be counter to how things work in the real world (trucks move, buildings don't).

With that in mind, we can create the following basic representation of the variable sets:

FHIPST ^{6}

X	Y	Z

Now, let's examine each rule.

Rule #1. The first rule establishes that Y is served by exactly three lunch trucks, two of which are F and H:

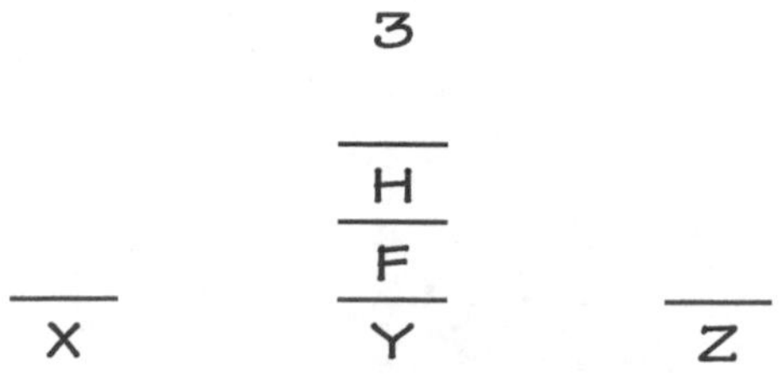

	3	
	H	
	F	
X	Y	Z

Rule #2. This rule indicates that F serves two buildings, one of which is Y, and the other is X or Z:

3

H

F/ F /F

X Y Z

Rule #3. Like the first two rules, this rule addresses a numerical relationship within the game. Given the open-ended nature of the truck assignments in the game scenario, you *must* look for rules that establish exact numbers, and, hopefully, a complete Numerical Distribution of trucks to buildings. More on this point later.

According to this rule, I must serve more buildings than S:

#I —— #S

So, at this point, I must serve either two or three buildings, and S must serve either one or two buildings (note that it *is* possible for I and S to serve the same building). This rule is worth tracking since other rules can (and will) impact these possibilities.

Rule #4. This rule, which states that T does not serve Y, can be added as a Not Law to our setup:

3

H

F/ F /F

X Y Z

T (crossed out, below Y)

Rule #5. This is a powerful rule, and one whose implications can be easily overlooked. First, the diagram for this rule is as follows:

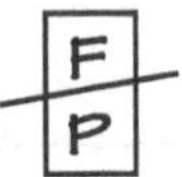

If F and P do not serve the same building, the obvious deduction is that P does not serve building Y. However, we already know from the second rule that F serves exactly two buildings. Since P cannot serve those two buildings and there are only three buildings, we can infer that P can serve only one building and that it must be the building *not* served by F. Thus, for example, if F is assigned to building X, then P would have to be assigned to building Z. There are several variations on this rule, but the gist in each case is the same: when one of F or P is assigned to building X, the other is assigned to building Z, when one of F or P is assigned to building Z, the other is assigned to building X. We can represent this with a dual F/P option on buildings X and Z:

3

H
F/P F P/F
X Y Z
~~T~~
~~P~~

Thus, numerically we have now established that P can serve only one building, and from the second rule we know that F serves exactly two buildings.

With this rule we have also eliminated several lunch trucks from serving building Y. With two trucks assigned to Y (trucks F and H), and two trucks eliminated from serving Y (trucks T and P), only two trucks remain to fill the third space at Y: truck I or S. This can also be diagrammed with a dual-option:

3

I/S
H
F/P F P/F
X Y Z
~~T~~
~~P~~

Rule #6. This rule can be diagrammed as:

I ⟷ T
2

The first part of this rule indicates that T serves two buildings. Since from rule #4 we know that T cannot serve building Y, we can infer that T serves buildings X and Z. The second part of this rule indicates that T and I serve two of the same buildings, and this means that I must also serve buildings X and Z. I could also serve building Y, but does not have to. With the information above, the diagram is:

	3	
F/P	I/S	P/F
I	H	I
T	F	T
X	Y	Z
	~~T~~	
	~~P~~	

Note that I can still serve the remaining building, building Y. This rule only specifies that T serves two buildings also served by I; I could serve all three buildings without violating this rule (or any other).

The setup above is the final setup for the game, but given all of the numerical rules in this game, you must examine the numerical possibilities for each variable before proceeding to the questions (remember, always examine rules about numbers!). Let's examine the options for each lunch truck:

F: As specified in the second rule, F serves exactly two buildings, one of which is Y.

H: H is somewhat of a wild card in this game. H must serve at least building Y, but there is no other rule limiting how many buildings H must serve. Consequently, H could serve one, two, or three buildings.

I: I must serve at least two buildings (X and Z), and possibly all three buildings.

P: Because of the interaction of the second and fifth rules, P can only serve one building (X or Z).

S: From the third rule we know that S is limited to serving either one or two buildings, but which buildings those are is undetermined.

T: From the third and sixth rules we know that T serves exactly two buildings, and those buildings are X and Z.

This distribution is critical, and having command of the numerical possibilities will allow you to easily solve several of the questions.

Reviewing the game, there are three elements of uncertainty that must be tracked throughout the questions:

1. The F/P dual-option.
2. How many buildings H serves.
3. The relationship between I and S.

Question #18: Global, List. The correct answer choice is (D)

This is one of the easiest LSAT games questions ever (proving that even if you miss the setup completely, you can still answer some questions correctly in a game just by applying the rules). From the first rule we know that F must serve building Y. Since answer choices (A), (B), and (E) fail to include Y, they are incorrect. From the second rule we know that F must serve exactly two buildings. Since answer choice (C) contains three buildings, it is incorrect.

Answer choice (D): This is the correct answer choice.

Question #19: Global, Must Be True. The correct answer choice is (C)

This question asks you to identify two trucks that must serve the same building (although they could serve other buildings as well). There are several pairs that should immediately jump to mind—including F and H, and I and T—but none of the obvious pairs is listed as a possible answer. Consequently, you should consider each answer choice on its own merits.

Answer choice (A): Although H and P could serve the same building, they do not *have* to serve the same building. For example, H could serve just building Y, and P could serve just building Z. Thus, this answer choice is incorrect.

Answer choice (B): Although T must serve both buildings X and Z, it is possible that H serves only building Y. Thus, H and T do not have to serve the same building and this answer choice is incorrect.

Answer choice (C): This is the correct answer choice. I must serve both buildings X and Z. From our discussion of the F/P dual-option, we know that P must serve either building X or Z, and thus there must be one building that both I and P serve together.

Answer choice (D): This answer choice is incorrect because it is possible for I to serve just buildings X and Z, and for S to serve just building Y. Thus, I and S do not have to serve the same building.

Answer choice (E): Although T must serve both buildings X and Z, it is possible that S serves only building Y. Thus, S and T do not have to serve the same building and this answer choice is incorrect.

Question #20: Local, Must Be True. The correct answer choice is (E)

The condition in the question stem affects the Numerical Distribution discussed in the setup analysis. From the discussion of the distribution we know that I serves either two or three buildings. If, as stipulated in this question, I is to serve fewer office buildings than H, then I cannot serve all three office buildings and we can deduce that I serves exactly two office buildings. This also allows us to deduce that H must serve all three buildings. In addition, from the third rule, we know that I serves more office buildings than S, so S must serve exactly one building.

With the above numerical information, we know that I serves only buildings X and Z, and that therefore S must serve building Y:

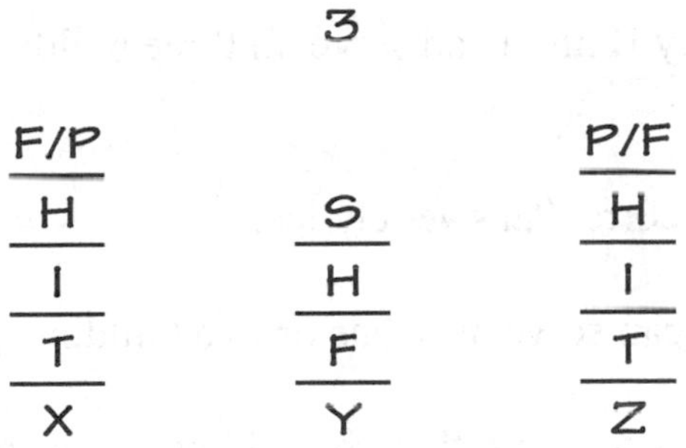

	3	
F/P		P/F
H	S	H
I	H	I
T	F	T
X	Y	Z

From this diagram it is apparent that I and T serve exactly the same buildings, and therefore answer choice (E) is correct.

Answer choice (A): Because F always serves two buildings and H serves three buildings in this question, this answer choice cannot be correct.

Answer choice (B): In this question S serves only one building but F always serves two buildings. Thus, this answer choice is incorrect.

Answer choice (C): Because P always serves one buildings and I serves two buildings in this question, this answer choice cannot be correct.

Answer choice (D): From the third rule we know that I always serves more buildings than S, so the two trucks could never serve exactly the same buildings, and this answer choice must be wrong.

Answer choice (E): This is the correct answer choice.

Question #21: Global, List. The correct answer choice is (A)

This question also trades on the Numerical Distribution established by the rules, so let's take a moment to revisit that Numerical Distribution:

F: F serves exactly two buildings.
H: H could serve one, two, or three buildings.
I: I must serve at least two buildings, and possibly all three buildings.
P: P can only serve one building.
S: S is limited to serving either one or two buildings.
T: T serves exactly two buildings.

The distribution proves that only H and I can serve all three buildings, and thus answer choice (A) is correct.

Answer choice (A): This is the correct answer choice.

Answer choice (B): Because S can serve only one or two buildings, this answer choice is incorrect.

Answer choice (C): Because T serves exactly two buildings, this answer choice is incorrect.

Answer choice (D): Because P serves exactly one building, this answer choice is incorrect.

Answer choice (E): Because P serves exactly one building, and S can serve only one or two buildings, this answer choice is incorrect.

Question #22: Global, Cannot Be True. The correct answer choice is (C)

Again, we can use the distribution to quickly and easily destroy this question.

As we have previously established, lunch truck P can serve only one building. Hence, P could never serve both buildings X and Z, and therefore (C) is the correct answer choice.

Answer choice (A): Because H could serve all three buildings, H could serve both X and Z. Therefore, this answer choice could be true and it is incorrect.

Answer choice (B): As established in the setup of this game, I serves both X and Z. Therefore, this answer choice must be true and it is incorrect.

Answer choice (C): This is the correct answer choice.

Answer choice (D): If I served all three buildings, then S could serve buildings X and Z. Hence, this answer choice could be true and it is incorrect.

Answer choice (E): As established in the setup of this game, T serves both X and Z. Therefore, this answer choice must be true and it is incorrect.

Game #7: December 2004 Questions 7-12

7. A 8. A 9. A 10. A 11. C 12. E

This Grouping and Linear combination game features six players who must form four groups of two players each. The Linear aspect of this game is that the four games are played consecutively. However, one benefit for test takers is that no individual seat assignments are made within each game, and this limits the complexity of the game. The Grouping element results from the rules governing the formation of acceptable two-person games. From the game scenario it is immediately evident that some players will play multiple times, and you should actively seek a Numerical Distribution while working with the rules.

Our initial diagram references the six people, and represents the four games:

L N O P S T [6]

___	___	___	___
___	___	___	___
1	2	3	4

Rules #1 and #2. The first two rules can be added to the diagram easily. The first rule is reflected by T split-option on the second and fourth games (plus the Not Laws on the first and third games), and the second rule is represented by placing L in one of the spaces of the fourth game (it does not matter which space L occupies since the game does not assign seat positions):

___	T/	___	T/
___	___	___	L
1	2	3	4
~~T~~		~~T~~	

Note that T could play in *both* the second and fourth games.

Rule #3. This rule establishes that N and P do not play in the same game, and it additionally establishes that N plays in one and only one game. The Grouping aspect of this rule can be diagrammed as:

We will discuss the numerical aspect of this rule during the discussion of rule #4.

Rule #4. With six players for eight spots, and with each player playing in at least one game, there are initially only two Numerical Distributions of the eight positions to the six players: 3-1-1-1-1- or 2-2-1-1-1-1. The first three rules do not provide us with any numerically useful information aside from the fact that T cannot be a player who plays in three games and that N must be a player who plays exactly one game, but the fourth rule is more useful because it eliminates one of the distributions. By establishing that S plays in exactly two games, this rule eliminates the possibility that a 3-1-1-1-1-1 distribution could exist. Hence, the eight positions must be distributed to the six players in a 2-2-1-1-1-1 relationship:

2: S (from the fourth rule, S plays in two games)
2:
1:
1:
1: O (from the third rule, O plays in one game)
1: N (from the fourth rule, N plays in one game)

Consequently, the three players not assigned above—L, P, and T—must be distributed in a 2-1-1 relationship, where one of the three must play twice and the other two play just once.

The fourth rule also creates a powerful horizontal block:

S O S

Because this SOS block requires so much space, it can only be placed in two positions: games 1-2-3 or games 2-3-4. Because this block is limited, and because there are several other powerful rules, you should make the decision to diagram both of the templates created by the SOS block:

Template #1: SOS in games 1-2-3.

With the assignment of the SOS block to games 1-2-3, and with the placement of L in game 4 (from the second rule), we now have one player assigned to each game:

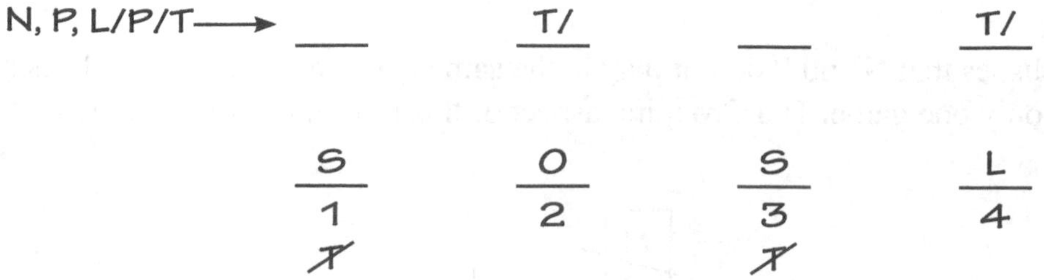

N, P, L/P/T⟶ ___ T/___ ___ T/___

S | O | S | L
1 | 2 | 3 | 4
T̸ | | T̸ |

Because each player must play in at least one game, we must still assign N, P, and T to games. However, assigning N, P, and T would only fill three of the remaining four spaces, and so, from the distribution discussed previously, we know that the remaining space must be filled by one of L, P, or T (that is, one of those three people plays in two games).

At this point in the template, we have placed the SOS block and determined which players must still be assigned. Since there is only one open space in each game, we can ignore the NP not-block rule since N and P cannot now be placed together. We have also fully addressed the second and fourth rules, and so the only concerns still present in this template is which game(s) T will play in and who, aside from S, will be assigned to play twice (L, P, or T).

Template #2: SOS in games 2-3-4.

When the SOS block is assigned to games 2-3-4, the fourth game is now fully assigned to L and S. This placement affects T, who can only play in the second and fourth games. Thus, T must play in the second game:

___	T	___	L
___	S	O	S
1	2	3	4
~~T~~		~~T~~	

The remaining three spaces must be occupied by N and P (who have thus far not been assigned to a game), and the apparent choice L, P, or T to play in a second game (someone must play twice and fill the final space). But, look closely at L, P, and T as possible two-game players: T can be eliminated because the remaining spaces are in the first and third games; P can be eliminated because selecting P would create the group of N, P, and P to fill in the final three spaces, and since two of the spaces are in the same game, the result would be that either N and P would play together (a violation of the third rule) or P would play both positions in one game (a violation of the stipulations in the game scenario). Consequently, we can conclude that L must be the player that plays two games, and that the group that fills the final three open spaces in this template is L, N, and P.

As if the determining the remaining players were not powerful enough, because two of the spaces are in the same game, we can also use the third rule to infer that one of N or P must play in the first game, and the other must play in the third game (if one of N and P does not play in the third game, then both play in the first game, a violation of the third rule). This forces L into the first game, resulting in a template with only two solutions:

L	T	P/N	L
N/P	S	O	S
1	2	3	4

The two templates give us an excellent overview of the general formations within this game, but because the first template has so many solutions, they do not give us complete information.

Question #7: Global, List. The correct answer choice is (A)

As with any List question, simply apply the rules to the answer choices. Given the presentation of the answer choices in this problem (the test makers have made them somewhat difficult to read), the easiest order of attack is to apply the second rule, then the first rule, then the third rule, and finally the last rule.

Answer choice (A): This is the correct answer choice.

Answer choice (B): This answer choice is incorrect because the first rule specifies that T cannot play in the third game.

Answer choice (C): This answer choice is incorrect because it violates both the third and fourth rules. The third rule is violated because N appears in two games; the fourth rule is violated because there is no SOS block.

Answer choice (D): This answer choice is incorrect because N can only play in one game, yet the answer features N in two games.

Answer choice (E): This answer choice is incorrect because L must play in the fourth game.

Question #8: Global, Could Be True. The correct answer choice is (A)

There are two ways to answer this question. The first way is to use the rules to eliminate each of the incorrect answer choices. The second is to use the templates to see which player could possibly play in two consecutive games. Let's examine both approaches:

Use the Rules

This is the easiest and fastest approach. The third and fourth rules tell us that N and O play in exactly one game, and so answer choices (B) and (C) can be eliminated. The fourth rule also indicates that while S plays in two games, those two games cannot be consecutive, so answer choice (D) can be eliminated. The first rule states that T cannot play in the first or third games, and so T could not play in consecutive games, and answer choice (E) can be eliminated. Thus, answer choice (A) is proven correct by process of elimination.

Use the Templates

When examining the templates, always look at Template #2 first because it contains more specific information. In Template #2, none of the variables could play in consecutive games, so we automatically know that the variable that plays consecutively does so under the parameters of Template #1.

Template #1 immediately eliminates all players except L, P, or T, because only L, P, or T could play twice and could conceivably be consecutive (although S plays twice, the template shows that S is not consecutive and is thus eliminated). However, P is not one of the answer choices, so the answer must be L or T. Of course, as shown on the template, T cannot be consecutive, and so L is the player who could play consecutively and answer choice (A) is the correct answer.

Answer choice (A): This is the correct answer choice.

Answer choices (B), (C), (D), and (E): The players in each of these answer cannot play in consecutive games, and thus each one of these answers is incorrect.

Question #9: Local, Could Be True. The correct answer choice is (A)

If T plays in the fourth game, then only Template #1 can apply to this question. Let's revisit template #1 with the addition of T in the fourth game:

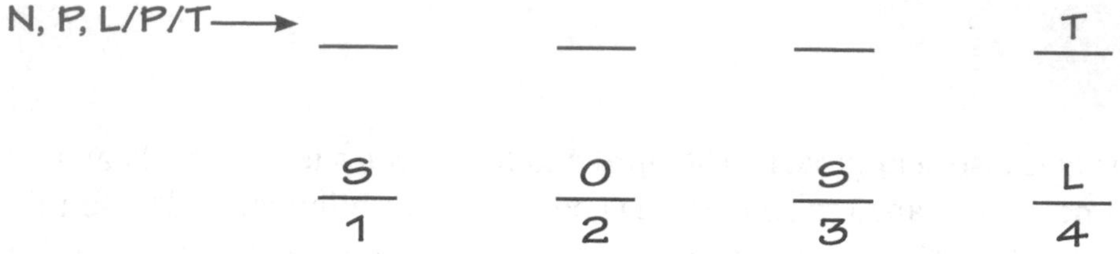

N, P, L/P/T ⟶ ___ ___ ___ T

S	O	S	L
1	2	3	4

The variables yet to be placed include N, P, and the choice of L, P, or T, but there is no way to place those remaining variables exactly. So, although you might wish you could derive more information as a consequence of the placement of T, there are still a number of possibilities and you must move forward and attack the answer choices without getting bogged down trying to assign every player.

Answer choice (A): This is the correct answer choice. N could play in the second game as proven in the following hypothetical:

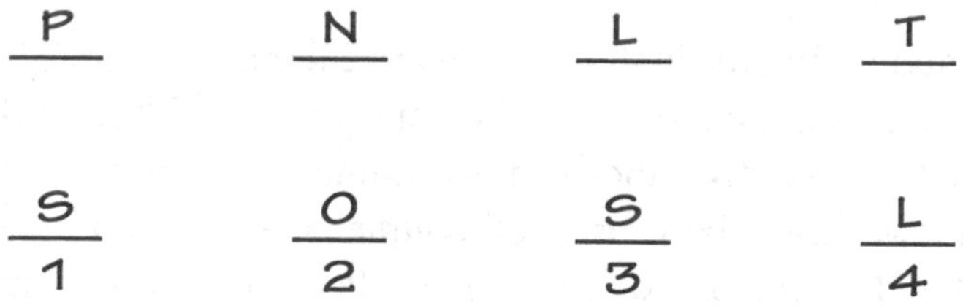

P	N	L	T
S	O	S	L
1	2	3	4

Answer choice (B): This answer choice cannot be true because O plays only once, in the second game.

Answer choice (C): This answer choice is incorrect because S must play in the first and third games, not the second game.

Answer choice (D): This answer choice is incorrect. N can only play in one game, and N's choices for playing partners are S or O (that is, the only open spaces in the diagram are paired with S or O). Thus, N cannot play with L.

Answer choice (E): This answer choice is similar to answer choice (D). Although P can play in more than one game, there is no possibility of P playing with L. As with (D), the only open spaces in the diagram are paired with S or O. Thus, P cannot play with L, and this answer is incorrect.

Question #10: Global, Could Be True. The correct answer choice is (A)

A Global question is made for the templates, and so you should immediately refer to the templates as you attack each answer choice.

Answer choice (A): This is the correct answer choice. P could play L in the first game as proven by the following hypothetical from Template #1:

L	T	N	L
P	S	O	S
1	2	3	4

Answer choice (B): As shown by the two templates, either O or S always plays in the second game. Thus, P cannot play N in the second game, and this answer choice is incorrect.

Answer choice (C): The fourth rule specifies that O plays exactly one game, and that S plays two games, one just before O and one just after O. Hence, O and S can never play in a game together.

Answer choice (D): As shown by the two templates, either O or S always plays in the third game. Thus, P cannot play L in the third game, and this answer choice is incorrect.

Answer choice (E): The second rule indicates that L must play in the fourth game, and hence N cannot play S in the fourth game.

Question #11: Global, List. The correct answer choice is (C)

This Global question asks for who cannot be paired with T. As with question #8, there are two ways to answer this question. The first way is to use previously created hypotheticals to eliminate each of the incorrect answer choices. The second is to use the templates to see who cannot play against T. Let's examine both approaches:

<u>Use Hypotheticals</u>

This approach has the benefit of eliminating several answer choices quickly. From question #7, answer choice (A), we know that T can play against O. Hence, any answer choice that contains O can be eliminated, and answer choices (B) and (E) can be removed from consideration.

The question stem of #9 places T in the last game. From the second rule, we know L plays in the last game, and thus T can play against L. Answer choice (A), which contains L, can therefore be eliminated.

At this juncture, answer choices (C) and (D) remain in contention, and both contain N. Thus, we need not concern ourselves with N and we can focus on the other variables in each answer: P and S, respectively. There are two different paths to the correct answer from this point:

1. Analyze the possibilities without writing them down. From a logical point of view, it is likely that T can play against S since S plays twice, and S can be placed in such a way as to conform to T's requirements (T must play in the second or fourth game). T and P, on the other hand, present a problem since they form a vertical block, and in order to make room for the horizontal SOS block, the TP vertical block would have to be placed in the fourth game. However, since L already plays in the fourth game, this cannot occur, and thus there is no way to reach a viable solution when T plays with P. Hence, answer choice (C) is correct.

2. Create a new hypothetical. Once you are down to two answer choices, you can simply power through the problem by creating a hypothetical to match one of the remaining answer choices. This hypothetical, for instance, shows that S can play against T, and that therefore answer choice (D) is incorrect:

1	2	3	4
L	T	N	L
P	S	O	S

The Hypothetical approach has the advantage of eliminating several answers quickly, and then it is not too difficult to eliminate the final answer choice.

<u>Use the Templates</u>

This approach is somewhat more logically attractive because it relies completely on work you did during the setup. In creating the templates, Template #2 paired T and S. Thus, we can eliminate any answer choice that contains S, and answer choice (D) can be removed from consideration.

Template #1 allows T to play against L or O, the players in the second and fourth games, respectively. Since there no limitations on variable placement in that template, both L and O can play against T, and any answer choice containing L or O is incorrect. That inference eliminates answer choices (A), (B), and (E), and thus answer choice (C) is correct.

Regardless of which method you use to arrive at the correct answer, the reasoning that underlies the answer is the same: placing T with either N or P creates a placement issue with the SOS block. The only way to successfully place the SOS block and a TN or TP vertical block forces the T block into the fourth game, which cannot occur since L already is there.

Answer choice (A): T can play against L, and so this answer choice is incorrect.

Answer choice (B): T can play against O, and so this answer choice is incorrect.

Answer choice (C): This is the correct answer choice.

Answer choice (D): T can play against S, and so this answer choice is incorrect.
Answer choice (E): T can play against O, and so this answer choice is incorrect.

Question #12: Local, Must Be True. The correct answer choice is (E)

If O plays in the third game, this enacts the scenario in Template #2:

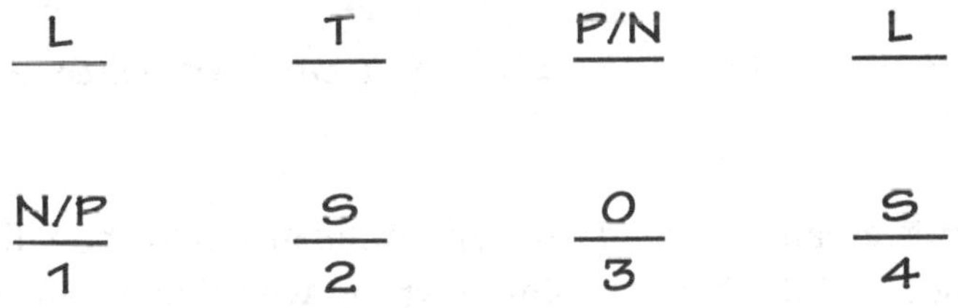

L	T	P/N	L
N/P	S	O	S
1	2	3	4

Consequently, T must play in the second game, and answer choice (E) is correct.

Answer choice (A): This answer choice is incorrect because L plays in the first and last games.

Answer choice (B): This answer choice is incorrect because although N could play in the third game, N does not have to play in the third game.

Answer choice (C): This answer choice is incorrect because although P could play in the first game, P does not have to play in the first game.

Answer choice (D): This answer choice is incorrect because although P could play in the third game, P does not have to play in the third game.

Answer choice (E): This is the correct answer choice. If you are looking for the reasoning of how we arrived at the diagram above, please go back to the discussion of Template #2 in the setup analysis.

Game #8: June 2003 Questions 18-23

18. D 19. C 20. C 21. B 22. A 23. B

This is a Defined-Fixed, Unbalanced: Overloaded Grouping game.

Monkeys: F G H
(* under G)

Pandas: K L N
(* under L)

Raccoons: T V Z
(* under V and Z)

9 ⟶ 6

___ ___ ___ ___ ___ ___
Six Animals

F ←|→ H

N ←|→ T

H ⟶ K ⟶ N

Inferences

K ←|→ T

H ←|→ T

Either 1 or 2 monkeys must be selected.

In the setup, some students create a second row within the group to show the type of animal—monkey, panda, or raccoon. While there is nothing wrong with this decision, operationally it has little effect as the questions focus more on the individual animals than on their type, and also, the questions can easily be answered without adding that second row.

There are more inferences in this game than might appear at first. Let us take a moment to examine the few inferences that can be drawn.

First, at the group level, we can deduce from the first rule that if two monkeys are selected, then G must be one of those monkeys (we know this by Hurdling the Uncertainty—since F and H can never be selected together, if two monkeys are selected then G must always be selected). As a corollary, we can conclude that at most two monkeys will ever be selected (and, from the second rule, we can conclude that at least one monkey must be selected: since N and T cannot be selected together, we cannot form a viable group from just the six pandas and raccoons, and therefore at least one monkey will always be selected).

Second, at the variable level, several more inferences can be drawn. By connecting the second and fourth rules we can infer that K and T can never be selected together. By recycling that inference and combining it with the third rule, we can also infer that H and T can never be selected together.

The last two rules form a chain linking H, K, and N. Consequently, H is an important variable because if H is selected then K and N must also be selected, and once H, K, and N are selected we can conclude from the first two rules that F and T would not be selected. At that point, any of the remaining animals could be selected because all four rules in the scenario would have been satisfied (and, as you might expect, the remaining variables—G, L, V, and Z—are randoms). Hence, the selection of H yields a number of ready-made hypothetical solutions:

H K N (G, L, V, Z)

~~F~~ ~~T~~

As with any conditional chain sequence, you should also consider what occurs if the final necessary condition is not selected. In this case, if N is not selected, via the contrapositive you know that K and H cannot be selected. At first, this may appear unremarkable, but remember that this is a "9 into 6" grouping scenario, and if H, K, and N are all eliminated, then there are no "extra" variables, and all the remaining variables must be used. This creates the following hypothetical:

F G L T V Z

Note that you should not just simply assume that such a hypothetical is valid; instead, quickly check the rules to make sure there are no violations (in the above hypothetical, there are no violations). If there was a violation, you would then know that the necessary condition—in this case, N—would have to be selected in every scenario and you would have gained a valuable piece of information (as it stands, since the hypothetical scenario above is workable, N does not have to be selected).

The other variable of note is T. Because T and N cannot be selected together, when T is selected there can be only one solution to the game (because N will not be selected, leading to the hypothetical discussed above).

Question #18: Global, Could Be True, List. The correct answer choice is (D)

Answer choice (A) is incorrect because N and T cannot be selected together.

Answer choice (B) is incorrect because F and H cannot be selected together.

Answer choice (C) is incorrect because if K is selected then N must be selected.

Answer choice (D) is the correct answer.

Answer choice (E) is incorrect because if H is selected then K must be selected.

Question #19: Local, Could Be True. The correct answer choice is (C)

According to the question stem, H and L are selected. From our discussion, we know that once H is selected, then K and N are also selected and F and T are not selected. This leaves the following situation:

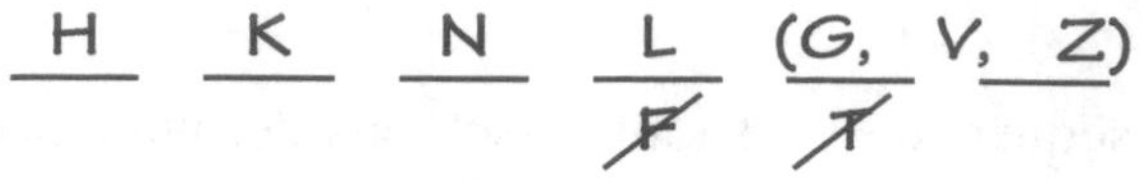

H K N L (G, V, Z)

Not: F, T

Answer choices (A) and (B) are eliminated due to the Not Laws. Answer choices (D) and (E) are eliminated because all three pandas must be selected. Consequently, answer choice (C) is correct.

Question #20: Global, Could Be True, Except. The correct answer choice is (C)

From our discussion of inferences, we know that K and T cannot be selected together (the combination of the third, fourth, and second rules makes it impossible). Consequently, answer choice (C) is correct.

Question #21: Local, Must Be True. The correct answer choice is (B)

This is the only question stem to contain a reference to the animal groups. If all three raccoons are selected, then T, V, and Z must be selected. Since T is selected, from the rules and inferences we know that N, K, and H cannot be selected, and therefore F, G, and L must be selected (see the discussion of inferences if this does not make sense):

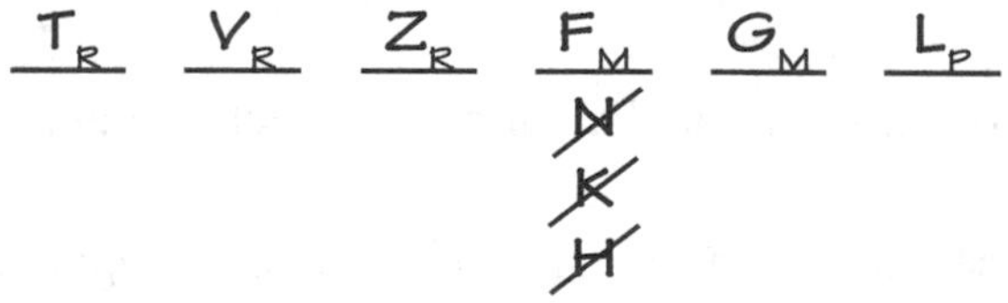

T_R V_R Z_R F_M G_M L_P

Not: N, K, H

Answer choices (A), (C), (D), and (E) can never be true. Answer choice (B) must be true, and is therefore correct.

Question #22: Local, Must Be True. The correct answer choice is (A)

Similar to question #21, when T is selected, from the rules and inferences we know that N, K, and H cannot be selected, and therefore F, G, and L must be selected:

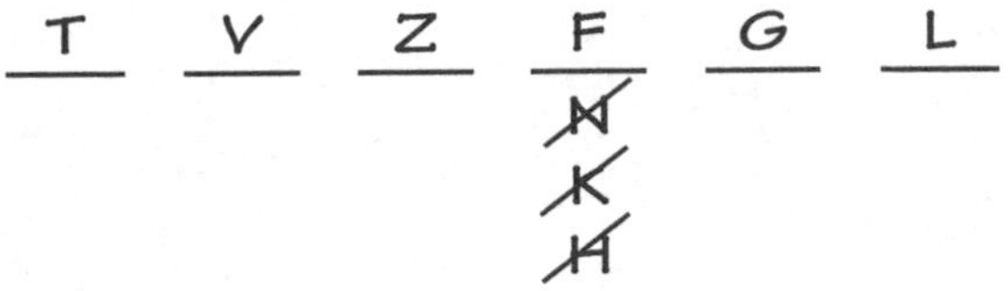

T V Z F G L
N̶ K̶ H̶

Answer choice (A) is therefore correct.

Another way of attacking this question is to eliminate answers that contain a variable that cannot be selected with T: use the rule that N and T cannot be selected together to eliminate answer choice (E); then use the inference that K and T cannot be selected together to eliminate answer choices (C) and (D); then use the inference that K and H cannot be selected together to eliminate answer choice (B).

Question #23: Global, Must Be True. The correct answer choice is (B)

At first glance, this appears to be a difficult Global question. Remember, if you do not have a ready inference to apply to this type of question, prepare to use hypotheticals and previous information.

Answer choice (A) can be eliminated by the question stem to #21.

Answer choice (B) is correct.

Answer choice (C) can be eliminated by the hypothetical produced in #21 (and in our discussion of what occurs when N is not selected).

Answer choice (D) can be eliminated by the hypothetical array we produced when discussing the selection of H, K, and N (when H, K, and N are selected, then any three of G, L, V, and Z can be selected, allowing for a hypothetical with only one monkey).

Answer choice (E) can be eliminated by the question stem to #21.

LOGIC GAMES EXPLANATIONS

Appendix

Test-by-Test Game Use Tracker

This appendix contains a reverse lookup that cross references each game according to the source LSAT. The tests are listed in order of the PrepTest number (if any). The date of administration is also listed to make the process easier. If a test is not listed, then no questions from that exam were used in this book.

Games listed under each test begin by listing the *Logic Games Bible Workbook* chapter the game appears in, the game date, and then the question numbers.

For information on obtaining the publications that contain the entire LSATs listed below, please visit our Free LSAT Help area at www.powerscore.com/lsat/help/pub_ident.cfm

PrepTest 40—June 2003 LSAT

Chapter 2, Page 258, Game #8: June 2003 Questions 18-23

PrepTest 43—June 2004 LSAT

Chapter 2, Page 246, Game #2: June 2004 Questions 1-5
Chapter 2, Page 250, Game #4: June 2004 Questions 13-17
Chapter 2, Page 254, Game #6: June 2004 Questions 18-22

PrepTest 44—October 2004 LSAT

Chapter 2, Page 252, Game #5: October 2004 Questions 7-12

PrepTest 45—December 2004 LSAT

Chapter 2, Page 248, Game #3: December 2004 Questions 1-6
Chapter 2, Page 256, Game #7: December 2004 Questions 7-12

PrepTest 51—December 2006 LSAT

Chapter 2, Page 244, Game #1: December 2006 Questions 16-22

Glossary

#

"5 if" Question:

In these questions, each of the five answer choices begins with the word "if," hence the "5 if" designation. These questions are basically five questions in one, and can be incredibly time consuming.

Advanced Linear:

Linear games that feature three or more variable sets are known as Advanced Linear games. As with Basic Linear games, one of the variable sets will be classified as the base, and the other variable sets will generally be "stacked" in rows above the base.

Answer Choices:

Each LSAT question is accompanied by five lettered answer choices, exactly one of which is the correct answer.

Arrows:

A representation used for both conditional relationships and certain sequential relationships. See also Conditional Rules, Double Arrow, Double-Not Arrow.

Balanced:

In a Defined game, when the number of variables to be selected is equal to the overall number of available spaces.

Base:

The variable set chosen as the foundation for the game setup. The base often has a sense of inherent order (in Linear games), and the other variable sets are placed above the base.

Basic Linear:

Linear games that feature two variable sets are known as Basic Linear games. One of the variable sets is classified as the base, and the other variable set is then used to "fill in" the row of spaces above (or next to) the base.

Block:

In Linear games, blocks reflect the idea of a fixed spatial relationship between variables. Blocks represent variables that are next to one another, not next to one another, or separated by a fixed number of spaces. Basic blocks indicate adjacency.

Cannot Be True:

Cannot Be True is the logical opposite of Could Be True. Cannot Be True questions ask you to identify the answer choice that can never occur.

Chain:

Any set of variables connected together, most often in a Sequencing or conditional arrangement.

Circular Linearity:

Games that consist of a fixed number of variables assigned to spaces distributed around a circle (usually a table). Essentially, these games are Linear games wrapped around a circular diagram.

Conditional Rules:

Rules involving sufficient and necessary conditions.

Conditional Sequencing:

Rules involving sufficient and necessary conditions paired with sequences.

Contrapositive:

Denies the necessary condition, thereby making it impossible for the sufficient condition to occur. Contrapositives can often yield important insights in Logic Games and in Logical Reasoning.

Could Be True:

Could Be True is the logical opposite of Cannot Be True. Could Be True questions ask you to identify the answer choice that could occur.

Defined:

In these Logic Games, the exact number of variables to be selected is fixed in the rules.

Diagram:

A visual representation of a rule, or of the game setup itself.

Double Arrow:

Indicates that the two terms must always occur together. The double arrow is typically introduced in any of the following three ways:

1. Use of the phrase "if and only if"
2. Use of the phrase "vice versa" (as in "If A attends then B attends, and vice versa")
3. By repeating and reversing the terms (as in "If A attends then B attends, and if B attends then A attends")

Double-Branched Sequence: See Multi-Branched Sequence.

Double-Not Arrow:

Indicates that two terms cannot occur together. The double-not arrow only prohibits one scenario—one where the two terms occur together.

Dual Option:

When only one of two variables can occupy a single slot. Represented with a slash, as in "A/B."

Either/Or:

For the purposes of the LSAT, the definition of "either/or" is "at least one of the two." Note that this definition implicitly allows for the possibility that both elements occur, and the existence of this possibility makes diagramming sentences containing the "either/or" term confusing. A careful examination of the definition of "either/or" reveals that a conditional relationship is at the heart of the construction: since at least one of the terms must occur, if one fails to occur then the other must occur.

Experimental Section:

An unscored section added to every LSAT. The experimental can be any of the three section types (LG, LR, or RC), and the purpose of the section is to test and evaluate questions that will be used on *future* LSATs.

External Diagramming:

When rules are diagrammed off to the side of the part of the diagram that contains the slots or spaces, this is known as External Diagramming.

Falsity:

Although most Logic Game questions are posed in terms of truth (for example, "Which one of the following could be true?"), some question stems are phrased in terms of falsity (such as, "Which one of the following cannot be false?"). Always convert a question phrased in terms of false into a question phrased in terms of true!

Fixed:

When used in reference to Grouping, Fixed means the exact size of each group is known. When used in reference to Numerical Distributions, Fixed means that certain variables are assigned to specific numbers.

Game Scenario:

In Logic Games, the game scenario introduces sets of variables, people, places, things, or events involved in an easy to understand activity such as sitting in seats or singing songs.

Global:

These Logic Games questions ask about information derived only from the initial rules, such as "Who can finish first?" or "Which one of the following must be true?"

Grouping:

These Logic Games require you to analyze the variables in terms of which ones can and cannot be together.

Grouping/Linear Combination:

Games that combine both Grouping and Linear elements.

Guessing Strategy:

There is no penalty for guessing on the LSAT, and therefore you should provide an answer for every single question, even if you do not have time to complete the question. However, because some answer choices are more likely to occur than others, you should not guess randomly.

Hierarchy of Game Power™:

The Hierarchy visually shows which elements are the most important in a typical game, and the order in which they should be analyzed.

Horizontality:

When a game is diagrammed in a horizontal line (or setup), the relationship between variables arranged horizontally indicates adjacency, while the relationship of variables arranged vertically indicates similarity. This is also true of horizontality in blocks.

Hurdle the Uncertainity™:

In Logic Games, during the placement of variables, situations occur where even though you cannot determine the exact variables being selected, you can "leap" that uncertainty to determine that other variables must be selected. This powerful technique can be used in many different games, and it attacks a concept frequently used by the test makers (it appears in virtually every Grouping game).

Hypothetical:

A possible solution to a question that you quickly create to gain insight into Logic Game answers. Hypotheticals can be the fastest way to solve a question, and sometimes they give you information that can be used to solve other problems.

I

Identify the Possibilities™:

In this approach, all of the solutions to the game are written out during the setup, before attacking the questions. This usually takes more time during the setup, but since it results in perfect information the questions can be answered incredibly fast.

Identify the Templates™:

Games that contain several major directions are often best attacked by Identifying the Templates, where the major possibility templates are diagrammed, but the exact possibilities within each template are not fully displayed.

In:

In Grouping games, the selected variables that meet the criteria of the rules in a question, and thus are part of the solution to the question. See also Out.

Inference:

In logic, an inference can be defined as something that must be true. In Games, inferences typically follow from a rule or combination of rules.

Internal Diagramming:

When rules are represented on the part of the diagram that contains the slots or spaces, this is known as Internal Diagramming.

J

Justify Question:

Justify questions ask you to select the answer choice that forces a specified result.

L

Law School Admission Council (LSAC):

The organization that administers the LSAT and oversees the release of LSAT scores.

Limited Solution Set Games:

Games that have a reduced number of total solutions. In these games, often the best approach is to diagram the solutions during the setup, before attacking the questions.

Linearity:

Involves the fixed positioning and ordering of variables. In every Linear game, one of the variable sets is chosen as the "base" and is diagrammed in a straight line, either horizontally or vertically, and the remaining variable sets are placed into slots above or next to the base. See also: Basic Linear and Advanced Linear.

Linkage:

Linkage involves finding a variable that appears in at least two rules and then combining those two rules. Often that combination will produce an inference of value. Linkage is the easiest and most basic way to make inferences.

List Question:

In Logic Games, List questions present a list of variables that can either fill a slot or possibly solve the game. The best technique for attacking a List question is to take a single rule and apply it to each of the five answer choices, one at a time. The first question in a game is often a List Question.

Local:

These games questions occur when the question imposes a new condition in addition to the initial rules, such as "If Laura sits in the third chair, which one of the following must be true?" Local questions almost always require you to produce a "mini-setup" next to the question.

Logical Opposition:

In truth and falsity, a logical opposite is the term that negates another term, and includes every possibility not covered by the original term. For example, Could Be True and Cannot Be True are logical opposites. Together, the two terms cover the entire range of possibilities on the "truth" scale. Logical opposition is distinct from polar opposition.

LSAC: See Law School Admission Council

Mapping:

These games either do not fix the physical relationships among the variables (Spatial Relations), involve a fixed point and all other variables are placed North, East, South, and West of that point (Directional), or the makers of the test supply a diagram intended to represent the relationship of the variables (Supplied Diagram). There are no numerical elements in a Mapping game.

Maximum/Minimum Question:

Maximum/Minimum questions generally ask you to identify the greatest or least number of possibilities in a certain scenario.

Mistaken Negation™:

Negates both sufficient and necessary conditions, creating a statement that does not have to be true.

Mistaken Reversal™:

Switches the elements in the sufficient and necessary conditions, creating a statement that does not have to be true.

Moving:

When an exact number of variables are to be selected (the Defined component) but there are still sub-groups within that set that are undefined, the groups are said to be Moving.

Multi-Branched Sequence:

When two or more variables are sequentially "ahead" or "behind" another variable, the variables are split into "branches," as in this double-branched sequence :

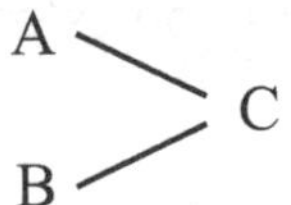

Must Be True:

Must Be True is the logical opposite of Not Necessarily True. Must Be True questions ask you to identify the answer choice that must always occur.

N

Necessary Condition (N):

An event or circumstance whose occurrence is required in order for a sufficient condition to occur.

Negative Grouping Rules:

Negative grouping rules state that two or more variables cannot be selected together.

Not Block:

Indicates that variables cannot be next to one another. Not-blocks only come into play once one of the variables has been placed.

Not Law™:

Physically notates where a variable cannot be placed. Not Laws are very useful since it is essential that you establish the events that cannot be true in a game. See also Side Not Laws.

Not Necessarily True:

Not Necessarily True is the logical opposite of "Must Be True." Not Necessarily True questions ask you to identify the answer choice that does not always have to occur.

Numerical Distribution:

Allocates one set of variables among another set of variables. Numerical Distributions occur in every game except Mapping games.

One-to-One Relationship:

In a one-to-one relationship, each variable fills exactly one slot and there are the same number of slots as variables to be placed.

Out:

In Grouping games, the variables that do not meet the criteria of the rules in each question, and thus are not in play for the question. See also In.

Overlap Principle™:

A principle that applies in some Logic Games (usually Advanced Linear, but possibly Grouping) that indicates that some variable set members must overlap, and share the same characteristic.

Overloaded:

Description of an Unbalanced game in which there are extra candidates for the available spaces. For example, "nine candidates for a five-person research panel." Some variables are then In, and some are Out.

Pacing Guidelines:

These guidelines present a basic plan of action for each section, including broad goals for certain timing points and question markers.

Partially Defined:

There is a minimum and/or maximum number of variables to be selected, but the exact number of variables selected in the game cannot be determined.

Pattern:

A variation on Linear games where the rules equally govern the general action of all variables, as opposed to the specific variable governance found in standard Linear games.

Polar Opposition:

A polar opposite is a statement that contradicts a given statement as completely as possible. For example, "sweltering" and "frigid" would be polar opposites on a temperature scale. A logical opposite includes the polar opposite.

Process of Elimination:

This is a question solution strategy that involves eliminating each incorrect answer choice, and thus the lone remaining answer choice must be the correct answer.

Pure Sequencing Game:

A game type where the rules do not fix the variables in exact positions but instead provide information about the relative order of the variables, as in "J was hired earlier than K." See also Sequencing Rule.

Question Attack Strategy:

The proper approach for attacking the question set in each game.

Question Stem:

Follows the stimulus and poses a question directed at the stimulus. Make sure to read the question stem very carefully. Some stems direct you to focus on certain aspects of the stimulus and if you miss these clues you make the problem much more difficult.

Random:

A variable in a Logic Game that does not appear in any of the rules. Because randoms are not referenced in a rule, they are typically weaker players in the game.

Recycling Inferences:

The process of combining a previously obtained inference with one or more of the original rules.

Restrictions:

Restricted points are the areas in the game where only a few options exist—for example, a limited number of variables to fill in a slot, a block with a limited number of placement options, or a slot with a large number of Not Laws. Inferences often follow from restrictions.

Re-Using Information:

In certain cases, information you have already gained in a previous question that might apply to the question you are working on. In those cases, re-using that prior information can sometimes solve the question at hand, and very often eliminates some incorrect answer choices.

Rotating Blocks:

When two variables are in a block formation, but either can be first, as in AB or BA, this is known as a rotating block. Often diagrammed with a circle.

Rotating Split Blocks:

When two variables are in a split-block formation, but either can be first, as in A __ B or B __ A, this is known as a rotating block. Often diagrammed with a circle.

Rule Substitution Question:

Rule Substitution questions are an unusual combination of Suspension and Justify questions. In a Rule Substitution question, one of the original rules of the game is suspended, and you are asked to select an answer choice that contains language that has an identical effect as the original rule.

Rules:

In a Logic Game, a set of statements that describe the relationships between the variables.

Scenario: See Game Scenario

Selection Pool:

In Grouping games, this is the group of variables available to be selected.

Separation Principle™:

A principle that appears in some Linear games where variables are separated by not-blocks in such a way that the exact position of certain variables can be established.

Sequencing Rule:

Establishes the relative ordering of variables. The key to differentiating a sequencing rule from a block rule is that block rules precisely fix the variables in relationship to each other (for example, one space ahead or two spaces in between) and sequencing rules do not.

Side Not Law™:

Physically notates where a variable cannot be placed. Not Laws are very useful since it is essential that you establish the events that cannot be true in a game. See also Not Laws.

Speeded Test:

The LSAT is a "speeded" test. The test makers presume that the average student cannot finish each section in the allotted time (e.g. that they are "speeded" up). So, most people do not finish all the questions in any of the sections.

Split-blocks:

Indicate that there is a fixed number of spaces between two or more variables.

Stacks:

In Logic Games, one set of variables is identified as the base, while the other variable set is placed in slots above the initial slots, essentially "stacking" the variable sets and allowing for the appropriate relationship between variable sets to be visualized.

Subdivided Variables:

If the variables in the selection pool all have different characteristics (for example, some are male or female, some are tall or short), the selection pool is known as Uniform. See also Selection Pool.

Sufficient Condition (S):

An event or circumstance whose occurrence indicates that a necessary condition must also occur. The sufficient condition does not make the necessary condition occur; it is simply an indicator.

Super Rule:

In Logic Games, when two or more rules can be combined to produce a single diagram. Super-rules tend to be quite powerful and often control the game.

Suspension Question:

Suspension questions always appear at the end of the game, and they suspend one of the rules of the game. These questions are relatively rare, but also very time consuming.

T

Templates:

In Logic Games, when certain variables or blocks have a limited number of placement options, the best strategy is often to show the basic possibilities for each option. This powerful technique can sometimes quickly solve the game, and at the least it tends to reveal important information about the relationship between certain variables.

Triple-Branched Sequence: See Multi-Branched Sequence.

Triple Options:

This occurs when a single space is limited to just three options. Represented as A/B/C.

Two-Value System:

When all variables must be used and each variable must be placed in exactly one of two groups, each variable has only two values—in one group or in the other group. Powerful inferences can be drawn from the fact that when a variable is not in one group it must be in the other group (these inferences often involve the contrapositive).

Unbalanced:

In a Defined game, when the number of variables to be selected is not equal to the overall number of available spaces. Unbalanced games are either Overloaded or Underfunded.

Undefined:

When the number of variables to be selected for the game is not fixed, and is only limited by the total number of variables. Undefined games are generally the most difficult type of Grouping game.

Underfunded:

Description of an Unbalanced game in which there are not enough candidates for the available spaces. This lack is almost always solved by reusing one or more of the candidates, or by creating empty spaces.

Unfixed:

In Numerical Distributions, unfixed means that certain variables or spaces are not assigned to specific numbers, and thus can be attached to any of the variables in the game.

Unified Grouping Theory™:

The classification and identification system used to keep track of the many different elements in each Grouping game.

Uniform Variables:

If the variables in the selection pool all have the same basic characteristics, the selection pool is known as Uniform. See also Selection Pool.

Unless Equation™:

A simple process for handling conditional statements featuring "unless," "except," "until," and "without":

1. Whatever term is modified by "unless," "except," "until," or "without" becomes the necessary condition.
2. The remaining term is negated and becomes the sufficient condition.

Variable Sets:

The sets of people, places, things, or events that are involved in each game. The variables will be involved in an easy to understand activity such as sitting in seats or singing songs. It is very important to always write down and keep track of each variable set.

Verticality:

When a game is diagrammed in a vertical line (or setup), the relationship between the variables arranged vertically indicates adjacency, while the relationship of variables arranged horizontally indicates similarity.